鄧惜華

A CHINESE TESTAMENT

THE AUTOBIOGRAPHY OF
TAN SHIH-HUA

AS TOLD TO
S. TRETIAKOV

MCMXXXIV · SIMON AND SCHUSTER · NEW YORK

Two people have made A Chinese Testament. *Tan Shih-hua provided the raw material. I put it into shape. To see one's own life in detail and to tell its story requires great skill. Tan Shih-hua did not possess this skill. He accepted with enthusiasm my proposal to write an accurate biography of a Chinese student. For a half year we conferred daily for four to six hours. He generously placed the depths of his wonderful recollections at my disposal. I dug into them like a miner. I was, at various times, his examining judge, father confessor, interviewer, companion, and psycho-analyst.*

What I have written in this fashion is really an interview. But as this interview embraces more than twenty-six years of a man's life, it might be called a "Bio-Interview."

Tan Shih-hua was a student of mine in the Russian Section of the National University in Peking. His home province is Szechuan in South China. The hoes of seventy million inhabitants work its fertile soil. Silently, on canvas slippers, he used to enter my room in Peking, and later in Moscow. A cone-shaped robe on his narrow shoulders hung in light folds over his sunken chest. Silently and unnoticed he went back again to his native land.

He was not a communist, the Kuomintangism of his father was transferred to him as an inheritance. He protested with bitter indignation the treason of the Kuomintang's generals, but he never left the party. His generation shows clearly the break-up of the social energies of the leading classes of the old China. The leaders of the new China will come from the depths of the new classes—classes which Tan Shih-hua had learned to shun from childhood.

Chinese communists, who have seen parts of this book, have

[v]

*said: "Here, indeed, is our childhood, our school, our life"—
so typical does this story of Tan Shih-hua seem to the young
Chinese intelligentsia today.*

S.T.

CONTENTS

[vii]

Contents

[viii]

Contents

PUBLISHER'S NOTE

The original of this book was written in Russian, not Chinese. Therefore it has been impossible to transliterate the Chinese words with more than a reasonable amount of accuracy. In many cases an arbitrary English spelling is used, calculated to offer the least difficulty to the American reader.

I

1. The House in Tan Tsia Chen

I AM CALLED TAN SHIH-HUA. I AM SHIH-HUA OF THE FAMILY Tan which comes from the Szechuan village Tan Tsia Chen on the river Yangtze. Hua is my personal name. Shih is the name of that generation of my family to which I belong. My sister, Shih-kuen, and the children of my aunts and uncles have this name. My father is Tan Ya-pu. Pu is the name of his generation. My elder uncle is Tan Sao-pu, and the younger is Tan Tsi-pu.

I was born in our big ancestral house in the month of January, when the magnificent Yangtze, grown shallow and blue, rushes noisily between its steep Szechuan banks. Our house—a chain of courts surrounded by rooms and terraces—spreads itself on the slope of a hill. From the upper terraces, through the tops of trees, you could see the blue body of the river. The shores of the Yangtze are of stone and clay. Clay and soft stone surround the docks where the boats of fishermen and ferrymen crowd. The Yangtze at this point is five times as wide as the Moscow River near the Kremlin.

In the spring the Yangtze is magnificent. The slopes of the

banks are not only green: they are red, yellow, blue with blossoms, and all these blossoms are reflected in clear, blue water. When summer nears, the Yangtze turns a rusty red, and swells with slimy, cloudy water—due to the heavy rains at its faraway sources in the wild mountains near Tibet. When the water of the Yangtze is blue, we drink it, after boiling it in our ovens. The coolies, the wandering harvesters, and the boatmen, tired out by their work and thirsty, drink it raw. They drink it with a bite of bitter onion, which, in their opinion, makes any water good.

On the slope, between our house and the river, there was a row of trees. Looking from the river, one could hardly distinguish our village through the black groves. Everywhere, around every wall in the village, trees were planted in orderly arrangements. The gardens were green and the air clean in Szechuan.

A large stone basin three feet high stood among the trees in the first big court of our house. Rain water accumulated in it, and gold-brown and silver-violet fish swam there. The vegetation inside the court was watered from this basin. Along the wall there were nutmeg trees. Being very expensive, they were planted under the main wall of the house to protect them from thieves. The house was built around three terrace-like courts. The uppermost terrace beyond them was used for a vegetable garden. Stairs led from court to court through the walls. Between the second and the third courts was a hall where guests were received. Behind the guest room was the last court, and beyond this court a row of main rooms. The *li tang*, a prayer-room, was in the middle. Next to it was the room of my grandfather, the head of the family and of the house. The other side of the li tang was occupied by his brother. Beyond the upper wall of the house, the vegetable garden was surrounded by trees, and hemmed in by a fence of live bamboo. This garden led into an orchard. There were mulberry, pomegranate, apricot, orange, peach, nut, and tangerine trees. The orchard and the garden,

[4]

including the house, covered about twenty *mu*—somewhat less than four acres. This land easily supported the seventeen people of the house. The vegetable garden was as rich as a museum. Cucumbers, radishes, bitter radishes, turnips, sweet potatoes, peas, lettuce, squash, and all kinds of Szechuan cabbage—these vegetables were brought in daily from the garden to our dinner table. Only the grown-ups might have meat every day. The rest of the family got a tiny bit of meat—and that only twice a month.

The elders lived around the family altar, in the topmost sections of the house, surrounded by storerooms. Then came the rooms of my father, my uncles, the reception room, and the kitchen. At the lowest end of the house were the rooms of the third generation and also rooms for visiting guests, the janitor's room and a big classroom where my uncle used to teach the village youngsters. The servants' rooms, no bigger than closets, were next to father's and grandfather's quarters.

In the prayer-room against the wall, facing the entrance, stood a big black altar. It was the *shen tang*. Its fancy wood-carving was inlaid with bone. On the black wood of its upper half there was a column of five golden hieroglyphics. They represented "The Sky", "The Earth", "The Emperor", "The Ancestor", "The Teacher". This column rested on a sixth hieroglyphic which read "The Altar". On both sides of this main column which we call *tang-li*, hung two small strips of cypress wood, twice the length of the palm of your hand. The names of the ancestors of the three nearest generations were traced on these strips—grandfather's, great-grandfather's, and great-grandfather's father. The strips of wood with the names of more remote ancestors had been put away in the village temple.

The lower part of the shen tang protruded and formed a shelf. In the middle of this shelf stood a porcelain incense-burner with handles. The fluffy ashes of the incense sticks accumulated in it. This lower part contained a cupboard. Incense sticks, oil for the lamp, strings of silver coin made of tinfoil, which are burned on the day of the dead, and the family book, *Chu-pu,* were kept here. The Chu-pu is a book of names, of birth dates, marriage dates, deaths, days of graduation, dates of promotion, and other important events.

Every day, at morning and at night, one of the little Tans would stick three incense candles in the ashes, and light them from a flame that burned at the snout of a small oil lamp that looked like a gravy-dish. When the family had money, this lamp used to be kept burning in the li tang day and night. When the Tans had no money for oil, they lit the lamp only for the night.

The incense candles would glow. Gay, blue threads of smoke rose toward the hieroglyphics and white, cylindrically-shaped ashes fell into the urn. When the urn was filled, the ashes were cast into the river under the house. "The holy ashes into the holy water of the river Yangtze," my grandmother used to say as she passed the heavy urn to her grandchild.

On both sides of the urn there were vases with flowers and a big copper bowl. This bowl was a gong. When hit with a stick, it would call the souls of ancestors to the festive dinner which was set on a table in the middle of the li tang every holiday in their commemoration. The best dishes were put on the table. There were meat and fish and fresh vegetables.

The grandchildren (the grown-ups had no time for this) drew the names of the ancestors accurately on little squares of paper, and put these visiting cards of the dead in front of the cypress strips of the altar. This meant that the ancestors had arrived and had taken their places at the table. Then the whole family knelt and bowed three times to the center column of hiero-glyphics, taking off their glossy skull-caps and holding them with both hands. Then the women would carry the dishes of food away, and the children would collect the visiting cards of the ancestors. They used to burn them carefully on the flat stones of the court, lest a spark fall on a paper window frame and burn the wooden walls of the house.

[6]

2. Uncle's Bad Luck

MY FATHER WAS IN JAPAN AT THE UNIVERSITY. I DID NOT know him. During my early childhood my older uncle was closer and dearer to me—he who might have become the pride of the family, but failed.

The ruling class of all China were the *Shihs*—the learned ones. Only after passing examinations and becoming a Shih, could you receive and put on a *Shen*—the formal belt of an official, a tight band inlaid with precious stones and tiny mirrors. Education meant government position and all its advantages. Shen Shihs were the nobles who possessed the land, and who could send their children to study in order that they, in their turn, could obtain government posts and, with the profits of those posts, increase their land.

We, the Tans, were also Shen Shihs, only we were poor. The Shens were rare in our family, which was in opposition to the ruling Manchu dynasty. But learned degrees adorned the names of our ancestors in our Chu-pu.

Long before I was born, my older uncle was graduated from high school and received the title of a university student. He spent three years in the main city of the district and passed an examination for his next degree. After three more years of study he went to Chengtu, the capital of Szechuan, to pass the examination for his second degree.

He often told me what it was like. All those undergoing the examinations were put into cages. This was done in order to give the examinations an appearance of irreproachable honesty. A man would take into this cage only some paper, brushes, Chinese ink, and his brain, swollen with a tremendous number of names, lines of poetry, aphorisms, commentaries, and dates. There were only written examinations.

The belief existed that if a man had loose morals or were a criminal, he would lose his courage in the cage and so fail to pass his examinations. In consequence, a scholar preparing for an examination had to be very careful not to commit even the smallest sin. He was supposed to walk in a special manner, lest he crush a beetle or an ant; and he also had to be careful with his gestures, for fear he might injure the microscopic beings floating in the air. So ran the Buddhist teaching.

He was forbidden even to think of love, of romances, of the courtesans in the tea-houses. When he met a woman on the street he had to lower his eyes. Only the pleasures of wine and opium were allowed him. If, after successfully passing his examinations, the scholar did not choose to become an official and so use his lofty title to the best advantage, the only profession open to him was teaching. The Tans seldom became officials, but there were many teachers among them. Many an hour had my father and both uncles spent teaching and training a new generation of short and serious little men in long robes.

My uncle was very able. His thesis was recognized as brilliant. It was printed at government expense and sent out to his relatives and scholars. It seemed evident that in three years he would come out from an examination cage in Peking as a scholar of the first degree. After that he might pass the test at the Emperor's palace for the highest title of an academician, Han Li.

But . . . a number of deaths occurred in our house. My uncle's grandfather died. My uncle put on the white mourning clothes. This severe mourning continued for three years, and during those three years the mourner was not allowed to marry or take examinations. Patiently my uncle waited. The mourning was nearing its end when his grandmother died. Three more years of waiting. After his grandmother, my uncle buried his father, then his mother, and his stepmother.

[8]

Fifteen years of mourning he endured and when it was over, the old system of examinations had been, meanwhile, annulled (1914). A few years later, the followers of Sun Yat-sen overthrew the ruling dynasty and abolished all academic degrees. My uncle could never forgive the new China, or my father, a revolutionary follower of Sun Yat-sen, for that.

"Your father is a traitor," he used to say, shedding drunken tears. "It is his fault that I did not get all my degrees."

When my uncle was sober he was always grumbling, but as soon as he had a cup of hot yellow wine at the table, he would become a gay, witty, and good-natured monarchist. He would have turned me, a baby, into a drunkard had it not been for the interference of my grandmother. I remember he put a chopstick, *kuei-tze*, in a glass of wine and gave it to me to taste. I didn't like it. It was bitter.

Most of his room was occupied by his bed, an enormous structure with its own ceiling and floor made out of boards. The ceiling rested on small wooden poles with a curtain attached to them. At the head of the bed stood a table, and next to it a small chest. When the weather was warm the whole construction, bed and all, could be easily moved out of doors and then moved back into the room again, like a photographer's camera into its box. This ceiling was very necessary. It sheltered you from the rain and it protected you indoors, too, from all kinds of beetles and centipedes that might fall from the rafters of the roof.

From the chest my uncle would take a fat bamboo pipe, as big as a flute. He would get out a jar of opium, not a bad opium, which is black as shoe polish, but a good transparent yellowish opium, thick as glue. Then he would take out a stone, a needle and a little lamp. It was a special kind of copper lamp with its flame protected by a glass cap. With the end of the needle my uncle would pick up a drop of opium from the jar and heat it over the lamp. The opium boiled and blistered with a white foam. He rolled it on the polished surface of the stone until it became a solid pill. Then he pierced it with a needle, as you would pierce a bead, placed it in the opening of the pipe bowl, and lay down on the bed, holding the end of the pipe to his mouth. He kept the little pill of opium hot over the lamp. As he inhaled the opium, he talked.

The revolting sweet smell pervaded the room. My uncle told a story; then he recited a poem. Under the little cap of the lamp burned a wick, floating in mustard oil.

My uncle stopped talking. His face turned blue; his mouth fell away from the pipe.

Later, it all changed. His grandfather, on his deathbed, forbade my uncle to smoke opium. He obeyed. But the force of the habit was so strong that every night he went to his room, took all the accessories out from the box, and spread them on the bed. Then he lay down beside his cold pipe. But he did not smoke.

---

3. Grandmother

Faces, words, objects, and the blue yangtze, in a setting of blossoming mountains emerge out of the grey, shifting twilight of childhood. When I was two (or one, as the Europeans reckon it) we removed to the village of Sian-Shih.

The house in Sian-Shih was much smaller than our ancestral house. It was crowded and poor inside. Father was in Japan and we had to economize. There was one servant girl for the house, and she came only when mother was sick. Instead of a vegetable garden, there were only a fruit garden and a tangerine orchard.

I remember grandmother feeding me sunflower seeds which had been dried in the sun. She shelled each seed and, passing

[10]

them to me one by one, she taught me to count: *i-ge, liang-ge, san-ge, si-ge, wu-ge*—one, two, three, four, five. She also told me fairy-tales. Grandmother was the second wife of my grandfather whose portrait hung on the wall in the li tang. She was my father's stepmother. Having no children of her own, she lavished all her affection on me.

Mother either worked in the kitchen or taught little village girls to read. I was very proud of her because in my childhood there were very few women in China who could read, to say nothing of being able to teach.

Grandmother is sewing, and I am sitting by her on a low stool. I have on a long robe, slippers embroidered with flowers, and white socks. One must not go barefoot—people would laugh at you. Only coolies went barefoot. The word *ku* means load, the word *li* means strength. Coolies were low people—dirty, rude, ragged coachmen, boatmen, porters, wandering reapers—in a word, all those who were willing to sell their big, brown muscles, hardened by labor and fights, for copper pennies. I was a little afraid of coolies, but they were treated well in our house, especially by my younger uncle (also a teacher) who was staying with us. For that reason, the well-off villagers were suspicious of him.

I am sitting by my grandmother, building houses, temples, bridges out of wooden blocks. I imagine that I am building my favorite bridge, the one that hangs over the little river flowing into the Yangtze, near Sian-Shih. It is a stone bridge, all sculptured. Carved dragons, six feet high, guard it. Three arches clutch the bridge with their paws. These arches are dedicated to the widows of Sian-Shih who remained faithful to their husbands even after the latter died.

This bridge was built fifty years ago by a rich man of the village. His only son was a cripple. At the sight of a woman he would throw a fit. No descendants could be expected from this feeble-minded son. The family of the rich man was dying out and, as he had no one to leave his fortune to, he built this bridge.

On its flat stones, the peasants threshed their grain in hot weather. There was no better threshing-floor in the whole district.

I am arranging my blocks and mixing them all up again at grandmother's feet, which are small and round, like ponies' hooves. Grandmother called them proudly her "golden lilies". Grandmother is sewing and singing, and teaching me a song:

> *Fly away,*
> *First pair of geese,*
> *Second pair of geese,*
> *Come back again*
> *To find grandmother.*
> *Grandmother does not like*
> *Rice with pork.*
> *Grandmother wants*
> *The egg of a wild duck.*

I knew why my shrewd grandmother wanted a wild duck's egg. It was rare, and difficult to get. We ate only hen's eggs. Mother and grandmother made a mush out of clay, mixed with the ashes of pea or rice straw, and smeared it over the egg. When it dried, the egg was as big as your fist. Then they buried it in the ground for twenty days. When such an egg was served at the table on holidays, its white was hard and had a brownish color. The yolk was soft and tasted as if the egg had been freshly boiled. Sometimes there were veins in the white of the egg that looked like cypress branches. "I had it kept in cypress ashes," grandmother used to explain to me.

The cool wind stirs the hot air. The blazing hearths are roaring in the kitchen and the plates are clattering in mother's hands. Far down, at the docks of the unseen Yangtze, the fishermen are shouting loudly, and children are screaming and

[12]

splashing. I want to go to the river, but I am not permitted. My mother is afraid that I may get hurt, be insulted, or pushed into the water. "All right," I say, "I'll just take a walk in the garden." Mother looks at me suspiciously. She takes me to the classroom, dips a brush in an ink-well, puts me on her lap, and paints, with a tiny tickling paint-brush, three-petalled black flowers on the palms of my hands and on the canvas soles of my slippers. Now I may go. Should I walk over a wet place, or splash water with my hands, the flowers will be washed off and I will be discovered.

I had seen other children being spanked by their parents as a result of these tell-tale signs. I did not go to the river.

Near Sian-Shih the river was terrifying with its bank dropping steeply down into deep water. The children of the fishermen and boatmen swam and dived near the docks, fighting and swearing. The fish-poles bent attentively toward the water. Yellow water broke over the rocks. Schools of fish swam by on their way to lay their eggs in the small upper streams.

4. Morning

I USED TO WAKE UP VERY EARLY, WHEN IT WAS STILL DARK. Roosters were crowing. Next to me my mother breathed evenly, her head resting quietly on the cube-like block of a pillow. The night before, she and grandmother had gone to bed late. I tossed and turned but this did not wake my mother. The pressed straw of the mattress made no noise under its cover of quilt. I loved

[13]

to watch how the grey smoke rose over each roof of Sian-Shih, in the blue light of dawn.

"I want to get up," I whispered to my mother.

Mother did not kiss me; she did not even press her cheek against mine. She patted my head, said a gentle word—that was all. Swiftly she got up and dressed. Her feet were just a little under normal size, the instep just a little too bent. I liked mother's feet more than the "golden lilies" of my grandmother. Grandmother walked too slowly with her small feet. She would waver from step to step when I wanted to hurry.

Quickly mother put on her white cotton homespun stockings and canvas slippers, thrust her legs through the little blue tubes of her trousers, and threw over her shoulder a short robe which reached her knees. Then she began to dress me. She buttoned my little robe on the side with buttons like beads, and washed me. She brought hot water from the kitchen in a copper bowl (the coal had been glowing all through the night under the big pots), put the end of a fluffy towel into the water, wrung it out, soaped it, and with this soapy end carefully wiped my forehead, face, neck, and ears. While I wrinkled up my soaped face, she rinsed the towel and took off the soap. Then she brought more hot water, and wiped me thoroughly with the same towel all over again.

When I was very small she used to clean my gums and my teeth, just cutting through, with a piece of cloth wound around her finger. Now that I was big, I had my own soft tooth-brush made of horse-hair. The salty tooth-powder drew the saliva. I rinsed my mouth again and again with water which had been poured from cooked rice. Four times a day I washed and cleaned my teeth: in the morning, at night, and after two meals. The teeth of Szechuan people are white and shiny. Everybody, even the coolies, even the ragged porters of palanquins, at least rinse their mouths, if they do not clean their teeth after each meal. And so we have very few dentists.

If the smile of a rich merchant reveals the gleam of a golden tooth, it does not mean that he has eaten too much candy, or lost his tooth in a fight. The merchant considers it smart and chic to have gold teeth. He lets his dentist file off a perfectly healthy tooth and put a fancy crown of yellow metal in its place.

My dressing finished, mother began to dress herself. On the table, by her bed, stood a bowl and a mirror. She combed her hair with a comb made of palm-wood. She wet her hair with oil, and parted it in locks. Then she wound these locks together on the back of her head, and fastened them with flat, spoon-like, silver pins.

My complicated coiffure I entrusted to my grandmother's hands. I entered grandmother's room and asked politely, "How are you?" The dull blue bald spot shone above my up-turned nose. My hair was shaved above my forehead, but it was long behind my ears. She braided my hair on each side of my head. The length of these braids was a great satisfaction to both of us. When I grow up, the long braid of a man will hang down my back. Grandmother took good care of my hair, washing it with hot water every third day.

Dressing was finished, but it was still a long while before meal time. The ways of mother and grandmother parted. Mother went to the kitchen. Grandmother and I, taking a bamboo basket from the kitchen table, went out into the street to buy vegetables.

The peddlers bent under their yokes. Cabbages, turnips, and cucumbers weighed down their shoulders. A delicate cabbage head and some blunt-nosed cucumbers were transferred from a peddler's basket into ours.

I liked especially the occasions when grandmother went to the store to get pork fat, and some brown, pungent soya-sauce, made from beans. These were mixed at home into a dark mush —my favorite dish. The store was narrow and dark like a corridor. Heavy pots on shelves contained soya, salt, vinegar, pepper, and other spices. Next door was an even more attractive store. Here you might buy indescribably sweet yellowish sand-like stuff, made from sugar cane. The green sticks of this cane

[15]

were soaking in large containers inside the store. There were also dried fruits, jam in earthen and glass jars, and walnuts.

The owner of the store, a relative of ours, used to offer me candy. Silently I would look up into grandmother's eyes. If she gave permission, I took the candy. But it often happened that, busy buying and smelling the goods, she would not notice my questioning glance, in which case I went away without the candy.

Never would I take candy secretly or without permission. My older uncle loved to say: "One must not take other people's things." Even when friends gave me a toy when we were visiting them, I would leave it unnoticed somewhere in a corner before going home. I didn't like candy, anyway. I was only four years old then, but I thought to myself: candy is bad for your teeth. The black stubs of rotting baby teeth in my schoolmates' mouths horrified me.

Over the flat stones of the morning streets of Sian-Shih, grandmother and I walked slowly home. The entrance to our house was through a drug-store. The stuffy smell of drugs coming from the dim closets, where little labelled boxes were piled up like honey-combs, made me dizzy. Branches, dried flowers, leaves, berries, roots were kept in these boxes. Poisonous insects —scorpions and flies—dried out in them and gave off unpleasant odors. They are used on boils to bring them to a head. White tiger-bone powder is drunk with brandy, or is mixed with fat, and smeared over plasters. Tiger-bone is used to treat rickets, broken limbs, and other bone diseases. A deadly odor came from the young stag's antlers—velvety cones, with congealed blood inside—which are boiled, then dried and powdered. The pills made from this powder are given to convalescents, to old bearded men, shaky with age, and to fathers who fail to produce children. A single antler may be used for many sick people. It is very expensive.

The upper shell of a turtle is also boiled the same way and

[16]

used to cure feeble people and the complicated and painful diseases of women.

Had a doctor thought of prescribing, for some sick rich man of our Sian-Shih, powdered ruby, amber, or the root of ginseng —which cost more than gold—or the dried heart of a criminal, our druggist would not have had it in stock. His store was just a small village branch of the prosperous drug-store of the district.

The druggist had two children, one of them a little older than I, the other my age. But I passed through the drug-store, clinging to my grandmother's sleeve, and not looking in their direction. They were quiet at that moment—something very unusual. They were the worst cry-babies. Before their crying abilities all the donkeys of Sian-Shih and its environments hid with shame. For this reason mother did not allow me to play with them.

The street, now warmed by the climbing sun, with its peddlers, housewives, and its children running to school, was left behind. I walked around a movable screen that stood in front of our gate, and entered our court, separated from the village, from Szechuan, and from the whole world. I knew why the screen was there. I would never push or pull it down. It protected our court, not only from the eyes of strangers, but also from evil spirits who swarmed in the wind, more numerous than flies over carrion, or mosquitoes over a swamp.

On New Year's day, the gates and the screens in front of them were plastered with red paper to scare the spirits away. This paper read: "Tsun Tai-gun is here". Tsun Tai-gun was a hero who managed to put under a lock all the devils and fiends of the other world. The spirits were afraid of his name, as flies are of a toad-stool. The name of Tsun Tai-gun did not appear on our screen. The grown-ups were not interested in him, and I was too small to write a hieroglyphic myself, because I did not even know how to hold a paint-brush.

We are sitting around a square table in the dining room—my

mother, my grandmother, my uncle, and I. We have rice, boiled green cabbage, soya-sauce mixed with pork fat, cottage cheese made out of bean-milk, pickled cucumbers, beans and radishes. All the dishes are on the table; in front of each person stands a white bowl and a couple of chopsticks—kuei-tze.

When I was small, I ate with a spoon from my bowl. I was very proud when I first got a kuei-tze and began to eat like a grown-up man. But the fact that mother or grandmother would put food on my plate was insulting. Once, burning with ambition, I got on the chair with my knees, and independently stretched my sticks out toward the bowl of fresh vegetables. I lost my balance and hit the corner of the table with my head. Everybody jumped up. My uncle grabbed me in his arms and, pressing mother's kerchief against my bleeding wound, ran to the doctor. The black-bearded doctor put a plaster on the wound. It stayed open for twelve days, and then healed. I still have the scar over my eyebrow.

I used to drink tea whenever I wanted it. I went to the kitchen, and poured it for myself from a copper tea kettle which was kept hot day and night.

All morning mother's eyes would water from the smoke in the kitchen. The flame rose in little curls of smoke from under the three kettles built into the stove. The chimney was too small for the fire leaping from the stoves. Enormous blocks of wood crackled under the kettles. They came from the tall forests on the mountains above Sian-Shih. They were floated over the mountain streams and dragged in from the river on the shoulders of peasants. Wood was cheap. A log three feet long and a foot across used to cost one *tung tze*—a cent. The coal came down the Yangtze river from the mines which are forty miles from Sian-Shih.

I hear a half-human, half bird-like twitter on the stairway. The girls have come—the pupils of my mother. Blinking her eyes, mother wiped her soot-covered hands, pulled up her trousers, straightened her blouse, and started the reading lesson. These girls were my only companions. I was their teacher's son, and they were very attentive to me, calling me their brother.

In summer time the girls were all in white. In the spring and autumn they wore blue blouses and trousers, and in winter they wore black. Each girl's braid was tightly wound on the back of her head with a colored string like the insulation of a wire. Short bangs fell over their foreheads, under which their eyes moved quickly, like baby mice.

The little girls did not talk—they whispered. They did not look at each other—they flashed glances. They did not laugh— they giggled. Everything seemed funny to them. They snickered in their handkerchiefs. Crowding in a circle, they sat and gossiped, passed judgment on who was pretty, who was plain, who was awkward, or miserly, or nicely dressed. In their free time, between lessons, they called me to play with them, but I did not know how to play their games. I came only to watch how they kicked the *tian-tze*, a kind of shuttle-cock. It flew back and forth through the air, rarely falling on the stone pavement. They used to make a ring out of a piece of cord and play cat's cradle.

They taught me chess, which differs from the European version. The board is divided into nine squares each way, and there are no carved men. There are white and red checkers with hieroglyphics painted on their tops. There are five pawns, two cannons, two carriages, two knights, two chancellors, two scholars, and one emperor. All this army is set out in three, instead of two rows as in Europe, and not on the squares, but on the intersections of the lines. Between the camps is the neutral zone—the "river".

The girls used to play the flute. Delicate, curly melodies, full of quick, sudden breaks.

I often sat on the burning stones of the court, watching the small yellow ants that formed a busy crowded stream between the cracks. Grandmother had told me that I must respect the ants as a model of social life. The girls killed fat flies with a horse's tail attached to a handle. They gave me the flies and I fed them

[19]

to the ants. I threw down a fly, and it was immediately covered with ants. In a second, there was nothing left but its wings.

Grandmother is sewing tiny slippers for her "golden lilies". I am tired of ants. I sit down on a small stool next to her, put my head on her lap and doze until it is time for dinner, which is served at noon.

At eleven o'clock the girls would curtsey to my mother, say *nin-hao*—good-bye—and, twittering, disappear, the whole group of them, through the court screen.

One must not sleep after dinner. It was Confucius who said to his pupils, "He who likes to sleep is similar to a rotten block of wood from which no statue can be carved". This did not concern me. I slept after dinner.

A breath of wind from the Yangtze quivers in the leaves of the trees, stirring the heat. In the court my mother and grandmother are washing clothes in a wooden tub. Grey soap, made out of a special kind of greasy clay, glides over swishing linen. The fame of Chinese laundries comes from this soap. We never use European soap made out of fat.

Heavy, wet shirts are hanging on thin bamboo poles. The sun will dry out the water which my mother's weak hands could not wring.

I wake up. Grandmother is calling me to take a walk in the fields beyond the village.

5. Fields

OUR SLIPPERS SHUFFLED OVER THE PAVED ROAD. CHILDREN flying kites rushed by. Some of their kites looked like monsters and centipedes; others like dragon-flies and butterflies. The children made them themselves with three tung tze worth of paper, and ten tung tze worth of cord. Their frames they cut out of bamboo strips.

There were no more than fifty horses to the five thousand inhabitants of Sian-Shih. Horses are not used in the fields. Rich people keep them for riding and carrying loads; wagons cannot travel over our mountain paths. Military people and innkeepers own horses; also horse-traders who rent them out with guides. Peasants own, not horses, but cows, which are raised neither for milk nor meat. Four hundred years ago a special law was passed forbidding the use of cow's meat. And long before that the teachings of Buddhism decreed against the spilling of animal blood. We use the cow to work the fields.

Small houses and cow-sheds are scattered on the outskirts of Sian-Shih. They belong to peasants who work in the fields. I looked up to them. Their caste—the *nuns*—comes right next to our caste of *shihs*. They are followed by the caste of *guns*—craftsmen—and below them is the lowest and least respected caste of *sans*—the merchants. Coolies and soldiers have no caste.

Along the sloping foot of the hill the clay edges of rice fields make patterns. A rice field is like a pond. It is flooded with water and then its bottom is broken up with a plough that looks like a bent dagger. A cow is hitched to this dagger and draws it slowly, kneading with her hooves and knees the yellow mud. The ploughman presses down with his hands and chest on the handle of the dagger. It rips the heavy bottom, turning out slippery clods of earth. These clods are broken with rakes, and then the soft, slimy bed is ready for sowing.

The copper green rice plants rise in the nurseries, scarcely covered with water. As soon as they reach the height of twenty centimeters, the plants are pulled out and replanted in bunches of ten in the slime of the pond fields. The distance between the bunches is a foot and a half. Straight, as if drawn with a ruler, the design of a chess board is marked on the field. The sunset gilds the water of the rice pond on which the green bristles of the rice plants are hardly visible.

Rice shoots up quickly. Then, in the middle of the summer, come the roaring rains. The water runs down the mountains like sweat off the ribs of an overworked horse. Small hollows dug out to irrigate the rice fields below them are flooded. Water spills over the edges of fields, washing away the clay walls and threatening the still ripening rice.

During this rainy season, the drenched and hungry peasants stand up to their waists in water, day and night, fighting its furious attack. They rush along the clay walls, patching the breaches made by the water, regulating the overflow by shutting and opening dams.

There are no women in the rice fields, for rice is a difficult job, a man's job. But there are many boys in the ditches that run along the fields, their pants rolled up above their knees, their arms in the mud up to their elbows. They grope under the rocks, searching for something in the thick growth of ripening rice. They are catching crabs. Every fall the crabs crawl out of their black holes above the stream, and come to eat the good, tasty rice which makes them grow fat. Then the boys grab them by their sides and throw them in a basket. The next day they sell them in the streets of Sian-Shih.

Rice fields bear only one crop a year. All other fields are worked the year round. In springtime the winter rye, which was sown in December, and beans, are maturing in these fields. In April corn is sown in straight rows in place of beans. Three months later the ripe corn lifts up its lances seven feet high, while on the ground, between its stalks, melons and cucumbers swell with sweetness and juice. We ate the corn, leaving the leaves and cobs for the cattle. The stalks are soaked in water, let rot, and then used to fertilize the soil. They are also dried and burned in the stoves. After the corn, in the midst of the summer, the field is ploughed over and buckwheat is sown. In the

[22]

late fall it is harvested, and again winter rye and beans are put into the ground. I used to love the fields most of all in the spring when the beans were in bloom. Their winged blossoms looked like a million butterflies resting on the green.

Where the fields change into the rocky slopes of mountains the olive tree flourishes. The third year of its growth it bears a greenish-brown plum-like fruit which contains a tiny pit. In the spring no wind is strong enough to carry away the fragrance of the white flowers of the *tun-tze*, which hang over the shores of the Yangtze river. In the fall its fat fruit is squashed open, and its pits are cracked in the press. The peasants crush them simply under boards. The clear oil—one of the splendid riches of Szechuan—flows off abundantly from the press. The ship-builders of the whole world, following the custom of the Szechuan boatmen, oil their barges, canoes, boats and ships to preserve them against the attacks of water and worms. We burn this oil in our lamps, thus competing with the product of the Standard Oil Company which comes to us from America in light colored tanks.

Above the olive trees the thick fronded woods climb the mountain slopes. There is wild game in these woods, hidden paths, and beehives made out of barrels by the foresters who try to lure the wild bees from their hives in the hollow tree. And where the forest ends, the grey-green meadows rise clear to the clouds. Flocks of slender, thin-tailed Szechuan sheep browse over them under the guidance of a boy shepherd and a goat, his assistant. I was afraid of the sharp, pointed horns of the goats, but I used to plunge my fingers into the warm, silky, impenetrable wool of the sheep.

The sun was going down. It was now about seven and supper time was near. On the way back my hand reached out for a golden mustard blossom. Grandmother pulled me back by the shoulder. "You mustn't do that! This mustard was sown by peasants. Don't you dare pick it; they will not like it."

The light inside the rooms was turning blue. I climbed on a

[23]

chair, and put my bouquet in a vase on the desk. Mother filled vases with water. I sat down on my little stool and rested in silence. I watched my mother as she set the table and brought in hot rice. All the dishes were steaming. No cold food today. We were having supper without my older uncle, who was the only one who had cold food. He liked it with his yellow whiskey.

Supper made me very drowsy. Mother undressed me. Gently she covered me with a blanket and said: "Sleep quietly, don't throw off your blanket, and don't muss it up."

The locusts were ringing through the darkness of the court like a thousand furious little bells. The whine of mosquitoes came from the corners of the room. Mother sat next to me, stroking the blanket with her hand, singing a song without words. I looked at the canopy which was made of fine linen. Branches of plum trees were painted on it—pink flowers and blue leaves. A basket was suspended from the boards of the bed-ceiling. White *yi lei san* flowers were in the basket. These flowers were lifeless all day, but now fresh fragrance breathed from them. Every Chinaman has a basket of yi lei san hanging over his bed at night.

Mother's song mingled with the fragrance of yi lei san. It mingled with the darkness, with the ringing locusts and with the far away slippery shores of the Yangtze. I fell asleep.

6. School

MY OLDER UNCLE WAS IN A PARTICULARLY GOOD HUMOR. HIS face beamed and his eyes squinted as if he were just about to say something funny. I was five years old (four, according to the European way of counting). My uncle took me to a room where four long narrow sheets of paper covered with beautifully written hieroglyphics were hanging on the wall. He pointed to one hieroglyphic and said "Fan". I repeated the word "Fan" after him. My uncle paused to let the word sink into my brain, and then named the next hieroglyphic, "Hsien". After I learned "Hsien", he read the last hieroglyphic, "Tin". Fan Hsien-tin. I said that word over to myself again and again, tracing in the air with the tip of my finger the lines of the hieroglyphics. Fan Hsien-tin was the name of a teacher, whose face I had not yet seen, but to whom I was soon to go. Fan Hsien-tin. I repeated the name with a vague feeling of respect.

Fifteen years later, in Peking, I was shouting the name of Wang Cheng-ting with great political ardor. It was on the occasion when a high Peking official with the same name signed a treaty between China and Soviet Russia, the first in which China was treated as an equal power.

At home I overheard conversations between my mother and my uncles about what school it would be best for me to go to— a public school where they taught you free, or a private school where the teaching was better, but where you had to pay heavily.

"Look, the sons of our neighbor pay only six *da yang* a year. And the nephew of the fat manufacturer, Tun, costs him twenty a year. Twenty da yang! We, four of us, do not spend that much a month, for everything—food, fuel, and laundry."

My uncle paced the room with noiseless steps, slyly squinting at my despondent mother. Then he said:

"We'll pay only two da yang a year for Shih-hua. The teacher, Fan Hsien-tin, is giving us a reduction, because Shih-hua is my nephew."

My uncle loved to point out how highly respected he was by the people of Sian-Shih.

The cold days preceding New Year's, dragged slowly by. The holidays were nearly over. There was no other talk in the house but of teachers and schools. My uncle was indignant.

"Sian-Shih is such a big village—5,000 population, and only one public school. Disgraceful! In other villages of this size there are both a high school and a preparatory school. Why, the Su-Tung must be fast asleep. (The Su-Tung were the officials who supervised education in the villages and appointed school directors.)

My uncle showed me a piece of paper. Three hieroglyphics were written on it. One of them looked familiar. It was "Fan," the name of the teacher, but I did not know the other two. He read them to me: Tzia wan. Wan was the name of a valley which was enclosed in a semi-circle of mountains. Tzia wan was the part of the village where my teacher lived. In a few days I had to go there.

I walked along beside the bluish bricks in the wall of our house. On them I traced curious signs with a stick, imagining: "Now I am studying. Now I know how to write well. I am a famous calligraphist, a painter of hieroglyphics, and for each letter I get a da yang."

Through the window I saw a dim light in the room. The window was divided vertically—half of it was glass, the other half was patched with a green semi-transparent paper. The paper was worn and torn and the wind fluttered the edges. Through the opening I heard the sound of voices. One, loud and rough, was my uncle's; the other, softer and gentler, belonged to my mother.

"Two da yang only—out of regard for me."

New Year's passed. The important day arrived.

"Hua, put on your *ma-gua*."

My mother put a black satin vest over my new robe. It had long sleeves which covered my hands. I gathered what it was all about. I had noticed that only on the most solemn holidays, or when they went to pay the most important visits, did my uncles put on these shiny dressy ma-guas.

My mother, both uncles and grandmother—an imposing escort—followed me to the gate.

"Now, you are a school-boy."

"No more idling."

"You must study. . . ."

My younger uncle went with me to the school. I did not look back at the gate where three pairs of eyes were watching me. I walked along, excited and happy. I had always been lonely at home, always attached to the apron strings of grown-ups. Now before me was a prospect of gay, interesting and boisterous comradeship. On my arm hung a basket in which were my first reading book, incense sticks, a pair of red candles and a rocket.

At the school entrance two dogs barked at me. They frightened me. I clutched my uncle's robe. He took me in his arms. The teacher saw us through the window, interrupted his lesson and came out to greet us. His face was covered with wrinkles. Head, eyebrows and chin were marked with strings of milk-white hair. There was only enough room on his face for the wrinkles and two serious eyes. No place was left for a smile.

My uncle and the teacher stopped at the threshold. They bowed at length to each other, pointing with one hand to the entrance, and trying to urge one another gently through the door.

While passing through the court I heard a rustle behind a window. Sticking to the window pane in the shape of a pyramid, like plums on the stand of a peddler, were the heads of the numerous pupils of the class. Their faces were burning with curiosity.

My uncle, the teacher and I entered the li tang, the most imposing room of the school. Before us was an altar with an incense burner, and vases with flowers. Beyond it on the wall was a long vertical inscription. The hieroglyphics said: "Here is the throne of the most perfect sage and teacher of the ancient days—Confucius." The interior suddenly darkened—the figure of a woman stood in the doorway against the light. The wife of the teacher entered the room and joined us. Again, for a long time, my uncle and the teacher bowed to each other, pressing their hands to their chests.

Then my uncle said, "Here is my little dull nephew. I entrust him to you, the best of teachers. Perhaps under your guidance he will have a chance to become a good boy."

The teacher answered: "I see that your nephew is a very intelligent boy, much more intelligent than other boys of his age. I am sure that he will grow up to be just as worthy a man as your highly educated brother." (He meant my older uncle who was known to everybody in the district as a writer of verse and a connoisseur of literature.)

After these speeches I bowed to the ground in front of the hieroglyphics of Confucius, then in turn kneeled down in front of the teacher and his wife. The teacher's wife was like a second mother to the pupils. While I was bowing, my uncle burned the incense sticks in front of the altar and lighted the two red candles. I got up from my knees, and with one hand wiped my nose which had suddenly started running; with the other I shook off the dust from the edge of my robe.

Tr-ra-p-p-PACH! The rocket went off in the court letting the whole world know the news: Tan Shih-hua is a pupil.

My teacher and my uncle lead me into the classroom. The twenty pupils I had seen through the window were seated around tables, different groups and ages all in the same room. Obedience and modesty shone from lowered eyes. The teacher introduced me to the class.

"Here is my new pupil. You see how small he is. You must treat him as a younger brother. Study companionably."

I sat down on a bench at one of the tables, trying to get near the teacher. On his table a whole collection of interesting objects was laid out. A stone for grinding ink-powder, a small porcelain cup for water, ink-brushes. Some of these brushes were standing vertically in copper cans—brush-holders—and some were resting diagonally on a stand, lifting above the table

[28]

their glossy, bristly snouts. There was also a slab of wood, thick as a big book. When the class become too noisy, the teacher would hit the table with this slab, making a sound like a gun shot.

In his hands he held a stick with which he pointed out the hieroglyphics in our reading books. On the wall behind his back hung a smooth, slightly-bent bamboo ruler. But this ruler was not for drawing lines.

The teacher turned to me with a question. Eagerly I slid off my bench, but found myself under the table. I was too little. As it is difficult to teach a pupil you cannot even see, the teacher permitted me to answer from my bench. In that way he could at least see my head.

The class was all attention. The book in front of me was open on the first page. I was very intense and excited. I looked around at the class—perhaps they were laughing at me. No, everybody was just as serious as I was. The teacher's pointer marked the first hieroglyphic.

"Tien," said the teacher— "Tien," I repeated after him.

I repeated it more or less out of politeness, because I could see from a picture to the right of the hieroglyphic that tien means sky.

The teacher explained.

"Tien is that part of the blue space which we see above our heads, over which the clouds pass, to which the stars are attached, and where the sun and moon travel."

The pointer moved toward the next picture. Without waiting for him to name the picture, I pronounced "Ti." (Ti means earth.)

His stick jerked down to the picture of a star.

"Hsing," I announced, very pleased with myself.

The wrinkles on the teacher's face grew fewer. He became animated. His stick jumped still lower down. The diagonal lines of rain I met with the word "Yü."

"En," I said at the moment when the stick was trembling over the black smoke of a bonfire. I had time to say "ping" before it touched the sixth picture which represented ice.

I had read six hieroglyphics in my first lesson.

"It is enough for today." The teacher was obviously pleased with me.

"You may go home with your uncle. Tomorrow my son will come to fetch you. You'll sit next to him in class."

He called to a slender lithe boy of about thirteen, almost twice my size.

"Ask him, if there is something you do not understand in your studies."

Without a word, I exchanged glances with the teacher's son, put my book in the basket, glided off my bench and came out from under the table. With quiet dignity, without once turning my head back toward the class, who were silently examining me, I walked out into the court to my uncle.

At home my older uncle, grandmother and mother all threw themselves upon me. As I put away my basket and took off my ma-gua, they besieged me with questions.

"Did the teacher question you?"

"Did you answer your lesson?"

"You didn't cry?"

I was astonished.

"Cry! Why should I? Nobody abused me or hit me."

I answered the questions of the annoying grown-ups politely but without enthusiasm. I could not understand why they were excited.

The next day after breakfast the teacher's son came to get me. Now, without fuss and without parental farewells, I went with him over the stony, hunch-backed streets of Sian-Shih, still cool in the morning. We talked about the school, wondered in how many days one could learn the whole book of hieroglyphics, discussed the slow-witted boy, Tun, who could learn the names of hieroglyphics without knowing which was which, and also the clever Liu, who remembered every hieroglyphic at first glance. I liked the teacher's son at once. He talked to me as to an equal. He did not look down at me nor bite off his words.

He respected me because I could learn as many hieroglyphics in a day as he could climb trees. He had a genius for climbing trees. Never in my life have I met another like him. His agility came close to that of the monkeys. He would climb the trunk, swing himself to the side branches, sway on them as though they were a trapeze. Then, aiming somewhere into the green thickness of a neighboring tree, he would catapult himself over, from one tree to another. Sometimes he would show the perfection of his skill by tying a handkerchief over his eyes and climbing a tree blindfolded.

A year after our acquaintance began he climbed to the top of a tree and began swinging . . . sprang off to fly to the next . . . and missed. He flashed downwards, tearing off the green leaves as he fell, hit the ground and died.

The second day of school. I did my first writing. The teacher passed over my first hieroglyphic. He drew a little circle beside the second. The old pupils stretched out their necks from their benches like geese, and whispered to the class: "An egg." The teacher would mark the well written hieroglyphics with an egg, the bad and blotted ones he crossed. Taking their papers off the teacher's table the pupils would show the class with their fingers how many eggs they had received.

At home my uncle, grandmother and mother surrounded me, asking: "How many eggs?" I received four eggs on my first day of writing.

"When you get eggs for each written hieroglyphic, I'll give you a real one," laughed my grandmother.

The days followed one another like a row of railroad ties. And I, like a diligent little engine, moved from one hieroglyphic to another, from page to page, passing the dull-witted boys, competing with the clever ones. In a month I had caught up with those who had spent six months in school. My work became more complicated. The teacher would draw a hieroglyphic, leaving a blank space above and below it. I had to write other hieroglyphics in this space and form a sentence.

The fat, lazy boys of the class were indifferent to my success. After three years of school, it must be frankly confessed, they had less in their heads than I after three months. For them the school was but one continuous yawn. Like blunt-nosed hens they would pick twenty or thirty times at the same hieroglyphic and still be unable to swallow it. Their eyes, gliding over the pages of the book, would stubbornly turn to the window through which they could see the pink, yellow and orange fruit hiding among the leaves in the teacher's garden.

But the clever comrades, whose ambition mounted no less than did mine, left me behind without any effort. I recall one of them. I could not compete with him. He used to remember the most complicated hieroglyphic, after looking at it only once. Through the elaborate thickets of writing he would pass smilingly, like a skipping child. Today he is begging in the streets of our village. He never finished school.

His mother, a widow, used to smoke opium. Life to her was worth nothing without opium. Her house, her garden, and all her fortune were smoked away through her opium pipe. At that time her boy was receiving an inheritance from his bachelor uncle. His mother had no rights to the property. In order to get her hands on his inheritance, she taught her son, a school-boy, to smoke.

He stopped studying. His eyes lost their brilliance, he grew weak. During the day he would be dull and sleepy. He livened up only toward night. The smokers of opium are like bats—they live at night. He forgot even how to hold a brush. He was thrown out of school. His eyes would brighten only at the sight of the opium pipe through which his inheritance was disappearing in light smoke. When the money was all used up, he went out to a street-corner of Sian-Shih and the first beggar-

pennies clinked in his hand. But these pennies were for opium.

Between lessons the "model" pupils would wander around with a book. The lazy ones would wake up and try to get to the garden, near the fruit. If the teacher's wife saw them she would only lower her eyes. She was too good-natured and too gentle to upbraid them. She would pass through the garden not wishing to notice anybody. The little thieves would noisily chew the fruit, rustle in the leaves and become more and more impudent.

Once the teacher brought one of them, caught red-handed, into the classroom. The teacher shook with anger.

"What is bad is not the fact that you ate my fruit—my garden is open for all worthy pupils—but the fact that you, such an irredeemable idler and ignoramus, steal my apricots instead of reading a book. I forbid all idlers, like you, even to touch the fruit."

Then he took the bamboo ruler from the wall and seizing the pupil by the fingers, beat him on the palms of his left hand and on his back. The pupil stamped his feet with pain and broke into a howl. But immediately his terrible yell was covered by a frightened scream which came from me. For the first time in my life I had witnessed corporal punishment. It was too much for me. Everybody was amazed—the class, the teacher, even the criminal.

"What is the matter?"

"I am afraid."

The whole class burst into laughter. Even the tortured pupil screwed up his wet eyes. Even the never-smiling teacher smiled. But not for long. He hit the table with the slab of wood, then he took me by the hand and led me over to his wife. When I came back to the class everything was in order, except the criminal who was sniffling over his paper.

Ever after that when he was about to punish a pupil, the teacher would send me to his wife. The gentle, sweet and quiet Sy-Mu would give me a candy or a peach, or taking me by the hand would lead me into the garden, away from the classroom where, under the singing blows of the bamboo ruler, the tortured pupil was wriggling and screaming.

7. Father

My YOUNGER UNCLE WAS A TALL, HUSKY FELLOW. HE TAUGHT children in a public school of Sian-Shih, and the children loved him. My older uncle was sly, intriguing, nervous. The younger was always clear, simple and straightforward. But there were days when the smile would vanish from his face. He would disappear from the house, and when he came back, he would go to the kitchen for advice from my mother. Sometimes I heard the tail-end of their conversations.

"The old Tun does not want to do it."

"What about the young one?"

"The young one was used last year."

"Why don't you ask Tchao as a third member? Or the one-eyed Fan."

"I am afraid of Fan. He is just waiting for an invitation in order to demand that I, in return, join his group."

Names piled on names. They counted on their fingers all the relatives and kin, of which there were hundreds in the district. My uncle disappeared again. Finally, entirely exhausted, he came to mother's kitchen and said:

"It's all done. I found all ten of them. Have the dinner ready."

And the peaceful smile again came to his gentle face. I knew what this mysterious running about meant. My uncle was trying to get money for father.

Father's education in Japan came to about 400–500 da yang a year. All we could squeeze out of our tangerine orchard and my uncle's earnings as a teacher, was about a hundred a year. In order to produce the rest of the money uncle organized mutual loan groups. Such a group usually consisted of about ten members besides the organizer. Each one would lend, say, fifty da yang. This made the five hundred needed by the organizer of the group. The following year the payments began. Every one contributed except the first invited. This time he would get the five hundred. On the third year the second invited would get his five hundred, and so on until in ten years all the indebtedness was paid.

The loan was not a free loan. The interest on it was quite large. The organizer, who got his five hundred, had to pay not fifty but sixty yearly. And the member who received his five hundred last, got his interest by paying only forty-five da yang instead of fifty a year.

The order in which the members received money was decided according to their needs. If one of them had to marry off his son the following year, he asked to be first. Another, who intended to repair his house four years hence, might take the fourth turn. And perhaps another who had some free cash on hand would agree to wait ten years. If a member happened to be in need of a large sum of money before his turn, he might organize a new group of his own with more members, and the organizer of the original group who had invited him to join, had to enter this new group.

This way we managed every year with the payment for father, collecting new loans and paying each year more and more of what was due, out of the hundred da yang of our income.

My older uncle entered the house swiftly, solemnly.

"Your father will soon be back. Sit down and listen to me."

Then, in a slow chant, letting the words fall, in a tongue which I could hardly understand, he recited an old poem of the time of the Tang dynasty. I watched his mouth and repeated after him the solemn lines full of pathos. They were dedicated to a man returning home after an absence of many years.

"As a young man you went away from your family.
As an old man you return to your family.
The native tongue is still the same,
But your moustache and your hair are grey.
The children do not know you when they see you.
They ask the guest, with a smile:
What is your name?
Where do you come from?
And what do you want?"

I smiled at the last line.

These were almost the exact words I used to say, with an obligatory smile, when representing the head of the family and replacing my tired mother. I remember how, as a tiny child, I used to totter out into the reception room to greet the large, grey-haired or bald and fat acquaintances who came to pay us a visit on New Year's day and the holiday of the Dragon.

"How is your esteemed family?
Whence have you been kind enough to come?
Whom might you wish to see?"

"You'll greet your father with this verse," said my uncle. And as he left the room, his glance was averted; he seemed unusually excited. What could the matter be?

Usually, when the name of my father was mentioned, he frowned and complained that father had given up a perfect job as his assistant in the school, and had left for Japan, without rhyme or reason.

Father, to pay his way, had borrowed some money from grandfather's sister's husband and with that money got as far as Shanghai. From there he had sent a letter to the family. It was from this letter that my older uncle learned, for the first time, where father was. Outraged, he had sworn that he would never give him a cent. That was why it was my younger uncle who organized the mutual loan groups.

Proud of his standing as a member of the learned professions, a monarchist and a connoisseur of antique poetry, my older uncle was furious because my father had left the old way of scholarship and had gone to study in a "barbarous" country. In spite of it all, now he came to teach me a poem of welcome. I went to mother's drawer and took out a photograph of a young man about twenty-five years of age. This quiet, austere face was that of my father. I knew him only by this photograph which had been sent to us from Japan.

Something, in the middle of the night, awakened me. The house was full of commotion.

An alarm? A fire? A death? An assault?

Mother's bed was empty. Grandmother was not there either.

"Grandma! Grandma!" I was frightened, ready to cry.

Grandmother came in elated, and said:

"Get up, your father is back."

My pants, robe, stockings and slippers flew through the air. In a moment I was dressed. Grandmother took me by the hand and led me to the li tang. The room was black with people. We pushed through them to the middle where there was a little more space. I stumbled over an open suitcase, almost pulling grandmother's arm from its socket. I lifted my eyes and saw father clad in a suit of European clothes, his hair cut short. The costume pleased me at once, also that he wore no braid, that he looked at me with cold austere eyes, that he made not a step nor a gesture in my direction. Opposite father were my two uncles and behind them moved the heads of the crowd.

Hands stretched out past uncle's robe to touch the material of my father's jacket. One hand in a torn blue sleeve, the hand of a fisherman or a coolie, reached out to feel the back of father's close-shorn head. Then it drew back, timidly.

My older uncle glowed with an unusual smile, like a bright oil lamp.

"Shih-hua, come here."

His smile continued to play irrepressibly over his face.

"Shih-hua, do you remember a verse I taught you to say?"

My mosquito voice sang out in the sudden stillness.

> *"What is your name?*
> *Where did you come from?*
> *Whom do you want?"*

I stopped. Uncle turned proudly toward my father.

"Well, Ya-pu, didn't I teach him well? Your son can already recite Tang verse."

My father bent down, lifted me in his arms and half-tenderly, half-mockingly asked: "Do you just recite this verse, or do you understand it, too?"

Without taking my eyes away from his cold inquiring glance, I answered: "I understand it."

"How?"

Looking past my father's ear I began to stammer.

"Talk more clearly."

"My uncle explained it to me."

Father let me down on a large suitcase from which I could see everything.

The crowd grew tired of being quiet. The shadows on the walls began to move. A gawky, hoarse voice shouted laughingly: "Yan Gu-tze, Yan Gu-tze" (a faked foreign devil). My father seemed an impostor to them. His face, speech, name—these were all native, but his appearance was that of a barbarian.

More and more people appeared from the darkness of the night. Buttoning their robes as they came, the neighbors entered only half-awake, but all excited. The boatmen who had brought

[38]

my father over the Yangtze stood about, their heavy arms crossed over their clay-covered shirts.

The bigfooted carriers of *tzao*—the stretchers in which people travel over our paths—gossiped in subdued voices. Even the night watchman, who guarded the sleep of the five thousand inhabitants of Sian-Shih, looked into the room over the shoulders of the people. The big gong he carried resounded softly as it struck his knee.

Almost crushed by the staring, pushing, breathing crowd, my father stepped forward and said, "Unfortunately my parlor is small and I cannot receive all my dear neighbors. But I can offer them a light amusement."

He bent over his suitcase, rustled the paper, dropped cardboard boxes on the floor and took out a shining box. A glistening black disk under an enormous metallic flower began to turn. Suddenly from the flower-like horn came the strong, hoarse measures of a military song. The crowd rushed to the doors. Somebody was trampled underfoot. Then they began to laugh, got over their fright, and surrounded the phonograph. While my father wound it up and turned over the glistening disk, their curious fingers got into the horn, touched the nickel surface, felt the disk and the point of the needle. Some nodded disapprovingly. My father lifted his hand and reassured the people.

"There is nothing inside this box. It is difficult to explain in a few words how this machine works, but I promise to tell you about it in detail at a more convenient time."

The crowd forgave the phonograph, for the time being, its human voice and howling orchestra. Leaving it under a slight suspicion, they turned to father's baggage. They fingered the canvas cover of his suitcase. There are no canvas suitcases in Sian-Shih where all our belongings are packed in leather and wooden chests. They tried to lift the heavy case. In vain. Their eyes met in suspicion, they frowned, I heard the whispered word, "Gold."

Father took out a key. The bulging pod of the suitcase popped, opened, and with a light rustle, glossy books slid out from its inside.

The people weighed them in their hands. What heavy books! Chinese books are as light as feather pillows. And they are made differently. In a Chinese book only one side of a long strip of paper is covered with hieroglyphics. It is then folded over like an accordion and bound. These foreign books were made of small separate sheets of paper printed on both sides. The hieroglyphics in these books were different too. They turned the books in their hands, looked at them upside-down and laughed, unable to read the Japanese words.

"What a barbarous language!"

The noise, the shuffling of feet, the boom of many voices did not stop until the grey dawn cut a square of light in the doorway of our room.

Sleep was closing my lids. I heard the voice of my younger uncle over my head.

"The boy should be in bed."

I clutched grandmother's hand and stumbled out.

My father managed to conceal from the neighbors the baggage that made his suitcase so heavy. Black, Japanese hand-grenades.

8. The Chief of Police

IN JAPAN MY FATHER HAD STUDIED LAW. THE LAW COLLEGE OF the university included the study of military science. Also in this college prospective police officers could take the necessary studies. My father chose the latter course.

It was in 1910, after a five-year absence, that my father returned to Sian-Shih. Shortly before that, in 1905, a group of revolutionary societies organized by Sun Yat-sen, had ordered its members to infiltrate the government institutions and to seek appointments to all available posts, especially the army and the police. The rifles were there, and rifles were what the revolutionists needed.

Sixty li (about thirty miles) from Sian-Shih lay our county seat, Teh chien. The *daoyin* (official of the prefecture) of Teh chien soon learned that an educated Chinese, who knew police work, had arrived at Sian-Shih from Japan. He summoned my father to Teh chien and offered him the post of chief of the county police.

"It is a newly created post," said the sly old man. "It is not in the budget, so I'll pay you only eight da yang a month."

"I understand," said my father.

"We must organize a school of instructors," continued the daoyin, "and teach our present cut-throats civilized manners."

"I understand," answered my father.

"Then we would not need to be afraid of all these lovers of disturbance and disorder," concluded the head of the city of Teh chien.

Father left the daoyin's office as chief of the county police.

When he brought home the news, mother, at his curt command, went to pack his things. Now he would have to live in Teh chien and could come to see us at Sian-Shih only once in a while. My older uncle was furious. Of the eight rules of polite manners he forgot the second, the fifth, and the seventh, which lay upon one respectively, the duties of brotherly love, politeness and disinterestedness. He ran back and forth in front of my father, raging with indignation.

"You are crazy! Eight da yang a month! It would be better to carry people in a tzao or to fish! You spent so much money abroad. You are in debt up to your ears. You have to pay it back. . . . Shih-hua will be put out of school unless his tuition is paid. . . . Your wife is all worn out without a servant. . . . The whole district will point at you. . . . Eight da yang a month, and you accept? . . . You must not accept this post."

Impassive, father watched the angry gestures of his brother.

"Why don't you say something?" continued the latter. "I tell you the truth. I, being older, must tell you this truth."

Exhausted, my uncle sat down, shrugging his shoulders and twitching his eyebrows. Father smiled.

"What can you tell me that's any good? You understand nothing."

Infuriated, my uncle ran toward the door behind which mother was bending over a suitcase. He waved his arms in despair and rushed out.

Father arranged two holsters on his belt and attached a long police sword. Now, I thought, he will come to me. Since the night of his arrival he has never even touched me. He walked toward me, looking straight at me. Worshipfully, I tried hard to guess what his eyes were asking of me—those eyes in which shone no hint of gentleness. I was mistaken. He looked me through. He passed by me swiftly, and the slight wind of his passing fanned my cheeks.

My younger uncle, large and radiant, noiselessly hurried after father. His warm hand remembered to stroke my stubbornly lowered head as he went by.

My father disappeared to Teh chien where he was organizing a police school. He came to see us rarely. Once, at most twice a month, a boat would bring him over from Teh chien. On these occasions his metal scabbard would ring over the flat stones of the court and two orderlies, their uniforms buttoned to the chin, would follow him.

I remember one of these visits. Briskly he nodded to my mother. My smiling uncle was already there, in front of him. My father, hearing the approach of my older uncle, who was in a hurry to greet the infrequent guest, whispered: "We must get Sao-pu out of here."

Then he walked toward the beaming Sao-pu. The latter, squinting his eyes ironically, preparatory to quoting a particularly exquisite verse of an ancient poet, was robbed suddenly of his irony, his verse, and his smile.

"Lao Sao, I want you to move to your school for two or three days, while I am here. The house is crowded; I have soldiers with me. I am sorry to inconvenience you."

The older brother threw a ferocious glance at the younger. Father interrupted him.

"I have already talked it over with Tsi-tze. He is also going to sleep at the school."

My younger uncle, with an air of complete despair, nodded his head affirmatively. But the lover of verse did not surrender. The respectful "lao" (old man) with which father began his speech to him, while addressing the younger one with the intimate "tze", did not work.

"An outrage! And why do you work in the police department for so miserable a salary? You should have found a better job and rented a better house, instead of this hole. I cannot even have a talk with you during your visits."

Father smiled. "I understand, I understand. Let us be patient. The time will come. We will have a large house. Then, permit me to hope, you'll stay with me always, and we'll talk all we want."

My uncle shrugged his shoulders and shuffled his slippers discontentedly. Meanwhile father was saying softly to the younger uncle, "Go and stay with him until sundown. Then come back to conduct the meeting, and I'll go stay with him. Otherwise, God forbid, he might get lonely and come to see us."

On such days mother had no time left to look at me, even when I dropped into the kitchen for some tea.

I remember, on another of his visits, hearing father talking to my younger uncle, in a low voice.

"Did anybody come from Sun Yat-sen?"

"Yes, two men."

"Did they stay long? Did you take care of them? Was a place arranged for them to pass the night? Were they fed?"

"Yes."

"When did they leave?"

"Late at night."

"The back gate does not squeak?"

"I oiled it."

Mysterious, unknown to any of us, these nocturnal guests would arrive from afar and enter our house with great precaution. They would ask for my father, stay in the back rooms and vanish in the darkness, when everybody in Sian-Shih was fast asleep, and only the night watchman rang his gong marking the five divisions of the night. After seeing such a guest off, mother would return to the bedroom. Careful not to wake me, she would gently set the lamp on the table. Noticing that I was awake and that my eyes looked like two interrogation points, she would bend over me, stroking my cover with her tired fingers.

"Shih-hua, do not tell anybody that strangers come to our house."

Days passed.

It was evening. I was washing my dusty feet. Through the sound of splashing water I heard careful steps and a light knock at the gate.

"Uncle," I said softly.

"Yes?" Through the thin papered walls his voice sounded as loud as if he were in the same room.

"Somebody is knocking at the gate."

Uncle almost ran to the gate. I heard his slippers shuffle. Father hurried after him. Making tracks with my wet feet, I looked through the crack in the door.

Opposite my father stood a strange young man. Father

looked at him without recognition, and then cried out in a restrained voice: "Le-wu, Chang Le-wu!"

That night I woke up often. In father's room the light burned till dawn and the indistinct mumbling of two voices did not cease all night. The guest left in the morning. His eyes were wet with tears when he said good-bye, and you could see the muscles move under the skin of my father's jaw.

After the revolution which overthrew the Tsing dynasty, Chang Le-wu became one of the two revolutionary governors who ruled the province of Szechuan. He was shot by order of the dictator Yuan Shi-kai, when the revolution broke down.

One night horses' hooves were heard at our gate. Father was home. We all rushed out. One of the new arrivals dismounted and, turning to his comrades, said gaily:

"You did not forget where each of you is to sleep tonight?"

"Who is that?" whispered my younger uncle, standing behind father's back and trying in vain to see through the dark.

"Sze Tin-chen." Father waved away my uncle and made a step forward. "Tin-chen, there is enough room for all your comrades in my house. Dismount. Bring your horses in."

The horde, dragging their feet, spread over the small courts of our house. The sound of hooves on the pavement, the smell of horse-sweat and of tired dirty human bodies filled the place. The horses were soon led away somewhere and only the men remained.

Sze Tin-chen was as modest as one of mother's girl pupils. I was impressed by his enormous black beard which hung down like tassels of a black silk shawl from his cheeks and chin.

The guests were seated around the table. They took off their heavy revolvers which had little chains attached to them, hung them on the backs of their chairs or laid them down on the table next to their chopsticks.

I whispered to my younger uncle, "I like him."

And uncle replied, also in a whisper, "Nobody can make better bombs in all Szechuan, than he makes. The daoyin is after him. He offers a thousand da yang for his head."

"With the beard?" The question almost slipped off my tongue, I liked Sze Tin-chen's beard so much.

The people at the table were arguing.

"Where can we find guns?"

"Make them yourselves," shouted Tin-chen and his eyes were lost in laughter. He took from his pocket a strange iron object and threw it on the table. Father immediately picked it up and examined it. It was a gun lock.

After supper, Tin-chen and his comrades made themselves ready for bed. They took off their jackets and sat around with only their shirts on, scratching their chests.

"But where are your things?" asked my uncle.

"That's all we have, what's on us."

My uncle was embarrassed. Father called to my mother. She came from the kitchen and listened to father's quiet order.

"You'll have to sew each one a shirt and do their laundry. They'll stay about five days. We must find them some money for the trip. Are there no more silk blankets left which we could pawn?"

I grew more and more interested in Sze Tin-chen. Waking up in the morning I immediately stole toward his room. I stopped short at the entrance. His splendid black beard was falling to the floor in big flakes under the serpent-like movements of his razor.

He greeted me laughingly.

"Hello, young Shih-hua of the family Tan."

His face was now entirely changed; last night's magnificence, together with his beard, was on the floor.

"Have you eaten today, O esteemed Shih-hua, first born of my friend Tan Ya-pu?"

He smiled at my amazement. Then he began to do something which I could not understand at all. He took out of a box some

[46]

hairy imitation warts and stuck them on his face. He opened his bulging suitcase, which was filled with funny little books that had amusing pictures on their jackets. He made sure that his revolver was loaded, and closed the blinds of the window, leaving only a narrow crack which let in a beam of light. Then he sat down and read, holding the open pages of his little book in the beam of light. Full of new impressions and bewilderment I backed out of the room. His laughing voice reached me from inside.

"Shih-hua, shut the door, and shut it tight."

That day I spent wandering in the garden, speculating about the beard, the warts and the half-closed window blinds.

A few hours passed. The closed room drew me. I opened the door a little, thrust my head into darkness, and with unseeing eyes tried to locate him. He found me first.

"What have you on your mind, my young observer?"

I summoned all my courage and said, "You are not lonely, sitting here by yourself?"

He laughed, lifted his book, and then pulled his suitcase toward him.

"Look how many of them I have. How can I get lonely with all these?"

He stayed at our house longer than the others.

---

9. Conspiracy

Dinner was over. The guests had finished their rice and wiped their hands and faces with hot wet napkins. Mother had carried the dishes away. Quite unexpectedly and unnoticed, as if they had been hidden in the same room under chairs, three new guests appeared from somewhere. They greeted our guest of the warts and his friends. Father seated them around the table and said, "Let's begin."

Noticing that I did not get off my chair, and was listening attentively to the conversation, father turned his troubled eyes toward me and with an indifferent glance, as one would look at a cat or a dog, ordered me out of the room. I began to slip off my chair. A strong hand took hold of my shoulder. It belonged to the man with the warts. He looked entreatingly at my father and said respectfully, "Let him stay at the meeting, Tan. He is our successor. Let him learn."

Father turned his eyes away from me. I was beginning to understand. This was a conference of the revolutionists. A man, who came from afar, from Sun Yat-sen himself, was anxiously inquiring from my father, how big a force he had assembled and whether or not it would be possible to come out against the daoyin with the latter's two battalions armed with European rifles. Father replied in a quiet, restrained voice, "I have recently sent a man with a report to Dr. Sun. I'll repeat to you in a few words how things stand. Our main support in this district comes from Go-Lao-Huei, the union of older brothers. When I came back here and received an order from the Committee of the party to get support from the Go-Lao I immediately became convinced that this ancient union with its definite slogan 'Down with the Tsing dynasty of Manchu oppressors!' had completely degenerated. It had become a mutual aid society and not an organization of militant revolutionaries. It was my task to transform this loose union of small landlords, professionals, soldiers, bandits, peasants, workers and tramps —this human dust—into something hard and inflexible, like a stone. I had to wake them up and fill them again with hatred for the Manchus—hatred which had been all soaked up by the grey ashes of indifference. At present I am a *da-ge* (the chief)— or as they also call me—the first old brother, for the all-eastern

[48]

part of the Szechuan. My assistants are: Comrade Kuen—the third old brother, whose days are entirely occupied by intra-union disputes, and the fifth old brother—Fu, who spends all his time on the road. He just missed you and is now on his way to Sun Yat-sen with my reports. Besides this principal trio, there are five other working brothers. Should a bullet or the ax of the daoyin find us, they will replace us.

"All the boys studying in my police school are members of Go-Lao. They constitute the most devoted group. Moreover, they have revolvers and swords.

"I direct all members of Go-Lao-Huei, who come to me and try to get into the school, to hire themselves out as soldiers and as staff employees in the army. There they will get a rifle and be ready for the signal. At present, in every village of Szechuan, the local committees of Go-Lao are at work. They are no longer clubs of rich and idle poets, nor gangs of brigands ready to rob every passer-by, nor pitiful, mutual-aid societies.

"The local committees are now becoming military units. There the members learn boxing, the use of the sword and the lance. The only thing we still need is rifles. I have ordered our bandits to try to get arms instead of money. I am afraid the daoyin will finally understand the meaning of all these assaults on the arsenal, on the military storehouse, and on the sentries."

"And are there no traitors in the union?" asked our friend with the warts.

"There were two. One of them was stabbed. The other was thrown into the Yangtze with a rock around his neck. This was exactly three hours after they had reported on the meetings held in my house."

"How did you escape yourself?"

Father smiled crookedly.

"Pure luck. The people to whom they had reported turned out to be also members of the Go-Lao. We have our people in the least expected posts. It was a very clever decision of Sun Yat-sen to get the union of old brothers into the work."

"Does it mean that we can regard the preparation period as finished?" asked one of the strangers impatiently.

Father frowned and shook his head.

"We cannot be in a hurry. We have not enough arms. We must intensify the organization. We need more discipline, and it is most important that we strike at the Manchus on the same day, the same hour, the same minute in every province. Only then will they fall, never to rise again."

"What is the state of conspiratory societies in other provinces?"

One of the strangers replied, "In the South things are going well. We are working together with a conspiratory union—San Ke-huei. Its membership consists almost entirely of peasants. Temperamental people. There are still some old people living who remember the time of the Taiping rebellion, when the peasants cut off their braids and declared an independent state over all southern China. The situation is more difficult in the North along the sea shore. The union of the boxers was very powerful there once. But they were so badly beaten by the foreign punitive forces for their insurrection of 1900, and also by the Manchu dynasty who provoked them to this insurrection, that even now they are still weak."

Father was no longer listening to the guests; all his attention was centered on the front door. He sprang to his feet, and unbuttoning the holster of his revolver on the way, pointed upstairs where a door led into the garden.

"Shih-hua, you'll show the way."

Then he ran rapidly toward the sound. In a second he was back.

"It is my orderly."

The guests, who had jumped from their chairs and crowded together, sat down again.

My head could hardly hold all I heard. I caught some fragments of whispered conversation between my father and the friend with the warts: "Tsing," "Manchu," "Sun Yat-sen," "daoyin," "rifle."

"The worst thing," said my father, with a frown, "is that the dead are holding us by the throat. Five million Manchurians conquered China three hundred years ago. All that is left of them now consists of just a few high officials, a gang of courtiers and several hundred thousand fat and lazy gendarmes scattered over the provinces. They have even forgotten their own language. The Manchurians and the officials are sucking the strength out of the living Chinese people. For three hundred years the Chinese people organized insurrection after insurrection and for three hundred years the Manchurians quelled these insurrections. Can it be that again the dead will prove stronger than the living? Will our heads roll over the stones of the *yamen?*"

While listening to my father, the friend with the warts was watching my face change according to every mood of my father. Interrupting my father's speech he suddenly said, "Tan, send your little Shih-hua to Japan to study acting."

Father, quickly glancing at me, asked suspiciously, "You do not believe in the success of the insurrection? Do you want to save him for the perpetuation of the family? Send him away from a place where he might get burned?"

The other replied gaily, "Why, not at all. Shih-hua will make an excellent agitator. An actor can get anywhere; into a city, into a village, into a private house—and no daoyin will ever be suspicious of him."

"Shih-hua, go to bed." Thus father ended my first participation in a political conference of the Szechuan section of the party of Tung Men Huei, which, under the leadership of Sun Yat-sen, united all liberty-loving Chinese intellectuals.

As I undressed and tossed and turned under my blanket, I heard the meeting disperse. Some footsteps came from the direction of the gate; others from the dark room with the closed blinds. There were also footsteps, lonely and firm, which seemed to be falling endlessly on the stones of our court. Then they stopped. There was the sharp clang of a revolver chain against the stone, and then silence. It was my father, the da-ge of eastern Szechuan thinking of his landlords, his bandits, his boatmen.

A few days passed. Another night had come. Suddenly I awoke. From far over the tile roofs of Sian-Shih, I heard the gong being struck three times. It was the night watchman announcing the third part of the night. I felt that our house was not asleep. Although there were no shouts, no sounds of dishes, no shuffling of feet, some indistinct mumbling in the direction of the reception room troubled me.

I slid out of bed, threw my robe over my shoulders, and, clinging to the wall, walked towards the reception room. I reached the window. I moved away the shreds of the torn paper and put an anxious and curious eye against a hole in the window. In the room a solid ring of people was seated around a table. You might have thought they were playing dice. Such a solidly set ring of people I had seen only at a county fair.

Candles were burning on the table, on window-sills and on the cupboard. They could hardly burn in the thick, warm, sweaty air. Clean-shaven heads wound in towels, and heads in glossy little caps were all turned toward the man sitting at the head of the table. He was the chief of all those people secretly gathered in our house. It was my father. One of the heads bent toward his and whispered something to him. Father thought for a moment in the silence. I heard bits of plaster drop, evidently knocked down by awakened rats, from somewhere in the attic. Then my father made a speech, dry and sharp as the bark of a revolver.

"Brothers, I have just been informed that brother Lo-han has been captured by the daoyin's guard. He was procuring rifles in the barracks of the guard. Tomorrow he will be cross-questioned, the day after tomorrow executed. Fourteen members of his family will follow him. But the main thing is, his loss means that our hands are tied. The supply of guns depends entirely on him. We need him. It is absolutely necessary that he should be at work tomorrow."

A voice—I could not see the man who spoke—interrupted my father.

"Some of the prison guards are members of the union. He can be free tonight."

Father went on.

"To free him means throwing fourteen innocent men to the hangman. It means, moreover, the revelation of the fact that Lo-han is connected with the organization. The daoyin must believe that Lo-han has been executed."

Again the same voice, as if continuing father's speech, concluded:

"Lo-han could be replaced by some other brother."

The circle of people around my father suddenly widened. Father quietly examined the ring of faces. The silence was finally broken by a dull, unfamiliar voice.

"Da-ge, say who must go in place of Lo-han."

For the first time I heard gentleness in my father's tones.

He explained that the ancient rule of the union of Go-Lao endowed the chief with the right to send a substitute for a brother who is to be executed. But he was not going to name him now. The night was before him. He would think about it. In the morning he would inform the one who is to go into the prison cell to replace the freed brother.

Two heads leaned toward father. I knew one of them. It belonged to the proprietor of a tea-house in the marketplace. The other man, judging by his dress, was a peasant from the mountain region.

The peasant complained, "Da-ge, I had nothing to eat for two days. I came to the tea-house, as I was instructed. I gave the password and poured my tea in the cups the way I was told to do when I want a brother to recognize me. But that man pretended he did not understand my signals, and threw me out of his house."

The tea-house owner tried to explain, "The brother gave the password incorrectly. I never saw him before. The spies of the daoyin are nosing about everywhere. How could I know that he was one of us?"

Father ended their dispute.

"Find him a place to sleep, and give him a good supper."

The peasant sat back in his chair contentedly.

One by one the heads leaned toward my father. He sat motionless and listened to the brief reports of those sullen-lookng, hard-headed people, who had come there from the cities, villages, castles, offices and fishermen's huts of eastern Szechuan.

When all the reports were delivered father said:

"We must get ready for the general meeting of the union. The local sections of Go-Lao-Huei should begin electing delegates. I and the old brothers will choose the mountain where the meeting will be held, and we will let you know. This year it will have to meet in an especially isolated place. The worst thing that could happen now would be our failure to overthrow the Tsing dynasty. Only one question will stand in the order of the day—the insurrection."

A few heads again interfered between me and my father's voice. They talked with restraint and humility as if asking for something. Lifting his head over their mumbling, father said something to my younger uncle who was sitting all this time at the table next to him, writing hieroglyphics on strips of paper.

"Tsi-pu, they lost their jobs. See that they get some money from the fund. And also remind brothers—" father named two very respectable families in Sian-Shih "—that the da-ge did not get any presents from them on the last two holidays. They have enough money and in these days we have to be particular about such matters."

Only then did I understand the meaning of all those boxes,

baskets, and packages, that were brought in daily and stored away in the cellar of our meager house, enriching it with piles of fruit, grain, materials, etc. They were the stock of the Go-Lao-Huei.

One of those seated around the table got up, a lanky man with big eye-glasses gleaming under his brow. He spoke of someone who wanted to be admitted into the membership of Go-Lao. He vouched for him as for himself. He expressed a hope that the da-ge would support his request before the assembly. But before father had a chance to say a word, a short, fat man rose in front of the bespectacled speaker. He seemed familiar. He looked like a merchant. He did not speak, he barked like a fat, hoarse dog.

"He must not be admitted! He must not be admitted! Only newborn babies do not know that his wife fools around with actors who often come to his house to give performances while he is away on his business trips."

Father made an attempt to interrupt the barking.

"But he belongs to a good family. His father and grandfather had a reputation for being almost the only government officials who never had their names connected with theft, speculation or the punishment of innocent people."

The barking continued.

"Everybody warned him—get a divorce, get a divorce, send your wife to her parents. But he is so weak that he goes on keeping this two-legged disgrace in his house. He is made of wax, and a member of Go-Lao should be cast in iron. I am against his admission."

The lanky man gleamed through his eye-glasses and sat back in his chair. He had nothing to say in defence of his friend.

A broad-shouldered fellow in a silk turban advanced from the crowd. I noticed the handles of two big knives in his belt. He leaned carefully on the table, as if he were afraid that he might break it, and said to my father: "The tax-collector will be coming this way in four days. My men will capture him in the canyon. Where shall we bring the money—here or to Teh chien?"

"Bring it here."

"How much money shall I give my men?"

"We'll discuss that after you bring the money."

Father stood up. He told the assembly about the Manchu dynasty. He told them how after the seizure of cities loyal to the Ming dynasty, Manchu armies slaughtered their entire population. They destroyed all that was alive in them to the last child, the last dog, the last hen. He told them about the powerful nation that inhabits the Eastern Isles—Japan, which has in its possession steel-clad ships, armies that can beat the Europeans, and newspapers which are read by hundreds of thousands of people. He explained to his listeners why the cost of rice was going up—because all the precious materials, coal, iron, cotton, tea, rice and pitch, bought for copper tung tze, were being exported from China in the greedy, capacious ships of the foreigners.

He explained how these foreign devils were tearing off one province after another, bit by bit from Chinese territory. Chinese railroads belonged to foreigners, Chinese custom-houses were occupied by foreigners, Chinese money poured into foreign pockets.

"Don't forget," he cried, "what the Canadian missionaries did to Comrade Tin. They bought land from him on which to build their church. And when Tin took the money they had given him to the bank, all of it was found to be counterfeit. He took his case to court. At the trial the Canadian priests smilingly asserted that Tin had lied, that they had paid him in real money. The judge said to Tin: 'I have no way of getting money from foreigners. Such is our ill-fate. I cannot help you.' I prevented Tin from jumping in the river. I said to him: 'The day will come when we will drag these Canadian priests over the hard earth which they cheated you out of.' "

Father's voice rang with anger—simple and convincing. With the story of these Canadians, which I heard that night, through the hole in the window, began my hatred of all foreigners in China.

In the heavy, stuffy air of the room, the serious heads listened to my father. I seemed to be in a classroom with a teacher.

"Until we overthrow the Manchus," said father in a clear, distinct voice, "nothing will change the terrible fate of the Chinese people."

Suddenly he pulled out of his black jacket a black watch. The meeting was over. Before the unbearably austere eyes of my father could find me, I ran away, through a little court, up a stair-case, through a passage and into my room. I got under the canopy and under the soft warm blanket, close to my mother.

Far away over Sian-Shih the watchman struck his gong five times, marking the last part of the night.

---

10. "How Dare You Lie to Your Father?"

I NO LONGER STUDIED WITH FAN HSIEN BUT ATTENDED MY younger uncle's school, which was an abandoned temple.

In one half of it a priest kept his tame wooden gods in their stalls, in the other half my uncle taught his crowd of noisy youngsters. The classes were held on the porch. Big stone steps led from the porch to the court, which lay between two tall tulip trees. Their four-petalled leaves looked like the tracks of some strange animal. I had just ascended those steps with my cousin Chan.

It was a crisp cold day in autumn. I was chilly even in my

padded robe. Books did not interest us that morning. My
father had come back from Teh chien the night before, and
everybody in the house was on tip-toes.

The four-fingered paws of the leaves glistened in the sun.
They were red, and were falling from the tree with a slight
rustle. They were very interesting to watch. A thick sap was
trickling down from cuts in the bark. This sap was used to make
the coiffures of the village women shine as though they had
lacquered heads. And stingy old women rubbed it in their hair,
reluctant to spend money for a real hair tonic.

The dull, subdued voices of the pupils in the class went on
and on. They were learning by heart the verses and exquisite
prose of ancient authors. We sat and looked at the falling leaves.
Counting those falling leaves was almost a game . . . it was
even more interesting than shooting with our bamboo blow guns.

"You idlers!" My uncle said it three times before we heard
it. I had never before seen his face so angry.

"I do not want to bother teaching you, go home! Let your
father (I felt cold all over) and your uncle (my cousin's eyes
looked somewhere outside of the porch) teach you."

We lingered as long as possible on the porch, slowly putting
our books back into our bags, but uncle was silent. The road
back seemed awfully long. Chan began to tell me all he knew
about my father. He told me that when he used to teach all the
pupils dreaded him as if he were a dragon.

"It's clear," he said, "that he's going to give us a beating.
And it'll be a real one, too. Let's stay out till school is over.
We'll go to the circus that's just come to town. When we get
home we'll tell your father that we just came from the school,
and we'll run out and meet uncle on his way and tell him that
your father had given us the lesson."

The plan seemed to me amazingly clever, so we went to the
circus. There were clowns in the circus, a big camel led on a
chain by a tiny little boy, an ostrich, which walked like a horse,
and a dirty, fuzzy, sad-looking bear. Father, uncle, school and

[58]

forthcoming punishment—all were forgotten. The way home was easy and short. We lied to father honestly, openly and enthusiastically.

"School is out."

"Why so early?"

I did not expect the question, and my mouth went dry. But Chan replied politely, "It ended so early today because you were home, uncle. The younger uncle let us off before the usual time."

"How much did you read today?"

"As much as yesterday, uncle."

We ran out into the street and waited for the younger uncle. When we saw him coming with his big stride, we rushed forward to greet him, looking gay and happy.

"Well, did your father teach you?"

"Yes," we answered together.

"And did it hurt?"

"No," we shouted together.

We followed him to the house. He entered the room and went straight to father.

"Well, how did they read to you?"

"Why do you ask me, don't you teach them?" my father asked.

"They were idling so much today that I sent them home to see you."

Father turned white.

Only once before had I seen him look so terrible. He was sitting at the table once, thinking. A startled chicken jumped on the table. Father sprang up, pulled out his gun and shot the chicken. Dripping blood, the poor bird ran all over the court.

Father's hands grabbed our shoulders like iron pliers. Shaking us back and forth, he shouted, "Scoundrels! Liars! Long ago in America George Washington cut the favorite tree of his father, just out of malice. But when his father, angry, asked him who had done it, Washington told the truth, not fearing the punishment. Why did you lie to your father? How did you dare lie to your father?"

He snatched a bamboo ruler and struck us each in turn on the palms of our left hands. He was particularly merciless to me. I screamed. Unbearable tears flowed out of my eyes. The face of my father quivered. It gleamed, swelled, divided in two. For four days I could not pick up a thing with my swollen left hand.

Even now, whenever I stretch out my left arm and open my hand, I remember father's shouts about George Washington, the whistling of the bamboo cane, the face of my cousin.

That time when my father killed the chicken on the table, mother had asked him: "Why did you get so angry? You like little fish and cats. I never saw you strike a dog."

Father had answered sharply and ironically: "Breeding birds is an idler's occupation."

11. An Unfortunate Suggestion

MY UNCLE'S SCHOOL MOVED TO ANOTHER TEMPLE—A LITTLE larger than the old one, but farther away from our house. To prevent me from getting too tired, walking to and from the school, he took me to live with him, and sent me home every Saturday. He adopted the European method of holidays. In his school, just as in the public schools, we had one day a week for rest. In private schools the pupils had to sit over their books from one Chinese holiday to another, and holidays in China are just as rare as springs in a desert.

One week-day I was called out from the class. Our maid was

waiting for me. I gathered that something must be wrong with my mother. We had a maid in the house only on days when mother was unable to work. I walked home in a great hurry. On the way the maid told me news which I had not expected at all.

"Your mother has borne you a sister."

I was glad; I had always been so lonesome at home.

The maid turned me over to my grandmother. Craftily and solemnly, the old woman led me into mother's room. Mother was lying silent on her bed. She was pale and thin. Her arms were stretched out on the cover. A funny little bit of a bed stood next to hers. Something wrapped in white and made entirely of little balls and wrinkles was in it.

"A little girl," said grandmother.

I wanted to touch my little sister, but grandmother would not let me. Having failed in this, I decided to go immediately to a store, and get her some candy. Grandmother sat down on mother's bed and released her high, thin laughter. She would stop, look at me, then laugh again. I paid dearly for that candy. Grandmother knew how to laugh at people.

I said to her, "It is nice to have a girl."

"No, it is very bad," she said. "Here in Szechuan, we have to give a dowry with the bride. It is just an expense. It would be different if we were living in Kiangsu—there people pay the bride's family."

I did not agree with grandmother. But she did not care. She was laughing again, probably remembering that candy.

Careful not to spill it, the maid brought my mother a bowl of boiled chicken. Every woman in China gets boiled chicken for a few days after her labor. Chicken is good. I looked longingly at the bowl. Mother put me next to her on the bed, and we ate the chicken together.

Taking away the empty bowl, grandmother looked at me, and said seriously and in a business-like manner, "Really, Shih-hua, it would not be bad if mother bore you a sister or a brother every year; then you would eat chicken quite often."

A month later, our house was buzzing with relatives. Such a lot of them. Mother was walking about, sweet and affable, but still white and thin, although she had not worked all that month. She entered the sitting room with my little sister in her arms, and all the relatives, one after another, came up to her and touched the little big-eyed girl whose small stomach was covered with a red flannel apron—a protection against the cold. The relatives argued about whose nose the little girl was going to have, whose eyes, whose mouth. They wished her good fortune.

"May she grow up to be as intelligent as her mother."

"May she become a good hostess."

"May she be the most beautiful bride in Sian-Shih."

"She will be a famous authoress."

This last wish was expressed by my older uncle. I knew it because, being himself fond of writing, he always said the same thing to every newborn baby.

The inspection over, the little girl was wrapped up again and carried away. The relatives presented mother with gifts. There were eggs in woven baskets, cackling hens, bags of sugar, selected rice—beautiful rice, which one would like to string on a thread and wear for a necklace, so beautiful it was—and candies. . . .

Grandmother glanced from the bag of candy to me, and began laughing again.

The procession of relatives moved to the dining room. At the table, the return gifts from our family were distributed, each relative receiving two red eggs. I was sad; we did not have enough money, so I could not stick a gilt-paper hieroglyphic meaning "luck" on the eggs.

A year later, on my sister's birthday, the same relatives again crowded into our house. A red table-cloth was put on a table in the sitting room, and all sorts of objects were spread out: a needle and thread, a sauce-pan, a tea-pot, a paint-brush, ink, a knife, a book of verses, a book of stories, a flexible fencing foil, a piece of printed silk.

Then the little girl, who, in her embarrassment, was trying to stick her foot in her mouth, was brought to the table, to see what object she would pick up first. If she takes a brush, she will be an author; if she grabs at a sauce-pan, she will be a housewife; if she touches silk, she will be a well-dressed woman; if she picks up a foil, she will make herself famous as a heroine or a chieftain.

I don't know what object my little sister chose. Judging by the fact that she is now in Peking University, and shows a great deal of interest in literature, she must have chosen a brush or a book. However, she was a niece of two teachers. So many books and stationery were piled up that day on the red cloth that the insignificant needle and thread had no chance of getting into the hands of little Shih-kuen.

In those days, she was the important person in the house. But I did not mind. I was grown up. I was six years older than she.

---

12. Illness

THE MOST DIFFICULT WEEKS IN THE MATURING OF THE REVO-lution—the time when rifles, military units, and fighting spirit were being marshalled—passed by without disturbing my in-flamed brain.

I was sick. A high fever tossed me from moist heat into sticky chills. All the time, an evil snout, belonging to someone who hated and wished to kill me, stared at me from under the canopy of my bed. The physician of Sian-Shih again and again inspected my tongue and felt my pulse. He could not understand what was the matter. Finally mother wrapped me up in blankets, and my younger uncle carried me down to the Yangtze. I dimly remember the covered top of a large row-boat which three oarsmen were pushing, with their heavy oars, along the mad, rough, and rocky Yangtze, toward Teh chien.

I was in bed for eight months, in a room of my father's quarters, sweating with fever. At times I could hear through my delirium his eager footsteps in the next room. He never came in. We were of no interest to him. My little, whining sister, crawling in mother's arms, meant no more to him than a dead, fan-tailed fish floating in a glass bowl. He lived wholly in the oncoming revolution.

A physician came to see me often. He had stopped looking at my tongue and feeling my pulse. He would merely lift his eyebrows, as though surprised: "You don't say, he is still alive?" and would write a prescription. The bitterest medicine would flow down my throat over my wooden tongue, and the fever would continue to torment my insides, unabated. My bed and I would separate from the floor, and the whole room, the beams of the ceiling, the windows, the bottles of medicine that stood on my table near the pillow would begin to circle around me. The sky, at night, with the stars nailed into it, circles the same way around the still earth.

The room would turn round and round like a wheel, my lips would mutter nonsense, and my mother, next to me on a chair, after rocking my sister to sleep and putting her in a cradle, would sit and suffer silently. The crisis was slow to come. The illness stretched ahead like an unending swamp. Through mist, weakness, and the turning room, I remember the dead nights, the unbearably fatiguing flame of the oil lamp, and my mother, her smooth, white forehead near the flame, sewing and sewing, night after night. She was sewing some pieces of white material marked with red prints or hieroglyphics.

I asked her once, "Mother, what are you sewing?"

Startled, she gathered her material together in a tight bunch and said: "I am sewing a new suit for you, Shih-hua, for your recovery."

I did not believe her, but I did not question her any more. First of all, why should I need so many suits, and secondly, I saw that sometimes during the day, and sometimes at night, people came and took away piles of the material sewn by my mother, and still the heap would grow no smaller.

The summer was over. My illness was slowly passing. No longer did I have my firm, red cheeks. My sickness had made me weak and transparent. To this day, though I am a grown man, I bear in my hollow chest the mark of that illness.

Yellow October passed over Szechuan. The revolution was near. It was no longer possible to keep it hidden. A gunshot, a knife stab, and it would break out. My father looked dreadful. None of our family dared to come near him. He grew much thinner. His eyes were sunken, his lips and chin dark with bristles; his hair hung down in long, unclean locks, like the hair of a monk.

My younger uncle came to take me to the country. Mother cried bitterly, uncontrollably. I did not want to go to the country. I wanted to stay with mother. Father shouted angrily, and commanded. I, thin and almost blue, swayed on my feet from weakness, almost as grandmother would stagger on her golden lilies. Mother stepped between me and my father and, stroking my hair, whispered, "Go to the country, I'll come there right after you."

Now I know why she wished to stay with me! I was crawling back into life with difficulty, while she was already quietly going away from it.

It did not take long to get me ready. Mother's swift hands put into a bag my textbook with pictures, a tin jar full of jam, my favorite chess set, and my friend—a jumping jack carved into the likeness of a little old man.

I waited for my mother a day, I waited another; she did not come. In her place, beside me, was my grandmother. I could not recognize her. She seemed to be listening continually to what was going on sixty li from us in Teh chien. She walked about like a mechanical toy; the smallest noise would startle her. I began to understand why they had taken me away from the city. Why did mother not come?

She never came.

There was excitement in the city. A rumor passed around that my father was a revolutionist. The rumor reached the daoyin.

"What? The chief of police—a revolutionist?"

The incredulous old man decided to verify the rumor. He began in a roundabout way.

The daoyin's wife suddenly came to see my mother. She had a quick tongue, sharp eyes, and well-trained ears. They had tea, a chat, and they gossiped. Mother was happy and hospitable. She was so glad to see the esteemed wife of her husband's chief. She was so delighted to sit and talk with her for hours, forgetting her rest and sleep.

The next day my mother returned the visit to the daoyin's wife, and again there was tea-drinking and mutual admiration and the expression of sincere friendship.

How could mother go to the country, when it was necessary to blind the daoyin's eyes with the sweet, sticky dough of flattery? It would have looked as though the whole family were being sent away to the country, before the decisive day of the insurrection.

The verification of the rumor by his wife did not seem sufficient to the daoyin. A fancy, red invitation card was brought to my father. The daoyin invited him to come to a banquet.

Should he go or should he not? What if, in the middle of

the banquet, he were to fall suddenly, black all over, after drinking a glass of wine in his honor? Or, what if, suddenly, in the midst of the dinner, after a most delicious dish of shark fins, the hands of the daoyin's bodyguard were to grab him under the arms, take him out to the yard, and put him to death, using the favorite method, invented by the cruel, old man—a slow beating with a thick stick. But to stay away—that would have meant the ruin of all the preparation for the insurrection.

Father went to the banquet alone, taking no bodyguard of his own, according to the etiquette. The conversation at the dinner table was amiable. It almost fully reassured the old man, but he ordered a watch kept over my father's house, nevertheless.

From that day on, strange people, standing and gaping at nothing, appeared in the streets adjoining father's apartment and the police quarters. Entirely new peddlers had taken stands on the nearby corners. Because of this, my father issued orders to hold all secret meetings out of town. The work became unbearably difficult.

Every morning father would enter the court of police quarters. He would close the door of his room, which was guarded by sentry, and give orders that nobody be admitted. In half an hour a slovenly dressed, black-bearded peasant would come out from the court of the police quarters, looking exactly like one of those simpletons from the far-away mountain farms. Hiding his face under a large-brimmed straw hat, accompanied by a policeman, he would go away, passing the yawning watchers.

In the evening of the same day, a policeman would bring to the same court a ragged fruit-seller, carrying on his shoulders bamboo baskets of peaches and grapes. The appearance of the man would show definitely that he had to get a license. A half hour later, from the gates of the police department, passing a sentry standing at attention, my father would come out. Clad all in black from toe to finger-tip, his hand on the shiny, nickeled scabbard of his sword, he was going home after a day's hard

[67]

work. The secret meeting had been conducted, new military units looked over, directions given.

Next day the dangerous game would take place again.

---

13. The Insurrection

IT WAS 1911, ACCORDING TO THE EUROPEAN CALENDAR, OR the third year of the reign of the Emperor Suan-Tun, according to the Chinese. The month of November was drawing near.

A comrade of my father's who, in accordance with an approved plan, was to start revolutionary action in his district simultaneously with my father, upset the scheme. He broke out two days before the appointed time, arrested the daoyin of his district, and the very next day, sent some of his troops to my father's aid. But news of the event travelled faster than his troops, and father's men were not yet ready.

Without telegraphic aid, as though brought by the wind, the terrible news reached the daoyin. He immediately instructed the commander of his garrison to arrest my father. The order was given to a detachment of soldiers. One of them was a member of the union of Go-Lao.

The entire detachment appeared before my father, and reported: "We have an order to arrest you. Tonight we will have to break into your house and seize you."

Father hurriedly mobilized the nearest military unit of Go-Lao, his entire Police School, and the detachment of soldiers that came to warn him. When, according to the daoyin's plan, he was to be arrested, my father was not in his bed. At the oppo-

[68]

site end of town, he was commanding his policemen, who were surrounding the house of the daoyin.

The daoyin was arrested and the rule of the Manchus in Teh chien ended that night.

Not until the next morning did the citizens understand that the revolution had come. The Emperor's yellow flag, with its black dragon, no longer flew over the daoyin's house. The revolutionary banners were fluttering on high bamboo poles over the insurgent Teh chien. They were white with a red circle. In the center of the circle a red hieroglyphic was sewn. The hieroglyphic read "Khan", the ancient name for China. That was what my mother had been sewing during the nights of my illness.

The gates of the prison were thrown open, but there were no revolutionists. The daoyin had not let them see the day of the revolution. All had been executed.

The hands of the revolution were still clean of blood. As yet there had been no executions. Even the life of the daoyin was spared, and he was simply kept under house arrest.

The town was bewildered. People spoke in low voices, wondered unbelievingly, whispered. The most anxious whispering went on in shops.

"Treason to the Emperor."

"If it goes on like this, we'll soon see executions in town."

The intellectuals, holders of lofty, learned titles, accused my father behind his back.

"A man with a degree, an intellectual aristocrat, how can he stand at the head of boatmen and bandits? How can he betray his Emperor?"

A week later the revolution received its first blow. The same comrade who had sent troops to father's aid, moved the rest of his soldiers against the town of Lan Shan, which was in the hands of a Chinese daoyin, loyal to the Manchus.

The revolution in Szechuan was not against the Manchus.

There were only a few real Manchus in Szechuan: the viceroy and two or three high officials.

The daoyin of Lan Shan was a sly fox. He greeted the comrade and his troops at the gates of the town.

"I am for the revolution," he said, bowing endlessly, and smiling sweetly. "Permit me, please, to place my garrison at your command, in order that you can carry on more successfully your victorious offensive."

The comrade was a trusting man, and the daoyin kept his freedom.

The comrade stopped overnight at an inn. November nights are dark in Lan Shan, and he and his bodyguard were tired by the long day's march. After midnight the daoyin broke into his room, accompanied by his soldiers. The comrade was killed in his sleep.

It was much harder for father to work alone. The daoyin of Lan Shan was now threatening from one flank, and the relations with the citizens of Teh chien also became more acute. People began again to say that it was not a real revolution, but just a bandits' riot. How could one prove to them that all over China the Tung Men Huei was overthrowing the Manchus?

Father put a fellow-revolutionist by the name of Li in charge of all his duties in town, and rushed to Lan Shan, at the head of his policemen and a regiment composed of "old brothers".

A month later, the treacherous Lan Shan and two other loyal Manchu districts were transformed into revolutionary districts. The garrison of the daoyin who had murdered my father's comrade joined father's regiment. The daoyin was captured and father ordered him beheaded over the grave of the murdered comrade.

The Central Revolutionary government gave my father a premium of one thousand da yang for his successful military operations.

Two days after the insurrection I was brought back to town by my father's messengers. Grandmother refused to come with us. She did not believe in the success of the revolution. Her nerves broke under the strain. She would either stand still for hours, staring straight ahead without blinking, as though she were trying to drill the wooden wall with her protruding eyes; or, tidying an empty room, she would suddenly start talking out loud.

I would run to the sound of her voice, and ask, "Whom were you talking to, grandmother?"

"I," she would answer, "talking? What nonsense!"

But she looked as though somebody had just awakened her from a sound sleep with a bucket of cold water.

The number of people flowing through our house overwhelmed me. I was bewildered. The town was wide awake. It buzzed with people rushing around, quarrelling, cautiously buying and selling, loudly sharpening weapons.

Braid-cutting was in full swing. Scissors clipped off my tiny braid, so carefully cherished by my mother and grandmother. I did not care. Let it fall to the floor. A braid on the back of a Chinaman's head is like a sign on his brow: "A Manchu slave".

The walls of houses were dotted with the white squares of orders:

"Those who have not cut off their braids within ten days from the date of this order will be shaved forcibly, at government expense."

At the city gates, where the country roads ran up to the walls of the town, posts of soldiers were placed, armed with rifles and scissors. A soft stack of braids grew high around the soldiers' feet. The swearing of the trimmed passers-by, who cursed the revolution and covered with one hand the backs of their heads where once had been a braid, continued around the gates all day long. They would have been less ashamed had the soldiers deprived them of their trousers.

The respectable intellectuals protested.

"An outrage! The filthy paw of a ruffian, who only yesterday was robbing people on the road, dares to touch our noble hair.

A braid is not a symbol of enslavement; a braid is a symbol of one's loyalty to the Emperor, to one's ancestors, to the great laws and the science of ancient times. They begin by cutting off braids, but they'll end by breaking up the sacred altars in our houses, and by evicting the best people like mangy dogs, from their estates. . . ."

The peasants were also indignant.

"Who ever heard of such a thing? We lived for centuries with braids. Our fathers and grandfathers had braids. . . . People in the villages will laugh at us as they laugh at tailless dogs. . . ."

But the coolies were glad to have free barber-shops at their service, and willingly placed their thin braids under the soldiers' scissors. They were glad to have them off. Less bother with vermin, and hair washing. They would have had them cut off long ago had it not been forbidden by Manchu law.

The buyers of hair were for the revolution. Never before had China brought them such a crop of cheap human hair.

Comrade Li, whom my father left in town in his place, was young. He could not successfully manage the chiefs of the troops. These chiefs, wearing turbans, or officer's caps, or civilian skull-caps were scornful of him. They pulled him this way and that, and demanded more than he could give. The hand of my father had held them to strict obedience. In his absence each of them thought that he should have been put in his place.

One of these commanders gathered all his sympathizers at a meeting, and announced, "We are tired of this youngster and his bossing. It is time to show him his place."

But they did not yet dare to overthrow the new government. Instead of arresting Li, they summoned my father. On New Year's Day, father returned to Teh chien.

The yamen was an enormous square with many houses on it, surrounded by a solidly built wall. Behind this wall lived the

[72]

daoyin and his secretariat, the commandant of the garrison and
his soldiers. The quarters of the chief of the military forces of
the district were also there, as well as the court, the house of
the tax-collector, and the high fence of the prison. The gates
of the yamen, which had always been closed, were now wide
open. Red strips of cloth were hanging down from the windows
of its houses. Chains of paper lanterns, red, yellow, and green,
like transparent accordions, swung in the wind. Their hooks
creaked slightly on the slender bamboo switches.

The members of the Military and Civilian Administration of
the County, or what should have been called more correctly
the Military Revolutionary Committee, passed through the gates
of the yamen in a dignified group. They were clad in new, grey
robes over which they had put on their black satin ma-gua.
Across their chests, ribbons were tied, each with an hieroglyphic embroidered on it, indicating their office.

My father had summoned all the discontented revolutionary
chiefs to arbitrate in their dispute with Comrade Li.

It was evident that the revolution had succeeded. Though all
the daoyins had not yet surrendered, the news from the Hankow
Revolutionary government was good.

Neighbors and relatives brought presents to father. He
politely refused to accept them, and sent back the bewildered
coolies with their heavy packs, packages and cases.

The time when my father used to earn only eight da yang a
month was past. His salary now was two hundred da yang.
Mother's eyes no longer watered from the smoke in the kitchen
every morning. She had a servant.

New Year's Day passed. The tumult of the holiday in our
town house quieted down. Mother went to the country to my
sick grandmother.

The old woman's health had grown worse. She ate nothing.
A little bit of milk crushed from beans would be her day's
nourishment. The physician looked anxious.

"There is no cure for old age," he said. "She is past seventy."

Grandmother lay in bed, her lips moving. Finally, they understood what she was trying to say.

"I want to see Shih-hua."

But she interrupted herself immediately: "No, don't let him come. I do not want him to see my dying face. I do not want him to cry."

Mother, alone, herself already incurably sick, was with her when she died.

Quietly they buried my grandmother.

Near Tan Tsia Chen, the village from which we get our family name, there are hills. In these hills is our family cemetery. Children and childless people are not buried there. Grandmother was not my father's own mother, but his stepmother, and she had no children. She was buried in the public cemetery among the numerous graves of the various Tans. The village sage chose the place for her body, which now had ceased to balance itself on those "golden lilies".

The graves in Szechuan are deep. The clay surface earth is broken all the way down to the underlying rocks. In the provinces at the mouth of the Yangtze, where the underground water is close to the surface, the coffin is usually placed on the ground and covered with a mound of earth.

My grandmother was buried.

Father left again for a new campaign. Before his departure, he sent us away from town, back to the quiet village of Sian-Shih.

14. The Leaders Split

ONE OF HIS REGIMENTS SUDDENLY ANNOUNCED TO MY FATHER: "Enough of this fighting. We have overthrown the Manchu Emperor; now we ought to put a Chinese one in his place. We have had enough of your command. We want no more orders from your revolutionary government, or from your Dr. Sun Yat-sen."

The regiment celebrated its independence with a massacre and a looting of the village in which it was quartered.

It was not difficult to trace the origin of the regiment's love for a Chinese Emperor. The commander was a member of the former Imperial bodyguard, and his mandarin's skull-cap was adorned with a brilliant red button—the insignia of an important court position.

Father was contemplating a way to crush the mutinous red button. But just at that time, he received an order from the Central government to advance against the *Tu tuh* (the governor) of Wanhsien, against whom the strong troops of Sung Ke-wu were already moving up the river.

Wanhsien is a big port on the Yangtze river. The Tu tuh of Wanhsien sat like a wedge between the two revolutionary provinces—Szechuan and Hupeh. The capital of Hupeh, Wuchang, was the seat of the revolutionary government.

There was none in Teh chien who could be left to replace my father except the same Comrade Li who had previously quarrelled with the commanders of the troops. It was Li now who had to bring the regiment of the red button to order. The red button's name, by the way, was also Li. One Li had to destroy the other.

Father gave these instructions to his substitute: "There must be no executions. Just put him in jail. There are many people, like Li, with the red button, among our troops. One cannot execute them all. Even now, ignorant people say in the markets, shops and temples that we are bandits and blood-spillers. Approach the regiment not with your fist, but with propaganda. Win them over, and then disarm them."

Li was young and quick in his decisions. He did not like the cautious advice of my father.

Father and his troops were far away. The Yangtze carried their boats down over its bumpy back. Li, the deputy, invited Li, the mandarin, to a banquet. Exquisite dishes followed one another, the chefs doing their best to please the guests. Endless cups of wine ran down their throats. In the midst of the feast the host gave his guard a signal. The soldiers grabbed the mandarin under the arms and removed him to the court. The sound of their guns told the guests that the possessor of the red button would never again be able to mention the new Chinese Emperor.

This shooting at the banquet caused an ominous rumble of resentment among the troops. The people whispered and called out: "We come from afar. We are fighting together. If we make blunders, explain them to us. You shock us with your death penalties, without trying out more moderate measures first. Such cruelty is likely to anger the hearts of our gods, and they may drink up all the water from our rice fields, or send the locusts over our wheat. They may destroy our corn with hailstorms and blight our families with incurable diseases."

So talked the fighters among the troops, who had come from distant villages, as they stood warming their hands in front of coal-burning ovens in the spacious courts of the temples.

Li selected a detachment of soldiers, brought them into one of these courts, placed them in front of the monstrous doll-like statues of the gods, and commanded: "Break them up!"

The soldiers moved back, startled. Li pointed his gun.

Under the heavy sticks in the soldiers' hands, the fragments of the broken idols fell ringing on the flat stones of the floor, filling the air with century-old dust. Before that day, this dust used to be carefully brushed off by the priests, with dusters made of hen-feathers.

The temple was godless. On the floor, beyond the cold incense burners, the broken gods lay crippled and mutilated. The rumble of resentment grew into a furious general uproar. In offices, where writing brushes ran fast over paper, in shops where the small abacus clicked, in gardens where the hoes rang as they hit rock, only one note was struck: "He has broken our gods. He has insulted our faith. He does not respect our habits. He shall not be the head of the town. He must go."

Again the gates of the yamen were opened wide, and again the delegates assembled. The possessors of large estates, the owners of shops, the insulted Shen-Shihs, and the troubled craftsmen all sent their representatives to the yamen.

The vain, angry, and frightened landlords took the power away from the party of Sun Yat-sen. The meeting elected respectable people to the important offices of the town—people notable for their shops, their learning, their gardens, or for the number of tenants on their land.

Li left Teh chien.

Now in 1927 he is still living in his native Szechuan village. He never again set foot on the streets of Teh chien. He hates Teh chien with a firm, sixteen-year-old hatred. He would never help a man from Teh chien. Every time conversation touches the subject the veins swell on the forehead of the veteran radical. He gets angry, runs excitedly back and forth in his room howling curses.

He spares only one inhabitant—my father.

My father left one battalion for the defense of Teh chien. One regiment and a battalion, armed with police rifles, he took with him against the Tu tuh of Wanhsien. Sung Ke-wu had more troops than my father; he had two regiments. He was the chief commander of the operation. Father was his aid.

The Tu tuh, whose name was Liu, with his staff, a battalion of soldiers trained in the European manner, and, what was more important, an arsenal of the most wonderful rifles, sat behind the thick walls of his city. These walls, which stretched up the mountain and then dropped down into the river, encircled the city like an impenetrable belt.

The revolutionary troops were flung out on the mountains of the opposite shore. Father had machine-guns, Sung Ke-wu had cannon. There was plenty of work for the artillery.

Thick fog filled up the glens, the roads, and the whole valley of the river. Over the narrow mountain roads, the soldiers pulled their heavy cannon to the summit. They groaned under the strain. They were forbidden to shout. Under heavy fog, the enemy might send boats across the river, and attack the weak revolutionary troops. My father and Sung Ke-wu went through the camp to inspect the machine-gunners, the transports, and pickets. They came to a rocky cliff. Everything in front of them was white. It was impossible to see either Wanhsien, the river, or the fishermen's huts on the shore. But they distinguished a figure, hardly visible through the bluish fog. It was climbing up over the ledges of the cliff, trying to hide behind the rocks.

"Give the password!"

Their words sank into the fog as into a soft pillow. The figure continued to climb. Sung Ke-wu said to his bodyguard: "Get him with a grenade."

The soldier detached from his belt a hand-grenade, that looked like a bottle, took it by its neck, and skillfully threw it down the path.

The grenade struck a rock, and exploded with a burst of flame. It tore out a big boulder. The boulder rocked once or twice, and then began to roll down—at first slowly, then faster and faster, till it made a great leap and fell on the shore. It

[78]

crushed a fisherman's hut, killing five quietly sleeping people.

While the boulder was rolling and leaping down, the figure continued to climb up. It was one of Sung Ke-wu's own officers. He had gone out to reconnoiter, but had forgotten the password.

The cannon were put in position. All day long their shells ripped out the innards of the houses of Wanhsien. Next morning the patrol brought the delegates sent from Wanhsien to my father. They were blindfolded. They had got secretly out of the town, and had made their way through the enemy lines to inform the revolutionary headquarters that the Tu tuh was safely protected from their shells, but that the citizens' huts, their shops and schools had suffered badly from the bombardment.

My father insisted that the bombardment stop, but the general was stubborn. What did a few shops matter? What if a few schools were destroyed? Let the inhabitants rebel and kick out their Tu tuh.

"If you want them to have an insurrection," said my father to his commander, "send down organizers and not shells."

The bombardment stopped. But the revolutionary troops did not have to wait for the insurrection. Tu tuh Liu was as incompetent as the rest of the Manchu daoyins. He had an arsenal full of rifles but he did not know how to use them. He had excellent soldiers but he was afraid of them. And one night he, his nearest relatives, and the staff officers, fled in disguise from the town.

Wanhsien surrendered. The civic council elected my father to be the judge of the town.

My father did not forget the hand-grenade of that first morning, the boulder rolling and leaping through the fog, the five corpses. He demanded that the family of the killed be recompensed with 500 da yang.

Sung Ke-wu was beside himself.

"What? You demand 500 da yang for a hut that was destroyed during an insignificant military engagement? And what would you want us to do if, in the course of a real battle, we should demolish scores of houses? We must not create such precedents. The whole of Szechuan will come to us for damages."

Not a word in answer came from my father. Next morning he wrote an order to pay 500 da yang from the military treasury to the family of the killed.

That was more than Sung Ke-wu could bear.

"There is no room in the army for people who have their own way. Subtract that half a thousand da yang from the salary of Tan pu."

Father was angered. He refused to work any longer with Sung Ke-wu and resigned from military service. His regiment he left to Sung Ke-wu.

Now Sung Ke-wu had four regiments—two of his own, one of my father's, and the fourth made out of father's battalion, and the garrison of Wanhsien. He became a division General.

The inhabitants of Wanhsien deplored the departure of my father. He went to Chengtu, the capital of Szechuan. The law school of Chengtu offered him a chair in civil and criminal law. But before he began his course of lectures the chief of police of the whole province of Szechuan, Comrade Tai, a member of Tung Men Huei, and his class-mate from the Japanese University, steered him another way.

"You are well experienced in police organization," wrote Comrade Tai to my father. "You know that general Yuan Shi-kai became the President of the Chinese Republic after Sun Yat-sen. We, the revolutionists, must be on our guard."

My father went straight north, and there received from the hands of Comrade Tai, in the yamen of the capital, the seal of the Lord Chancellor, the symbol of his new office.

In those alarming days, when revolution was already feverish, Sun Yat-sen created the Kuomintang. Kuomintang was the party of the builders of new China. It had three slogans: "Nation", "Democracy", "Socialism". The Tung Men Huei was a military organization. It had only one slogan: "Down with the Manchus".

The Tung Men Huei party which organized the revolution

of 1911 ended its existence. The fat bewhiskered general Yuan Shi-kai, a former commander-in-chief of the Imperial army, and now the President of the Republic, began to gather China into his hands, appointing his generals and colonels as rulers of its provinces.

The paths of my father and General Sung Ke-wu, which had crossed on the streets of Wanhsien, were never to meet again.

---

15. Motherless

AT NIGHT, A CRIMSON-BREASTED BIRD CRIES IN SZECHUAN gardens: "Quee-quee-yang!" "Quee-quee-yang!" The name of the bird is Tu Tiu-en. Her cries are poignantly plaintive. People say she cries until blood comes from her throat, and that in the morning she will be found under a tree, dead, with blood-stained beak.

I did not believe these stories. But, when in Sian-Shih, I heard in the night the cry, "Quee-quee-yang!", it seemed to me that it was the weak voice of my mother. She coughed blood, and languished. Silent she was then, as she had always been, because my father was far away on his dangerous duties, and my sister and I were so small.

I am now twenty-six years old and a father myself. I have travelled around half the world. I read many books in many languages. Yet it is hard for me not to shed the tears that fill my eyes when I remember my dear, pathetic bird that lost her blood and her life on the shore of the greenish Yangtze.

I know; you call it sentimentality.

She took care of my little sister, and received a crowd of guests daily. She was getting things ready for the marriage of my younger uncle. Every morning she coughed timidly, turning away from me. Then, suddenly, she would shrink and stop coughing.

She went to our tangerine orchard, past the kitchen door, over which the curly, bluish smoke rose in the air. The buyers were coming to purchase the future yield of the trees. If a tree was not sound they paid only a da yang; for a good one the price was a da yang and a half.

A man, bending down under the short tree, inspected the leaves, the roots, the branches. He was looking for the harmful black fungus or the red bug. With an experienced eye he noticed tiny holes in the bark, and pierced the tree with a long needle, killing the bug. He also cut out the sickly growth with a bent knife.

The high voice of the servant called to my mother—the match-maker had come.

The match-maker entered the house with quiet dignity and a sweet smile. She wore gold earrings. Not a hair of her slicked coiffure was out of place. In the South they say a woman's hair must be so slick that even a fly will slide off it. Her face was hot and fat. She held a handkerchief in her hand which she constantly lifted to her nostrils. Sometimes she tucked it up into her long sleeve, close to the arm-pit.

She came with a man. He was as humble as a messenger boy. He was her husband.

My younger uncle, already thirty years old, was late in getting married. He had tried his best to escape it, pleading poverty. But now there was no excuse. We had, in addition to our tangerine orchard, 200 da yang of father's salary, plus the untouched capital of 1000 da yang—my father's premium. Relatives who lived on the same street, and those who came from the nearby village, listened to the conversation between my mother and the match-maker.

Every day some relative, on the way downtown, would come in and ask: "Well, how is it going?"

More often they went to my older uncle. "We hear that your esteemed brother is going to marry such and such a maiden from the village of Sian-Shih. Will you be so kind as to satisfy our stupid curiosity and tell us if you have given your wise consent to this marriage?"

My older uncle was drunk, and angry about the revolution most of the time. Everything displeased him—the campaign of my father, the health of my mother, and the fact that he, a learned man, happened to be the brother of the fool and the rebel, Tan Ya-pu.

He would stare at the relatives, and say ironically: "But, excuse me, we have the revolution. What difference does it make who is the oldest in the family? What can I have to do with the marriage of my brother, Tan Tsi-pu?"

Our living room was crowded with merchants. The dry-goods peddlers undid their packs of silk materials on the floor; the seamstresses tried on colorful robes; the jewellers took boxes out of their pockets. The gold of their rings and earrings, the silver of the clasps and pins, gleamed in front of my mother's eyes. We had to have gifts for the bride.

The business men came. They sat down, drank tea, and named figures. They talked about the weather, about the neighbors, and named figures again. Mother was trying to rent a special house for the wedding ceremony because our own was too small.

One could not get through the kitchen, nor through the pantry. There were big kettles filled with sour green cabbage; there were glassy, transparent chunks of salt, with which pork was salted. There is no better salt in the world than the salt of Szechuan.

The wedding took place in the clear, hot days of summer. Guests swarmed about the tables. The married couple went around serving wine. The guests greeted the bride and her bridegroom with wishes and congratulations. My mother stood up. The noise stopped. She said, addressing my uncle and his wife:

[83]

"Perhaps I shall not live very long. If I die, I beg you, take care of my children, as you would your own."

A protesting murmur interrupted my mother. The guests objected: "Today is a red day. Today is a happy day. One must not mention such things today."

And then they shouted to her: "Let yours be a happy fate!"

My older uncle looked sullen and discontented. Less than half a year had passed since the death of my grandmother, and now a wedding was being celebrated in the house. Where were the strict rules of mourning? This revolution was breaking all too quickly the backbone of the old customs. Had he not sacrificed all his examinations for the sake of proper mourning?

The wedding was over. The tables were put back into the rooms. The borrowed dishes were returned to the neighbors, and the hired chefs left our kitchen.

Every day the doctor came to see my mother. He would repeat endlessly: "Rest, rest, rest! You should not work!"

But the young wife of my uncle did not know how to do a thing, and the quiet feet of my silent mother went back and forth over the steps of our courts. Her practical hands were mending our finances, which had been badly shaken by the wedding. They were doing it as skillfully and as quietly as they used to in the difficult days when father was studying in Japan.

My aunt came to visit us in the fall. She did not like the appearance of my mother. Her skin was stretched too tightly over the bones of her face. My mother, a bit solemn and nervous, said to my aunt: "I know what will happen to me soon. Please take care of Shih-hua and Shih-kuen. Tsi-pu's wife has too much to do. She'll soon have her own children. It will be easier for you. Your children are all grown. Please take this money—I have saved it, penny by penny. Ask a dozen of your friends to form a mutual aid group and invest these savings. Let Shih-hua have a little pocket money every month. Who knows what his life may turn out to be? His father may never come back. He may become poverty-stricken. He may bring back a step-mother, and she may not like the boy. He is so small, only nine."

Frowning, my aunt took the money. The two women sat for a long time in the fading light of the room, talking about the living and the dying.

Weakness was overcoming mother. Every day it became more and more difficult for her to get up, more and more difficult for her to walk across our little courts without holding on to the walls. The time came when she could no longer arise from her bed. Her face and forehead were purple-red. Sometimes I saw drops of sweat on her brow. She did not like to have me come into her room as she was afraid I might get infected. A servant girl stayed with her continuously, fussed about with cups and rags, wiped off the sweat, washed up the blood-stained towels, carried away the bowls of untouched food. Besides the servant, a physician also stayed with my mother. My younger uncle installed him in the house. After a month, the doctor said, "Her condition is hopeless. There is no use in my staying here. I shall come to see her from time to time."

I had been brought home from the house of my uncle, where I had been living, in order that I could be closer to mother.

A month passed this way.

One morning, the doctor, who came to see mother, said: "She is much better."

I was sent to school. Three hours later, the director of the school sent for me.

"What is the matter?"

"There's someone here for you. Hurry home."

The passers-by stopped and looked at me as we panted along the streets. From the brief words of the man running beside me, I knew that mother was dying. I did not feel my feet, only the whistling of the air in my ears, the pounding of my heart, and fear—the fear that I would not get there in time.

The flat stones of the street echoed under my feet. My thoughts flew back home. I remembered mother's room, her bed, the lighted windows, mother herself, thin and wasted. I remembered how, a week ago, I had watched her bluish hand trying to lift a juicy pear to her mouth. She accomplished it with great difficulty, as though it were not a pear, but an iron weight. I remembered how she smiled at me with her lovely, luminous smile, and said softly, more softly than usual (I had never before heard her whisper so softly):

"Study faithfully, Shih-hua. Listen to your uncle and to your aunt. Never swear and never fight."

I rushed into the house. My uncle's eyes were red as though he had been rubbing them for a long time. My aunt, her face hidden in her handkerchief, was sobbing by the window.

I had come too late.

Mother lay on a long, narrow, wooden bench, her face covered with a sheet of paper, soaked in alcohol. The faces of people who die of tuberculosis are always covered in this way. There is a superstition that the germs that caused the infection fly out through the nostrils.

I tried to lift up the paper. How dare they hide my mother's face from me! My uncle rushed toward me.

"You mustn't! What are you doing?"

My three-year-old sister, holding on to the bench, pouted disapprovingly, and pulled my sleeve.

"Don't wake her up, naughty boy. Mother's asleep."

16. The Funeral

THE HOUSE WAS CRAMMED WITH WOMEN RELATIVES AND neighbors who suddenly had mysteriously appeared. Throughout the night the noise of preparations and the shuffling of their feet never ceased. Now and then water splashed; they were bathing the body of my mother. The women dressed her in a new garment, conversing in whispers.

"How different things are now. When the first grandmother died she was buried in the uniform of a mandarin, as the title of her husband demanded. She had a hat with a shiny button."

The women's voices grew louder. They shouted, chasing someone out of the room. It sounded as if they were chasing a dog. A pregnant woman, obviously discontented, bore her enormous stomach out of mother's room. A pregnant woman may not come near a dead person.

A silk-covered cotton-wool mattress was spread on the bottom of the coffin, and a soft pillow put at its head. One of the women busily looked over the ready coffin, and remembered: they had placed an amethyst in the mouth of the dead grandmother, and a piece of gold as big as three drops of water. Jewels keep the dead body from decaying.

Sighing politely, the woman threaded a needle by the light of an oil lamp, and sewed her last garment on my mother. This garment had been secretly made while mother was still alive. It had no buttons. It was sewed up once and forever. A servant put slippers on mother's feet. They would be no good for walking. She tenderly stroked their soft, canvas soles. Then mother was lowered into the deep box of the coffin, her arms stretched down along her body. A thin blanket covered her up to the chin.

Only the head of a clan could be taken into the li tang after death without special permission. Dead servants, their children, and dead concubines were not allowed to be brought there. To remove mother to the prayer room permission had to be had from the shaking, white-whiskered brother of my grandfather, and from my older uncle.

A white curtain, hung across the room, separated the house-altar from the coffin. On the hither side of the curtain a long table was set out. A large porcelain bowl for burning prayer sticks was on it, and two bronze incense burners with sandal-wood glowed in them, so that the fragrance would kill the odor of the dead body. Next to the incense burners were two candles. Behind the burners my mother's picture should have been placed, but there was none. She had always refused to be photographed.

"First of all," she used to say, "the time now is a hard, revolutionary time; it is dangerous to have portraits in the house. Luck might turn against us, and our enemies will have a photograph to help them find us. And secondly, if I die, the children will look at it and cry. I don't want them to cry."

In place of her portrait there was put on the table a large tablet with the following words written on it, vertically:

> "Mother
> Beloved
> Legitimate
> Tan (name of the husband)
> Liao (maiden name)
> Lady
> The throne of the soul"

To the right of this column, the year, month and date of her death were stated and, to the left, at the very bottom of the tablet, my name and that of my sister were written in small letters.

For two days and nights people continued to pass through the prayer room. They stuck incense candles into the ashes of the bowl, and put their gifts on the table: whole necklaces of gold and silver money, made of tinfoil, strung like beads on a string. They also brought beautiful gowns made of paper, paper horses and wagons, and a paper model of a house thirty-five inches high. Again and again, bunches of paper money flared up with yellow flame—some superstitious relatives were sending it to my mother, that she might have enough to live on in the other world.

People crowded our house to its limit. Their chatter of sympathy tired the ears. From distant villages came various Tans, relatives of my father, and numerous Liaos, relatives of my mother, whom she had probably never seen in her life.

My younger uncle went over the surrounding hills looking for a burial place. He had to find a spot where the ground was dry, and covered with flowers; where one could see the distant mountains, the white, delicate clouds, and the loud Yangtze. According to Chinese belief one must find a place for the grave, that will please the spirit of the deceased. Otherwise it may happen, that many years after the funeral, a village sage will appear who will prove that the place was chosen incorrectly, and that the soul has been suffering, and should be buried elsewhere.

Mother lay in her coffin in a room full of the sweet fragrance of sandalwood. White, the color of mourning, distinguished our parting. The revolutionary government had decreed black the color of mourning, but the will of the relatives had been stronger. I was dressed in a white robe. White threads were hanging from my unhemmed sleeves. My uncle, my aunt, my little sister, and the rest of the people staying in the house were similarly clad. We were not allowed to eat meat, butter, eggs, or milk for forty-nine days.

Unfamiliar, insistent, and numerous Tans and Liaos led me into the room where my mother lay. They drew me to the table and put a Buddhist prayer book in my hands. I saw my uncle frown and shake his head deprecatingly. He attempted to get near me, but I was well surrounded by the dense crowd of relatives. . . . In those days, they, and not my uncle, laid down the law in our house.

"Read, Hua Sao-E," they said, ceremoniously. "Read. You know how to read. You don't want to compel us to invite some monk to read over the dead body, do you?"

"Read, Hua-tze," the servants and coolies repeated after them, addressing me in their simple way.

Tears tickled the corners of my eyes. The hieroglyphics quivered. Then the lines became familiar, and I uttered them without looking in the book.

". . . The good ones will be happy, and there will be no end to the misfortunes of the bad. . . ."

I read the consoling words, but I did not believe them, and my tears were tears of anger.

Mother's body stayed in the house only a week. It was too costly to keep it there longer and money was spent fast as new guests continued to arrive. They had to be given a place to sleep. They had to be fed. They burned incense sticks, candles, and fragrant wood. It is true that some brought these with them, but not all.

The day before the funeral new sounds shook our house. It was the funeral orchestra, blowing its trumpets, whistling through its flutes, roaring through its metal pipes, pounding its barrel-like drums, copper gongs, and the melancholy little bells. In such an orchestra monks of different religions get along quite peaceably. A Buddhist, beating his drum, may sit next to a Taoist, who plays his sad melodies on a many-piped flute shaped like an artichoke.

The monks sang sad, Buddhist psalms in unison. Their singing made me want to strike my head against the polished top of mother's coffin. Then they broke off, to be replaced by the mutter of drums and the clink of cymbals. Then the joyless melodies of the monks' chorus was renewed.

[90]

In the morning, as I came out of the house, I noted a sad sign was hanging over the gates: "No greetings, no farewells". It meant that the guests were not to feel offended by their hosts if, during these sorrowful days, they did not receive the full attention demanded by etiquette.

The coffin carriers had set the bamboo bier against the wall and were arguing in front of our gates. Their rags were not hidden under new robes, for to have provided them all with ceremonial garments would have been too costly. The servants distributed white towels among them. These towels, their only mourning dress, they wound around their shaven heads which were covered with sores. They kept them after the funeral as presents.

We all knelt down beside mother's coffin in complete silence. The cover was put on and a piece of soft material spread on top. Then it was carefully hammered down. Along the rim of the coffin a white ribbon was tied, and a brush dipped in lacquer paint was passed over it two or three times.

If mother's body had been waiting for someone hurrying to find her for the last farewell, the coffin would have been only tightly covered. It would not have been tied around with a ribbon, and it could have been opened whenever necessary. If the body had had to wait a very long time, the coffin would have been half buried, right there in the room, under a pile of sand. Sand consumes the bad fumes of decay. And had we been very rich, the coffin would have been filled with quicksilver. The body would have been attached to the bottom of the coffin to prevent it from floating on top. But mother had nobody to wait for. My father was in faraway Chengtu, ignorant of mother's death, but knowing that her death was imminent. His cause, building the revolution, was more important.

The heavy coffin was carried out of the house on ropes. The bamboo poles bent under it, the shoulders of the carriers bent under the bamboo poles. The distance to the grave was long. A white belt, forming a long half-circle, was attached to the front of the bier. Harnessed to this white belt, and holding it with both my hands at the height of my stomach, I, the eldest son of the deceased, led the procession, the rest of the relatives following behind me, all holding the belt. We were like teams of white horses, carrying mother's body. The carriers behind us were the wheels of the swinging bier.

Finally we came to the hills. The day before grave-diggers had dug a deep hole there under the supervision of my uncle— so deep they could hardly throw up the last shovelful of earth.

"Now even if a railroad should pass by here, it will not disturb her," said my uncle, measuring the depth of the grave with his eyes.

The coffin was lowered from the shoulders of the carriers and set down noiselessly on a soft pile of earth near the grave. The carriers rested, wiping the sweat from their brows with the ends of their towels. Their rags, wet with perspiration, stuck to their backs. The crowd of relatives was quiet.

The beat of the drum, like a gunshot, the metallic screech of a trumpet, the scream of a woman. The ropes groaned, as they were pulled under the coffin. Swinging the black lacquered monster, the carriers, with grunts and whispered commands, lowered it into the grave.

I had been pushed back from the grave, and I tried to make my way nearer to it, but the feet of the crowding relatives and their heavy rears separated me from the stony sound of the falling earth, dropping in time to the quick drum-beats of the orchestra.

The pit was soon filled up, and a high, sharp-peaked mound of earth rose over it. Carefully bending over this pile of freshly dug earth, my uncle planted limp, helpless flowers in it. On the very top he put a slip of a tree, a dark-green branch of a cypress.

The orchestra was now silent. In place of its gongs, there was a sound of dishes. Smoke rose from a small kitchen, which had been built near the grave beforehand, and people hustled about, serving guests with bowls of cooked rice, meat, and vegetables.

A servant loaded with dishes gave me a bowl. I passed it to a man next to me. Meat was not allowed me.

Moody and tired, we returned home, the relatives walking in scattered groups, talking over their affairs, looking appraisingly at the crops in the fields, consulting one another as to the price of tangerines.

At home—fire and smoke. On the flat stones of the court, mother's things were being burned: the dress she had worn when she died, her sacrificial paper slippers, dresses, wagons, and the model of the house. Grey ash-flakes floated in the air over our roof and did not drift down.

The guests left. My uncle stood at the gate, seeing each one off.

My uncle's wife and servants took down the curtain in the prayer room, and put the table with the incense burners in its usual place. The house seemed cold and empty. My uncle put his big, warm hand on my shoulder, and said:

"In two weeks, Hua, you'll go to Teh chien, to a high school there."

---

17. My Girl Friends

IT BECAME IMPOSSIBLE FOR ME TO STAY IN THE HOUSE. THE moment I entered mother's room or saw any of her things, I would go to a corner and cry. Still frail after my last year's illness, I felt particularly wilted after the funeral. My uncle arranged for me to stay in a boarding house near his school. The room cost me nothing, and I paid a da yang and a half a month for my board.

Days went by. My uncle lived in our house, and I near his school. To distract my thoughts, my older uncle often took me to visit his school for girls. I had a friend there, who used to study with my mother before she went to school.

I was ten years old. My friend was older than I. Skillfully, she drove from my head the persistent thoughts about my mother. She would sit down on the stone steps of the court, and I would lean my head, which I could hardly hold up straight on my weak neck, against her knees, and listen to the legendary tales she would tell.

She was five years older than I, and maybe she might become a famous authoress. I thought, surely she would become one if she drank wine. The ancient poets say that only a drinker can be a genius. (For instance, the poet Li Tai-po always used to be brought to the court, completely drunk.) She wrote poems, played the flute and the *tsin,* an ancient lyre, and knew how to talk to people with such intelligence and charm that the faces of the most sullen and wrinkled old men would light up with smiles. Snuggled near my friend, I would look up into her face, and watch her moving lips shape the words of a poem. She seemed to me most beautiful—so beautiful that there could be no one more beautiful than she, not only in Szechuan, but in all China.

I say in all China because outside of China in foreign countries, no face, of course, could seem beautiful to me. How could one even talk of beauty, looking at those long-nosed, pop-eyed *wai-kuo-jen,* those foreign women, with piles of feathers and material on top of the fuzzy wool of their heads. I had seen them pictured in the pages of the illustrated magazines which occasionally happened to reach Sian-Shih.

You could not call Tchen thin. Compactly built, she rolled like a joyful little ball from one door to another. She willingly took care of me and of her own brother who was my age, but two classes below me at school, and looked like a fat woodchuck. Phlegmatic, touchy, and thick-necked, he was slow-moving and slow-thinking. His sister was continually explaining everything to him, repeating her words over and over again scoldingly. He would only move his thick lips in answer, and snort loudly.

I called her my "third older" sister. My own sister was younger than I, and I called her the "first younger". I shall tell you later about the "second younger". She was about eight years old, with mischievous eyes, and was always laughing. She was the sister of my "third older", and her name was Tchen Tsai-in. She resembled both her sister and her brother. I met her much later than her sister.

Although Tsai-in was two years younger than her brother, she was far ahead of him in all subjects. Before he could solve one problem in arithmetic, she would be through with three; while he was learning two words, she had mastered five; while he, with great effort, amid snorting and lisping, read one line of verse, she had finished reading the whole poem. The awkwardness and slowness of her brother kept her laughing all the time.

We used to recite our poems by heart. He could not keep the lines in his head, and tried to glance in the book. Very politely, Tsai-in would suggest that we close the book. We smiled. The fat boy recited his poem, stammering and blundering, as though he were climbing over a fence. We laughed. He shook his head discontentedly.

"Ah, you! You think I care about your stupid verses? Let's play cards, instead."

After three minutes the happy cries of Tsai-in would inform us that he had lost there, too.

The last few months before mother's death, and almost all the days between the time of her funeral and my going to the high school, we spent together. Either I was in their school, or they were visiting me, or I went to their house.

At their house I met their slow, fat father who walked about the house with an air of importance and spoke with long intervals between his words. It was as if I were looking through a magnifying glass at his only son. But the father was seldom at home. He could be found, generally, visiting, dining, or playing cards with bankers, rich men, and high officials.

Their house looked like an antique shop, such a lot of very old things were in it. I was afraid to stay long in their parlor. The things were too precious. Had I broken anything, I would never have been able to pay. My hands behind my back, I would examine with particular respect a wine tumbler, with two bent handles, all covered over with tiny hieroglyphics. I had a great reverence for this tumbler. It was 500 years old, and I was only ten. Narrow, faded, silk pictures hung on the walls, in pairs or in fours. They represented birds, wizards, or peasants coming down the mountains. Some had traced upon them, in exquisite handwriting, the hieroglyphics of wise aphorisms.

The room of my girl friends was full of musical instruments. They could play all the ancient ones. There was a *ku-tzin*, a two-stringed violin, which can be bought in the market for forty cents. On the wall hung a long-necked banjo, *san-hsien*, which blind men play, pressing its snake-skin with their hands. This skin is stretched over the instrument to give it a more plaintive tone. There was also a pear-like *pi-ba*, a kind of four-stringed guitar. A long wooden trough with seven strings stretched taut over its convex side, and having thirteen keys—a *wu-tzan* was the most expensive of all the instruments. There were also flutes, *di-tzi*, which you blow into from the side, and the flutes called *sao-tzi*, which you blow into at the end.

Tsai-in and her sister felt very much at home in their musical kitchen. There were many di-tzi, and sao-tzi, which they had made themselves out of bamboo sticks. The whole village knew of their love of music. I heard the rumor that their father, fat old Tchen, was not a son of Tai-tai—the legitimate wife of his father—but a son of E Tai-tai, an additional wife, who had been brought into the house, and who had been an excellent singer and musician. It was from her, through her dull, slow son, that her grandchildren had inherited their gift for music.

My friends tried to teach me to play the flute. It was easy, and I liked it. They made a special flute for me. But their mother pulled the flute out of my mouth, and said: "You mustn't do that. You have a weak chest. You forget what the doctor told you."

My younger uncle did not like my friends' family.

"No good plant comes from a bad seed. One cannot forget how their father and grandfather made their fortunes. They used to be the daoyins. The entire district suffered from their peculations and graft. The girls are being brought up on money drawn from peasants and craftsmen."

"But is it the girls' fault?"

My uncle did not answer. When he met Tchen, he was as sweet, as smiling and as gentle as usual.

My older uncle came to my help; the sisters Tchen were his favorites. Who could read the classical verses better than they? He protested, "The girls are not responsible for the sins of their father. Love for the arts redeems the crimes of the ancestors. Go, Shih-hua, to your friends, and play with them.

The chill of the coming winter.

Sian-Shih, Tsai-in with her flutes, mother's grave—all that was left behind the stern of the boat that took me to Teh chien.

I was going for my examinations.

18. High School

EXAMINATIONS OVER, I BECAME A STUDENT. I WAS THE youngest boy in the school. The voices of the noisy fourteen-year-old boys, and of the serious seventeen-year-old students, whose upper lips were already fuzzy, resounded over the school courts. There were three hundred of us, all living in a dormitory. Every afternoon between five and seven we went outside the school walls to the shore of the Yangtze, and there watched the boats bobbing over its whirlpools. We talked, and looked at the outlines of Teh chien, which lay scattered over the hills on the opposite shore.

Multitudes of people danced before my eyes. The noise they made was in my ears from morning till night. This rushing, running, banging, and shouting stopped only during lesson hours. It grew especially strong at dinner-time, threatening to break the walls.

In our preparatory school we used to dine quietly. Servants brought food from home to some of us; the rest used to eat in small street-kitchens. Here, in high school, all three hundred students would burst into the dining room at once. Three hundred throats, demanding food, laughing and shouting, six hundred feet scratching the floor under the tables and benches. Eight students, two at each side, sat around each square table. The kuei-tze sounded like the nervous ra-ta-tat of a drum, as the hungry boys knocked them on the tables to even them before they clutched the food with these claws.

Four bowls of boiled vegetables and two bowls of soup, steaming in the hands of kitchen coolies, were brought to each table. Grabbing with my right hand the hot, steaming cabbage leaves, I carried them over the table. At the same time, I held an empty bowl with my left hand, so as not to drip the water on the table. Appetites were great, the gluttony unsurpassed, for weren't we all boasting to each other about the black marks on the doors of our rooms, which showed every month how much we had grown? In four moves of the chopsticks, the bowls were emptied. The contents of the bowls of soup were quickly disposed of with porcelain spoons.

Bending under its weight, the servants brought in the second and last dish. Two large tubs full of rice, each containing a hundred and fifty portions. The tubs were put on a bench and a furious stamping mob immediately surrounded them. Rushing from their tables like herds of wild animals, the students tried to fill their bowls as full as possible. I was so small that the edges of the tub were on a level with my eyes. It took me a long time to get enough rice, groping in the tub with my hand, without seeing. The rice was bad, hard, insufficiently cooked. Its color was not white, but yellowish. This showed that it was stale, old rice. The cook had probably bought it as a bargain. We were all continually getting indigestion. The vegetables were also bad. Boiling could not kill the smell of mould and cellar. The cabbage leaves were canary yellow. In our village we used to feed such cabbage to the pigs.

We chewed the tasteless hard rice and hated the cook. The whole school was engaged in a continuous warfare against him. We knew that he was making good money on our dinners, but there was no possible way of getting rid of him—he was related to the director of the school.

We used to have terrible battles over these tubs of rice. Without planning it beforehand, we would wink at each other, and cough expressively; then all of us would take only a slender portion of rice, leaving quantities of it in the tubs. Overnight the rice would get sour. But the cook would serve it over again the next day. Then a murmur of resentment would pass over the dining room, soon swelling into a storm of shouts: "Give us new rice! Take away this swill!"

The cook would bide his time in the kitchen. Perhaps the boys would get tired of shouting in vain. After a while he would give an order to carry out the stinking tub and to bring us fresh rice. Again we would eat but a little. And overnight the rice would get spoiled again.

Trying to economize, the cook would serve the tubs only half full. Then a signal would be passed over the dining room: "Eat more, boys!"

The first lines around the tubs would take out all of the rice, and the rest of us, empty bowls in hand, would roar: "Rice! More rice!"

The angry cook would add more and say nothing. Our board had been paid six months in advance. His position was stronger than ours. Nevertheless, this continuous fight suddenly came to an end with a scandal. I was the hero of it.

It happened this way. Pushed back by the students, I could not reach the tub from the floor. I went around the crowd, climbed on the bench, and bent over the tub to get my rice. I lost my balance, and overturned the whole tubful. The cook came running out of the kitchen, saw that the guilty student was a small boy, and decided that he could relieve his annoyance without fear of the consequences. His curses filled my ears.

"Get the hell out of here! Who are you, anyway? You should be thrown out of school! Crazy fool! You knocked it over on purpose!"

My fellow-students became suddenly silent and began to move slowly toward the cook like a solid wall. One of them, a tall broad-shouldered boy, came close to him, and watched with interested sympathy his screwed up, cursing mouth. With a wide swing of his arm he gave the cook a resounding slap.

It was as though a dog had been hit with a cane. The stream of curses changed rapidly into an unintelligible barking. He was cursing all of us. We were scoundrels and brigands! We were a shame to the school! We were ruining him, a poor working man. All three hundred boys ran back to their tables. Three hundred bowls were grabbed and raised in the air. The bang of broken dishes brought the inspector flying into the dining room. An investigation began. The broken dishes, the tubful of rice on the floor, and the red face of the cook presented sufficient testimony to the crime.

It was not to the cook's advantage to blame it all on me. I was too small. All that could be given me would be a slight calling down. The cook passed his vengeful glance over the row of stu-

[100]

dents. He chose two of them: the one who had slapped his face, and another.

"Those two broke the dishes."

It was a base lie. All of us had broken the dishes.

I came out to the middle of the room, and stood in front of the indignant but stupefied inspector.

"It is my fault. I knocked the rice-tub over. The cook is lying about them."

The same day three squares of paper, covered with writing, were pasted on a bulletin board which hung in the corridor. It was an announcement about me and the two comrades accused by the cook. All three of us had a da-ge, a black mark, charged against us. If a student had a da-ge charged against him three times, he was expelled.

The summer days were getting hotter and hotter. The feast of the Dragon was near. It was just as big a holiday as New Year's. We had three days' vacation and I was in a hurry to get to Sian-Shih. I was confused by the school and longed to see my uncle, my aunt, and my girl friends, the Tchens. Especially the younger one, Tsai-in.

The morning was cool at dawn. The sun was still hidden behind the mountains. The heavy oars squeaked in the hands of the sun-burned oarsmen whose skins glistened with sweat. I nodded to them as to old friends. How many times had this big boat carried me back and forth from Teh chien to Sian-Shih! I knew the owner of the boat also. He sat in the stern, clad in a light blue jacket, firmly holding the steering wheel. The owner's assistant, the pilot, smiled at me, showing all his teeth. His place was in the bow, where he could see all the dangerous rocks hidden under water.

In places where the cliffs of the steep shore pressed the body of the river from both sides, the strong current held us back. The boat pulled up to the shore. The oarsmen got out. Splashing water with their bare feet, dragging their soles over the gravel, they pulled the boat along the shore by heavy ropes.

"Hi-ho! Hay-he! Hi-ho! Hay-he!" The sailors chanted their song in time with their steps. Dragging their hands over the ground, almost transformed into quadrupeds, they pulled up bunches of grass and brush from the shore, made fluffy wreaths, resembling crow's nests, and put them on to protect their heads against the hot, white summer sun.

At times the oarsmen could no longer pull the boat. They would stop again and again and look back. Then the owner and the pilot would jump out on the shore, and say loudly and meaningfully, "Well, let's try to pull it, together!"

The passengers understood what was required of them. They all climbed out and took hold of the ropes. The empty boat, digging its bow into waves, dragged heavily behind its walking load. The swift current was passed, the oars squeaked and splashed again.

The sailors sang a song, the words of which could not be found in any dictionary. It was a simple, peasant language, unknown to me, an educated boy—the language of a coolie, who knew not a single hieroglyphic. I could hardly understand one word out of ten. I would have been delighted to join in their singing and felt sorry that in school I was not taught to understand the language of the coolies.

The day was burning hot. The owner of the boat and the pilot took from under their seats their straw hats, large as wash-basins. They tied them with ribbons under their chins. They were really not hats, but umbrellas without handles.

At eight o'clock, we stopped at the village, half-way to our destination, and at noon we pulled up to the rocky dock of Sian-Shih.

19. Tsai-in

I FELT AMAZINGLY GROWN UP. VERY MUCH PLEASED WITH myself, I looked down on the little boys who found it amusing to scream, romp about, and talk nonsense. I was very meticulous about my linen uniform.

I enjoyed being addressed respectfully as Lao-Tan (old Tan) but I did not like it when ordinary people called me, in a nice but not exactly respectful way, Hua-Tse, which meant something like "young fellow Tan".

I used to walk along the streets of Sian-Shih, bowing with dignity to left and right. In the dark, cool caves of shops clerks moved back and forth, unpacking barrels and wicker boxes, while the owner of the store sat on a high stool, towering over them like Buddha, the god of the rich and the well-fed. Fanning his fat face, he used to bow to me, and I would return the bow with quiet dignity.

I went to visit the Tchens, whom I hadn't seen for six months. They were all in the drawing room—the mother and her three children. With great propriety I bowed to the mother who was sitting in an armchair. She got up and said:

"Su-Tun" (to be called Su-Tun was a compliment. Su-Tun was a divine boy of the ancient legends). "How able you are! You see, you already go to high school, while my son, although he is your age, is still struggling through elementary school."

The boy, standing behind her chair, snorted heavily. He did not like to have people talk about him. I did not grant him a smile, but said to my hostess:

"Tsin-an, how are you?"

"How is your esteemed family," she returned.

"Thank you, very well, indeed."

"Tell us about your school. Are your teachers very strict? Do you think my boy has a chance to get into your school?"

I felt that these questions actually troubled her. I glanced at her boy as a merchant might weigh a melon in his hand, and answered seriously in a grown-up manner, "Well, after he finishes elementary school, he might try to pass the necessary examinations."

"How many boys of your age are there in the school?"

"I am the only one. The rest are much older."

"Do the older boys ever hurt the younger ones?"

I remembered how my comrades defended me in the fight against the cook and firmly denied such a ridiculous suggestion.

I could understand how much she wanted to see her son a student, fearing at the same time that her fat boy, her first-born child, might be hurt by the big boys of the school. And even though he was sitting right next to her at the moment, and had not yet finished elementary school (would he ever finish it?) she was ready to cry over the possible bruises he might get in that terrible high school.

The tension of the situation was relieved by the older Tchen. "Wait, mother, perhaps he will not pass the examination."

Tsai-in was standing behind her mother's shoulder, laughter dancing in her eyes. Looking at her snorting brother, she began to scratch her cheek. This meant "shame, shame, shame". Fatty could stand it no longer. He pouted, his eyes narrowed, and he trotted sourly out of the room. His mother did not expect such an outcome. She thought the boy was hurt by the remark of his older sister, and called after him, "What is the matter? Nobody said anything against you. Aren't you ashamed to run away like that when we have guests?"

To run away feeling insulted in the presence of guests meant to lose face. Fatty did not want to lose his dignity. He stopped at the door, his back to his mother, but would not turn his sulky face toward us.

The older sister made signs to her mother, showing that Tsai-in was to be blamed. The mother smiled.

"Turn around, don't be angry with Tsai-in. It's nothing. You are big and intelligent, and she is younger than you are."

Laughter was still dancing in the eyes of Tsai-in. His mother went to the sulky host, took him by the hand, and invited us all into the dining room for tea.

I approached the table with unusual satisfaction, for children were never asked to have tea. They were given candy and that was all. I was asked because I was big, a high school student. The table was set for the holiday. Porcelain bowls and silver vases were filled with candies, fruit cakes, yellow apricots, fuzzy peaches. Along the sides of the table, in front of each chair, cups were placed on copper saucers. A pinch of green tea had been put into each cup, a dash of boiling water had been poured over it, and the cup covered with a lid. Now the lids were taken off and the cups filled with fresh boiling water from a small tea-pot.

Ah, how pleased I was with myself. No jokes, no giggles. My answers were well thought out, my intonations serious. Had you closed your eyes, you would have thought me sixty years old and the wisest old man in Sian-Shih. How wonderful to be a grown-up person!

After the tea Tsai-in invited me to her room. She opened some boxes and, rummaging in them, said without looking at me, "Forgive me, Shih-hua, if I have no expensive presents. Please take this. I made it myself."

She passed a book-mark to me, shaped like a beetle, with a long tail made out of thin silk threads. Then she put it in a white card-board box, so it would not get wrinkled. She said, "I know a hundred different patterns for book-marks. I learned them in school. But it seems to me this one is the most beautiful."

[105]

I answered solemnly, "I thank you, Tsai-in. To me there could be no book-mark more beautiful than this beetle."

I then asked my girl friends to come over to my house for a visit.

It was two o'clock. The burning air quivered over the tile roofs. The walls of the houses were like the walls of a bakery shop oven from which the coal has just been swept. Over the walls banana palm-trees draped their torn leaves, like the ears of green elephants. A peasant walking ahead of us tore off the end of a leaf almost as large as a newspaper page. He rolled it up into a cone, pinned its ends together with a bamboo splinter, and put this green cap on his sticky, perspiring head. The green texture of the banana leaf cooled his skin pleasantly. Toward evening, the leaf would wilt and be thrown into a gutter.

The locusts screeched out their song from every tree as though they were being paid for it. It was hot enough without them, but with their continuous ringing, which seemed to fill the entire atmosphere, the heat was absolutely unbearable.

Peddlers offered passers-by fresh water with honey. On their tables each had a china bowl with a spigot, surrounded with heavy cut glasses. The hands of men exhausted by the heat stretched out toward these glasses. A brownish stream would pour into a glass and clothe it in mist. We did not go near these tables. We were forbidden to do so for fear of disease.

Around the glasses were piled fresh leaves. These the man sprinkled with water from his hand, freshening the fruit kept under them.

It was difficult to walk even on the shady side of the street. In the blazing sun, alongside of us, in the middle of the pavement, the coolies bore on their bent backs bags full of rice, piles of wood, and bunches of yellow paper. This paper was being carried from the bamboo groves which overgrew the narrow rivulets flowing into the Yangtze beyond the village. In these groves small, primitive factories made thick paper sheets from the bamboo stalks.

Walking along, the older Tchen said to me, "Don't you think these last few days your younger uncle seems less gentle and attentive than usual? It seems to me something is troubling him."

"No, I haven't noticed. But I only arrived here yesterday morning."

"You watch him." There was a note of anxiety in her voice which I had not remarked before.

We entered the house. There was my uncle. Big and friendly, he stood in the door smiling and greeting us. I stared at him, listened carefully to the tone of his voice. All seemed to be as before.

My uncle watched my friends make their curtsies.

"Do you know what the ancient rules say? When good girl-pupils meet their teacher they should get down on their knees to greet him."

Before he had finished his speech the older Tchen dropped on her knees and, folding her hands, looked up meekly.

"What are you doing? What are you doing?"

And my embarrassed uncle hurried to lift her up.

My aunt poured hot water into the tea cups. Again we drank tea. Bending my head over the cup, I did not take my eyes off my uncle. I could not notice a thing. She had probably made a mistake.

The girls got up from the tea table. They had to go back. I did not want to leave them yet, and went to see them home. I was ready to walk all day long back and forth along the streets of Sian-Shih, just to listen to the wise conversation of the "older third", and see that brown laughter in the eyes of Tsai-in.

Next morning I bought some black ink, a fan, and the finest rice paper, the kind used for drawing portraits of famous actors. It was my turn to give presents to Tsai-in. But I could not visit her until after a banquet which I had to attend. I could not get out of going to it.

It was the custom during vacation time for pupils who had

come back from high school to have dinner with the teachers of the elementary school of the village. There were three high schools in Teh chien. Two or three scores of pupils who went to the same preparatory school that I did were studying there.

All the teachers who ever taught in our school attended the dinner. The banquet was planned to last for many hours. Slowly dish after dish was served. The noiseless waiters poured pale rice wine into our cups. The first morsels of food were chewed with great eagerness. The conversation lagged because our jaws were busy. But when the fourteenth, fifteenth, and sixteenth courses arrived, the guests fell away from their bowls over which up till now their mouths had been hanging. The sound of the kuei-tzes being laid down on the table next to the bowls was heard frequently.

The teachers, raising their wine cups, made speeches as long and dull as the rope of a boatman by which he pulls his boat. The chair under me was burning. I wanted to get home as soon as possible, to have a look at my uncle again, and then go to the Tchens and ask the older sister about the mystery concerning my uncle at which she had hinted. At last the waiters brought in bowls of steaming rice. I hurried home, only half saying my good-byes and farewells.

There was a cool room between the two courts of our house. You could hardly call it a room. It was just a covered passage— two walls and an awning—but it was the airiest place in the entire house, and it was pleasant to receive guests there on a hot day.

Under the awning my uncle lay on a bamboo sofa, lost in thought. I had never seen him lying down in the day-time before. Obviously something was wrong. I asked him if he was feeling ill. Pulling himself out of his reverie with obvious effort my uncle said, absent-mindedly, "It was so hot. I got tired and lay down."

That my uncle, the tireless worker, should suddenly become

exhausted! My giant uncle laid out by the heat? It was hard to believe. I went to my aunt. She was sewing by the window. Without lifting her head, she answered, "You think he is sick? Perhaps you are right. I told him to go to a doctor, but he won't do it."

Having found nothing at home, I took my presents to Tsai-in. The older Tchen looked at me inquiringly. She asked me about my uncle. I said, "Your suspicions are just. My uncle is in bed and does not leave the house. My aunt agrees that possibly he is sick."

The older Tchen looked aside and did not say a word. I began to distribute the gifts. The first present was for the fat brother. I was a clever diplomat. If I had presented all my gifts only to Tsai-in even his fat head might have grown suspicious. He might have run to his mother and started gossiping.

Tsai-in took my fan and the new brush, opened her box that stood on a desk, and put her presents there.

"I love your presents very much, Shih-hua. They come in very handy. My gift box was not full enough."

The box was closed and placed on top of another larger box. It was the box of Tsai-in, the future housekeeper, wife, and mother, and was full of spools of thread, needles, and bone thimbles. It also contained dresses, pantaloons, hats, and slippers, the latter so tiny they might have been made for a sparrow.

We went to the court, and sat in a shady corner. Tsai-in smoothed out her fancy holiday silk skirt which reached down to her knees. She was not used to it. On week-days she always wore long blue trousers. I looked at her.

"How dressed up you and your sister are today."

On her flat chest were embroidered disks of a silky pattern. The blouse was buttoned on the side with small round buttons. Wide sleeves reached the elbows. Deep inside, near the armpit, flickered a little white handkerchief. An evenly trimmed bang fell over her fine, long eyebrows—hair close to hair.

Where the hair was gathered into a braid, a tortoise comb shone with a gilded design. White stockings glimmered in the sun, and on the blue silk slippers was embroidered a whole procession of boats.

Tsai-in saw that I was looking at her. She smiled and shook her head. My admiring glance passed over her small teeth and the little holes in her ear lobes. The school had removed the earrings from them.

Four of us played cards. The one who lost got smacked over the palm of the hand. The fat brother suddenly awakened. He deftly shuffled the cards. He did not snort and he surprised us all with the cleverness of his play.

Tsai-in and I exchanged glances. We must put an end to the skill of this ground dog. She began to raise her hand to her left cheek, then to her right, then to her nose. This way she let me know which of the three suits she had. Every suit had nine cards, and I quickly deciphered her finger-signs. The little brother was astonished. He lost every single move. We smacked his hand with great zeal. He tried to play back. My moves were unbeatable. Again he stretched out his hand, and again we smacked it till it swelled, till tears began to pour out of his eyes. Then he ran shamefacedly back into the house.

It was exactly what we were waiting for. Now, without putting the cards down, Tsai-in and I could sit next to each other, could explain our moves and study card combinations. Our voices sounded falsely serious. Our fingers were tenderly intertwined. The arrival of her mother interrupted us. We moved away from each other, blushed, and loudly said something that had nothing to do with the card game. But her mother went back into the house, and again we found it necessary to put our heads together over the fan of cards.

We were not afraid of the older sister for she was our ally. We invited her to play with us long before the brother had run away. Looking at her brother's red hands, she had demanded neutrality.

"One condition: if I win, I will not smack you, but don't you dare touch me, either."

How could I dare to hurt the "third older"?

---

20. Final Examinations

On the first of june the school year ended and the examinations began. The class rooms were no longer quiet during lesson hours. They resounded with studying pupils. The lazy ones, kindled with belated diligence, buried their noses in their books, put their fingers in their ears, and swayed from side to side, learning names, words, and rules. The good students had a much easier time. During the school year they had learned all that was required. Now it was necessary for them to stay away from the buzzing class rooms, because there they were immediately attacked by the lazy pupils who swarmed around them.

"Please, explain it to me! Show me how! Solve this problem! Help me!"

Some of the head pupils earned a lot during this examination fever. These enterprising boys tutored the backward pupils in exchange for new notebooks, paper, money, or a fine dinner in a restaurant.

Four different classes were to sit together during the examinations in order to prevent pupils from copying from one another. Because of this arrangement the inventors of "ponies" had been working at full speed. They cut up a great number of long narrow strips of paper, narrow as telegraph tape, and covered them from top to bottom with the tiniest hieroglyphics. They worked day and night like diligent ivory carvers, not even using a magnifying glass. This first task done, they folded the tape like an accordion and placed it between their fingers. Then they practised the involved technique of reading from this complicated apparatus.

Some of the students wrote their subjects down on classtables, in the hope they might have the good luck to sit at the same table. Others tattooed the formulae and rules on the palms of their hands and would refrain from washing for fear of destroying their learning. The disadvantage of this system lay in the fact that during the examinations they were likely to perspire from excitement, and their hands, tattooed with such care and effort, might then present only a picture of stormy clouds.

The inspector walked about on his noiseless soles, watching, remembering, moving his fingers. On the day of examinations, the possessors of "ponies" and the "cuff-writers" might be thrown out of the class by those fingers.

We hated the inspector unanimously, even more perhaps than we hated the cook. We hated him because he was always like a somber prison guard to the new young pupils. The frightened little boys never heard a good word from him; but when he had to deal with the older boys who would get unruly, he would approach them with a sweet, soft smile, reassuring gestures, and a honey-like voice.

We used to say, "The inspector is a fox—he treats the older boys like lions, and the younger ones like rabbits and goats." I was high in the front lines of this hatred. Because of my size I was nothing but a goat to him—perhaps just a kid. He was stupid and ignorant but as he was related to the director of the school he kept his job.

The final examination was to be given the next day. A wave of unusual excitement passed over all the school. Everywhere there were conspiratorial gatherings of pupils, subdued negotiations and the ringing sound of money being collected.

We started out in a very orderly manner for our afternoon

walk between five and six o'clock. As soon as we reached the gates of the school we scattered in great haste to all sides. Some of us were in a hurry to get to town and back; others ran toward the trees of the nearby village. We came back in groups, concealing the runners in our midst. They walked in the center, their hands in their pockets, the tails of their robes bulging grotesquely. That night there was a clinking sound of glass under our beds in the dormitory, and a faintly perceptible smell of rice-wine and strong rice-brandy. Only out of habit did we turn toward the door at every sound of the soft steps of the inspector. All that day and the next the inspector's eyes were shut tight. Such was the law of the school. These nights belonged to us, to those who had passed the examinations.

Our dormitory was in the outside addition of the main building of the school. Small and large rooms, each containing from three to ten beds, had windows and doors which looked out on the terrace. Between the porch posts you could see the waters of the Yangtze.

Usually we did not dare lock the doors for the night. They were left unlocked in order that the inspector, stealing in the dark along the terrace, could, if he found it necessary, suddenly enter any of the rooms. He would jerk off the blankets which the youngsters had pulled up over their heads, so that they could read by the light of a lantern worn-out paper novels, or pornographic booklets bought in the marketplace. He would listen eagerly for the rustle of cards, or the knocking of dice, or the sound of coins. Most of the time we knew when he was approaching. He usually found only a peaceful and orderly breathing but as soon as his steps faded away beyond the far corner of the terrace, the blankets would fly off, and a group of gamblers gather around a one-eyed night lamp.

A small copper *tsan* (you get ten tsans for a copper tung tze, which is equivalent to a quarter of an American cent) has four hieroglyphics on each side. On one side of the tsan, the hieroglyphics are Chinese, on the other, Manchurian. In America, you say "heads" or "tails", we say "tse" or "man". Some of the gamblers had wonderful luck.

I gambled also, but my bets were small. I received the two da yang of my allowance, willed to me by my mother just before examinations. I was careful with money and besides I had absolutely no luck.

The very last night, the inspector did not even come near our rooms. The doors were locked anyway. The students were gay and noisy. The amount of wine and brandy in the bottles decreased rapidly. With hot burning eyes each of us boasted of his success in school, and formed plans for the future. I was excited also. My speech was elevated. I told my friends that, as soon as I was graduated from high school, I would go to Japan to the university, because my father had done so in his time. My imagination, warmed by the brandy, went on working in bed. I was already in Japan; I had finished the university. I was back in Teh chien, elected the head of the town. Surrounded by devoted soldiers, I punished the scoundrels and peculators—first of all, the inspector of the school and the cook. I also punished the director because both of them were related to him.

---

21. My Uncle's Secret

THE FINAL EXAMINATION WAS OVER. WE DECIDED NOT TO USE the regular boat for our return, but to hire a private one for three da yang, each of us paying about ten cents. The coolies either rowed, throwing their bodies back with each splash of their oars, or pulled us joylessly along the shore. We did not notice them; they interested us very little. There was not a single son of a coolie among us in the school. Only the children of merchants, teachers, rich peasants, and officials went to a high school. The children of coolies went to a different kind of school, to the free charity institutions.

The bench on the boat was as wide as a table. Small parcels of all sorts were spread out on it. Pickles were in great demand. We were all still slightly nauseated after last night's brandy. The ku-tzins rang and moaned in the hands of our musicians, who sang a favorite old song, in a very high voice, exactly the way professional actors sang it. Old women washed their linen along the shore, beating it on round rocks, slippery pieces of soap glistening in their wrinkled hands. They rubbed the bluish wet piles with hard brushes made of bamboo and bristles.

The river at this point was too shallow to float the boat. All of us, thirty strong, piled out on the shore. We shouted, yelled, and, picking up multi-colored pebbles, about an inch in size, threw them into the river, trying to hit the water exactly under the noses of the old women. Water splashed into their faces. They turned around, furious, and called us monkeys. As soon as the coolies had pulled the boat out of the current into the quietly flowing river, we jumped aboard.

In Sian-Shih a big crowd was waiting for the boat. I was in a hurry to jump off. My uncle was waiting for me. He looked troubled. What was the matter? Could it be possible that he was worried about the result of my examinations? But I had written to him that everything was all right. Perhaps he did not believe my letter, and was afraid that in some subject I might have received that awful mark—60. A mark of 60 in Chinese, English, or arithmetic meant repeating the class. With great pride I passed him my school paper signed by the director.

All of the first day I spent lying around the house like a fish in stagnant water. No wonder. One night I had spent drinking, and the night after I had been packing my things. Besides I had been unable to sleep because of the excitement of going home.

The second day the usual visiting of schoolmates began. Either I was at my friend's house or he at mine. Putting all reading and notebooks aside, I hung my intense brow over a chess board, or studied the strategy of a game called *we-ti*, checkmating and capturing adroitly the pieces of my partner. We arranged chess tournaments, imitating the grown ups who played in temples and clubs. I was flattered by the fact that I always won. Shih-hua, the chess champion of Sian-Shih.

Evenings my friend and I used to go rowing in a boat along the bamboo groves on a river flowing into the Yangtze.

The night was clear, the moon round and white, as it usually is in the middle of a Chinese month. Its light made the shores and the bamboo groves look black. We rowed the boat into a dark cave of the shore. The white moon danced upon the river. We unrolled our lines. My friend attached his bobber high above the hook, and put a worm on the hook. He was catching fish that live at the bottom of the river. I was after the dancing fish which, like jockeys in a European circus, broke, with a light splash, the circles of the moon's reflection.

The bobbers were sharply outlined by the moonlight. They would quiver on the water, then dive in, and in a second a fish would flap on the bottom of our boat. If the fish were no bigger than a finger, we pulled the hook out and threw it back into the water. But the big fish, as big as your hand, we would take home to the kitchen.

The moon moved slowly through the knife-like blades of the bamboo leaves. The bobbers seemed dead. Evidently the fish had gone to sleep. We rowed on a little farther. Fishermen's nets, stretched between large bamboo trunks, hung high above the water, big enough to hold two elephants. We got out on the shore, lowered our net into the water, kept it at the bottom for a while, and then quickly hauled in. In the center of the net, quivering and dancing in the moonlight, lay small silver fish. The drops of water fell down loudly.

I returned home late, walking through the quiet streets of Sian-

Shih. At the sound of my steps my younger uncle came out from his bedroom. He was barefoot, dressed only in his white underdrawers, his shirt unbuttoned at the collar.

"Where were you? Why do you come home so late?"

"I was in the boat up the river. We went far into the bamboo groves to catch fish."

I passed him the live necklace of fat fish, glistening like tin. My uncle paid no attention to them. I had never seen him so somber.

"It's a bad business to come home so late. Aren't you having too good a time, my little man?"

I stood, my head lowered, picking scales off the fish.

"Do you know what has happened to your father?"

I had a sensation of swallowing boiling water. The fish dropped to the floor. I turned whiter and colder than the moon.

"He is in prison in Chengtu. By the order of the Tuchun he is to be executed. A friend who is trying to help him wrote me."

I was frightened, crushed, frozen. I was to blame. I was a scoundrel.

"Uncle, why didn't you tell me before?"

"I didn't want to upset you. I was afraid the others would find out. It is a dangerous time. Too many ears around."

Father . . . Prison . . . Hu . . . Execution . . . The white face of my mother . . . The blood of the wounded chicken . . .

My feet stuck to the ground, my body became wooden. My uncle patted me on the back. He was sorry for me. Had he patted me once more I would have burst out shrieking, as though my father's coffin were already in the next room. But then the old, white-whiskered brother of my grandfather, who was visiting us at the time, would know. He was too old. A shock like that might kill him.

"Go to sleep," said my uncle.

But I could not sleep.

Father's friend was hopeful about my father's fate. But what if he had lied? Perhaps, now, while he was trying to console us, my father was lying flat, like an empty bag, his face against the stones of the prison court.

My eyes wide open, I lay in bed, remembering the figure of my father to the last detail, from the stitching on his official hat, set so straight on his head, to the cuffs of his black trousers. I remembered him walking across the room silently, looking over the heads of people, his hands folded behind his back, his bearing erect and military. I remembered how, striking his sword against the stone, he would sit down on the steps of the court to think about the old brothers, about Sun Yat-sen, his Police School, the mandarins of Yuan Shi-kai moving against the revolution. I saw him pacing the room excitedly, and telling a guest from afar—his voice going up at the end of each sentence, as if he were speaking at a meeting—why it was necessary to have a revolution, how to make it. I remembered how he would speak mockingly to my older uncle, and how my uncle would reply, at first slowly savoring his sentences; then, as he would get drunker and drunker, how his words would run ahead of one another, like the spokes of a rapidly turning wheel. And by the window near the light, my mother would sit, sewing, sewing, without ever saying a word or looking up at my father. . . .

Again the letter came to my mind. How will we live if they kill my father? I was still a little boy. Would I be able to finish school? Perhaps, like a cousin of mine, I would have to work as a clerk in a shop. And my sister was so small. What about the debts my father had contracted for his university education? Who would pay them off? If we delayed the payment I should be regarded as dishonorable. The grown ups would turn their faces away from me, boys in the streets would point at me with their fingers and throw orange peels and banana skins.

I was trying to imagine the execution. A sword . . . A shot . . . Blood . . .

But these were just words. I had never seen an execution.

I knew it was dreadful, but how dreadful I did not know. What was I to do? The lines of the famous poet Tu-fu came to my aid. The poet's grandfather, a high court official, was falsely denounced by an enemy mandarin who hated him. Accused of treason, Tu-fu's grandfather was imprisoned and was awaiting execution, just as my father was now awaiting his. A thirteen-year-old son of the imprisoned man—almost exactly my age—and the younger uncle of the poet Tu-fu, hid a dagger under his official robes, arrived at the banquet given by his father's enemy, and stabbed the mandarin to death. While his bodyguard was killing the boy-avenger, the dying mandarin said: "I did not know that the old man had such a son. I regret now that he was arrested. He is innocent. If I die, set him free." He died, and the boy died, but the boy's father left the prison. So said the poem.

I dreamed that I was the thirteen-year-old son of the mandarin. I hired a palanquin and went to Chengtu. I bought myself a dagger in a store. It was so sharp that it cut wood as though it were a boiled potato. I entered Hu's reception room. I lifted the dagger, clenching my teeth. Hu was on the floor, dying. The sabres of the bodyguard were whistling over me, and through their whistling I heard the voice of the shaken Tuchun: "Free Tan Ya-pu!"

I was getting lighter and more and more transparent from loss of blood, but to die for my father was a joy. Joy was sweetly sucking life out of my body. The sharp, firm steps of my father walked over my body, stretched on the floor of the reception room. I could see only his chin. He walked away swiftly, looking above me.

The windowpanes grew blue against the brown darkness of the wall. The dream fell apart. Father with his firm steps floated back into his prison. I, still bleeding, was transported from the floor to my bed. Hu flew back to Chengtu over the black mountains. He was still alive. The problem had not been solved. The curtain of illusion collapsed like an immature and

[119]

unprepared-for insurrection. Anxiety, fear, hope, anger, insomnia, and helplessness, clear and inexorable, were again at their posts.

How many times that night I died for my father in my thoughts! How many times father, executed, white and limp, fell face down in front of me under the fatal blows! That night I remembered the name Hu more firmly than one remembers the name of the beloved. I must kill him. I will avenge my father. I will meet Hu, I will find him.

The knife which cut without effort the silk robes and ribs of my dream had in it for me more steel than the knife with which my aunt was cutting off the heads of my fish in the kitchen.

In the morning I came out of my room, pale and new. That night split my life in two. That night I think my childhood ended.

---

22. Father in Prison

WHILE STUDYING IN THE HIGH SCHOOL ON THE SHORES OF THE Yangtze, I had missed the important political developments which hung now like an avalanche over the heads of the Kuomintang and its members.

The Kuomintang stood for the French form of government. The followers of the President of the Republic, Yuan Shi-kai, formed their own party, which advocated the United States form of government. Yuan Shi-kai, headed for the dictatorship, favored the latter form.

The governor of the province Tsan-Su, and the governor of the province Tsan-Se, both members of the Kuomintang, moved troops against Yuan Shi-kai. They were defeated. Their soldiers and officers lost their heads, and the governors themselves sought shelter in the foreign settlement of Shanghai. The Tuchun of Szechuan, a follower of Yuan Shi-kai, Hu-Tsin, received instructions from the President to clean his province of members of the Kuomintang. At the same time his assistant, the governor of Eastern Szechuan, Sung Ke-wu, was instructed by the insurgents to get rid of Hu. Hu began his cleansing activities with the Department of Police.

The whole complicated story of how this cleansing process had affected my father was to be told me many months later by the woman my father had married in Chengtu and whom I was to come to accept as my step-mother. This is the story, as she told it to me.

My father's chief, the little Tai, could not understand why all these spies and sentries, composed of soldiers of the Governor's Guard, suddenly appeared around the police department. He could not understand the mysterious whispering about town. One thing was obvious: something was going wrong and it was necessary to flee. Father suggested that they go together, but Tai said, "If both of us leave at the same time, then the last remnants of our influence will be destroyed. The revolution has already lost the greatest part of its strength. One of us must stay. Your post is less conspicuous. Hu has nothing against you."

Father remained in Chengtu.

The next morning a little, plump-chested Chinese lady, all rouged and powdered, came out of Tai's apartment. The husky guards, standing at their posts around the house, stepped aside and let her pass, winking at each other understandingly. They were convinced that Chief Tai was having a good time before his arrest. A dao, waiting for her in front of the house, carried the Chinese lady away. Ten minutes later an officer with a warrant for his arrest entered Tai's house. It was empty. In his room they found a pair of man's trousers on the floor and an open box with make-up on the table.

Over the mountain paths and over the river the sound of the hooves of the troops of Sung Ke-wu reached Chengtu. A few days after the flight of Tai, my father entered his office and found a strange man who smiled at him when he came in. This man presented to him a paper signed by Hu. It was an order for Tan Ya-pu's resignation. Father immediately went to see Hu, and informed him that he was leaving Chengtu. The governor was very amiable.

"I am very sorry to inconvenience you in any way," he said, "but the bands of the traitor Sung Ke-wu occupy all the roads at present. I cannot have you risk your precious life on the mountain paths or here in Chengtu. I must protect you."

Hu's gendarmes were placed around father's house, and they kept him there under guard. Only my step-mother could leave the house. The gendarmes regarded her as a little dog that gets underfoot. A woman, in general, was to them a being devoid of brain, and quite harmless. All she was good for was gossiping and bargaining with store-keepers. How could a woman have anything to do with revolution? The guards would glance at my lively step-mother with long, lazy glances, and turn away scornfully. In the meantime, she would run to see the members of the party and find out the news.

Sung Ke-wu was surrounded by the troops of the generals of Yuan Shi-kai. He had only one division under his command. It was true, though, that his soldiers were brave, that they would not lay down their arms, or sell them to the enemy, and that they would not run away from battle. There were stories about how, when losing a battle and being forced into the woods and up the mountains, they had cried tears of anger, and had not let go of their arms. Sung Ke-wu was not easy to conquer. It was possible, perhaps, to down him, but he would always get up again. He

[122]

clung persistently to his power in Szechuan and to a rich silk mill which belonged to him and his enemy and boss, Hu-Tsin. Five punitive expeditions had moved against him from five different sides and forced him out of the Yangtze valley. He was compelled to break through the hostile provinces to the South, toward Canton.

Arrests were made all over the city. Hu, now unafraid of vengeance, was cleaning Chengtu of the Kuomintang. His policemen took father to prison. Father asked his guard, "What is the reason for my arrest?"

"The secret alliance with Sung Ke-wu."

Father's apartment was searched for several days. All his clothes were turned inside out, the soles of all his shoes ripped off, his pillows inspected. They even shook each bamboo chair and bed-stead to see if papers were hidden inside of them. Had my step-mother dropped a hair from her head in a crack of the floor, they would have found it. They left the house empty-handed and angry. My father was too cautious a revolutionary. All the papers had been burned in time, and as to his brain, none could see what was hidden there.

An editor of the Kuomintang paper, *Tsao-San*, was laughing at the punitive fury of Hu in biting articles. He mocked the "American doctrine"; he demanded that political climbers keep their dirty hands off the not yet completed revolution. He was put into prison for spreading inciting and dangerous theories. Then he was taken out to the prison court and shot down. My father heard these shots and knew that his turn was next.

The spies were searching the city listening to all rumors, trying to catch in them the name of my father. All they needed was the smallest strip of paper, the slightest mention of father's name, in order to dispatch him after his comrade.

Father's cell was a mere hole in a brick wall. A window no bigger than a port-hole was reinforced by iron bars. A chair, a table, and a couple of boards for sleeping. The stench of a clay pot in the corner. Bedbugs. Twice a day a guard, a gun on his

hip, would bring him a bowl of old rice. Books were not allowed, not even the most ancient verses. Every day my step-
mother stood at the warden's door:

"Could you please let me see Tan Ya-pu?"

The warden did not answer. He looked down haughtily, his
eyes half closed, and shook his head.

"Would you tell me, at least, if he is still alive?"

A shrug of the shoulders.

"I will say nothing. I can do nothing. I know nothing."

My step-mother took measures of her own. Buyers came to her
house. They handled the chairs, tapped the carved surface of the
tables with their stony fingernails, rustled the rolls of pictures
taken from the walls, shook heavy robes, and passed their hands
caressingly over the silk blouses. One by one the pieces of furniture left the house. Step-mother was selling her possessions.
The walls of the rooms became bare, and the rooms square and
large. Big chests waddled out of the house like fat people. There
was nothing left to be kept in them. Only one change of clothes
remained. The coolies loaded their carts with chairs and tables.
A few bamboo pieces were left in the house in order that there
might be something to sit or lie down upon.

The furniture was moved out of the house, but silver coins
and brown bills with an impressive English signature of the
bank director filled my step-mother's purse. She collected altogether two thousand da yang. But what could she do with only
two thousand, when her task was to free Tan Ya-pu, whom Hu
would not release from his grasp for anything in the world.

She had an important acquaintance in Chengtu, a quiet and
impressive-looking official, contented, amiable and rich. People
respected him, and bowed low and smiled when they met him on
the street. He used to go to the same class as my father in high
school. My step-mother went to see him. She spoke excitedly, but
in a low voice, urging, explaining, proving her point. The friend
was silent. He had just had his dinner. Once in a while he would

belch. He stroked the fat fourth layer of his chin, then he got up and nodded affirmatively.

"Of course, it is very sad that Tan Ya-pu got mixed up in this revolution, that he got in wrong with important people who might become dangerous—but I must help my friend. I'll take care of the warden. I know him very well. He is gluttonous and stubborn. It will be necessary to soften him. People of that sort melt best at the sound of money. And my wife will do her part with his wife."

"I have two thousand," said my step-mother.

"Two thousand is too small a ransom for an important life. Still, we'll try to do what we can."

Day after day went by. Father's friend courted the warden and the overseer of the prison. He took them to the best restaurants and ordered the most expensive dishes in Szechuan, shark-fins, which had to be brought from the sea-shore three thousand miles away. The warden sucked in the well-cooked fins, closing his eyes with pleasure, and melted. After tasting different kinds of light-colored yellow wine, he became good-natured and meek, and ready to embrace the entire world. And when his fingers felt the firm and glossy texture of new bank bills, he was transformed into a god of gentleness and mercy who spent his time thinking of the happiness of people. His eyes became so small that at times he did not see the door of my father's cell. The overseer did not look so frequently into the peephole of the cell, and the guard who came after the dishes was agreeable and willing to take a note to the outside world with the precious word "alive" written on it.

But how could my step-mother buy my father out of the greedy paws of the suspicious Hu? It is true that she knew the richest antique store in Chengtu. One could go there and pay five thousand da yang for a vase that cost fifteen at most. Then, succeeding in getting an audience with a secretary of the powerful governor of the province, she could put it at his feet. Let people call it a bribe. It was really not a bribe, but a simple expression of amiability and appreciation. Who was going to prove that the store belonged to a group of high officials and that the vase was but a receipt for the money paid to them?

The way to the Tuchun's yamen was closed to my step-mother anyway. He would not have granted her an audience, nor would he have spoken to her. And the way to him through the antique store was also closed. Everything that belonged to them, from her earrings to the best official robe of my father, lined with fox fur, had been sold. But there was a door that led into Hu's house. It was the door to his women's quarters. This way lay past the room of the Tai-tai, his legitimate wife, an old and prim lady, who would not condescend to talk to my mother. It led into the pretty and strongly scented rooms of his E Tai-tai—the concubine of the ruler—a young, clever, and beautiful singer, for whom he had paid twenty-five thousand da yang.

It is easier to put a young woman in good humor, and once she is in good humor, it is easy to get her sympathy and use it. But my step-mother had to play sure. Hu might not listen to the twitter of his superficial E Tai-tai.

Hu had an old secretary, a grave and learned man. He knew my older uncle. They had sat together in the examination cages for their degrees. His name was U, and his E Tai-tai was younger and even more fond of laughter than the concubine of his chief. On these two women the wife of father's friend concentrated her attention.

She had never had much use for the concubines of high officials, but now a friendship that was rare to see grew up between them. Every day a tea-table was spread out in the women's quarters of the house of my father's friend. Every day the two made-up young women, clad in silk, and twittering endlessly, were brought to the house in their palanquins. The hostess praised their coiffures, their complexions and the exquisite shape of their hands. She wanted to know where they got such remarkable silk for their dresses, and who painted that unique embroidery on their slippers. The concubines were pleased. They told her all about the stores in which they shopped, the things that were bought in Chengtu, and about the wonderful singing of a new actor who had arrived from Hankow. When the tea cups were empty and the charcoal under the tea-pot went out, the tiny bamboo bricks of the mah-jong-game, inlaid with ivory, were scattered on the table. What bad luck their hostess had! One could think that she was blind, or that she had never played mah-jong before. She lost systematically. Again the concubines were pleased. They exchanged glances. Tomorrow they would have a few extra dozens of da yang for shopping. That was fine.

The game was finished and the guests were saying good-bye. The hostess could not bear to let them go. She was so used to them. She became so sad when they were away. She would love to stay twenty-four hours in the company of such charming women. Only with them could she be completely happy, were it not for a little "but".

"What 'but'?" demanded the beauties.

The hostess turned melancholy and would not reveal for anything her little secret. She apologized for letting fall these absolutely useless words.

Now there was no way to stem the curiosity of the two women. They begged their hostess to tell them her worry, patted her on the head, snuggled close to her, caressed her, and finally learned the sad news that a friend of her husband, Tan Ya-pu, a modest humble, ill-fated man, was unjustly in prison, and that was what made her husband feel so terribly unhappy.

"Tan Ya-pu has little children who are now left without any means of support. Every day they cry from hunger. How can you help feeling sorry for children—you are sorry for little birds with broken legs, or for a small fish when it turns its white stomach up before death."

The concubines were moved.

"Is it impossible to help them? Why can't the man be released from prison?"

Solemnly and humbly the hostess answered, "All is in the hands of the highly wise and merciful Lao-Hu."

"Let's go to the theater," said one of the ladies. "We must hear the singer from Hankow."

But the sad hostess did not lift up her head. They tried to console her.

"Don't think of such sad things. I'll talk to Hu. We'll save the man. We cannot bear such cruelty. Let's go to the theater."

They sent for the daos. The long poles of the palanquins squeaked on the shoulders of their carriers. In the theater the hostess bought the best seats and delicately pushed aside the hands of her guests holding money.

"No, no! I'll really be insulted if you don't let me take you."

On the stage an honest courtier was represented confined behind prison walls. His charming daughter, singing coloratura, (the part taken by the famous male actor from Hankow), made her way to the Emperor himself, and kneeling before him begged him to pardon her father. The concubines were touched to tears. Their hostess was crying. They bent over her and whispered, "We'll talk to him without fail. Do you hear, without fail."

The next day the hostess sat with my step-mother and gave her an accounting.

"Yesterday cost me sixty-seven da yang. I had to lose forty-six da yang at mah-jong, and I paid twenty-one for the theater tickets, the tea, and the daos. But it was a remarkably successful day. The concubine of the Tuchun agreed to interpose for your husband. My husband is writing to Sian-Shih to that effect. Let them stop worrying. Now it's just a question of days before Tan Ya-pu will be free. We cannot count on the first few days, because Sung Ke-wu is not out of Szechuan. But as soon as his last soldier steps over the border of the province, the door of the prison will open. Today I invited the ladies to dinner. Unfortunately, they liked it so much at my house that they told all their friends about it, and they also want to come. I'll have to ask them. If you only knew how tired I am of these stupid, painted faces."

My step-mother took money out of her purse for the current expenses of the hostess and listened to the next task.

"Take about a hundred da yang and buy two presents."

My step-mother made a suggestion: "I saw a lovely box for rouge and eye-paint."

"No," said the hostess. "A box would not do. You have to look for something unusual. You must find a bolt of Indian silk and a bottle of French perfume. Only see that you don't spend more than a hundred for both. It is enough for those ducks."

One concubine was smelling the perfume. The other was feeling the soft silk and whispering to the hostess.

"Smile, please smile. I give you my word that I'll talk to him today about freeing poor Tan Ya-pu."

"I am afraid that he is too severe," the hostess answered sadly, "and it is doubtful that you can influence him by mere persuasion."

An angry frown.

"You think he will not listen to me! You think he would dare to disobey! We'll see. I know him very well. He does not like to stay alone evenings, and in that case he will have to spend his time alone, even if he is my lord and master."

But the hostess sadly shook her head and said, "I believe in your charm, and would not think for a minute that the most esteemed Lao-e could refuse you anything. But men do not like to pay attention to women's opinions. They think that we do not understand things. They must have a man's advice."

The other thought for a moment and then, remembering something, said joyfully: "How did you guess? U Lao-e received a letter yesterday from the older brother of the arrested Tan Ya-pu. It seems that they used to study somewhere together. You can cut off my head if tomorrow my husband does not go to the governor and tell him that Tan Ya-pu is innocent and that he must be let out of prison."

Then the E Tai-tai of Hu came up to the hostess and said, "I have already told Hu that he has an innocent man in his prison. He was interested in knowing who it was. When I told him that it was Tan, he did not answer. He only smiled. But don't you worry. I know him. He is nice, but very slow. You always have to wait a long time for his answer."

The next day the hostess again sat with my step-mother. My step-mother thanked her, "I'll never forget what you have done for me, and I'll write it in my will to my children. It seems to me that never in your life have you been so tired as you are these days. To listen to the chatter of these rich women for several hours a day must be very painful. I see that you have a head-ache. Will you permit me to paint a red circle on your fore-head? It will make you feel better."

But the hostess had already entered into the excitement of her well conducted chess game. She was now herself interested in its success.

The next day the old and learned Wu was making reports to his master and friend, the Tuchun Hu. After they had decided about six different questions he said, "I looked over the case of the former secretary of the Police Department, Tan Ya-pu."

Hu was very much interested.

"Did you find a letter from Sung Ke-wu among his papers?"

"We found no letter," continued Wu. "Not only did we find no letter, but we found no evidence of any sort against this man. I think that his revolutionary activities in Teh chien were inci-dental. He and Sung Ke-wu parted at one time as enemies. At present he is only an ordinary citizen, not interested in politics. To keep such people in prison might create a bad impression."

"Then you also think that he should be freed?"

Wu thought for a moment and then nodded with conviction.

Hu wrote down "set free", and put a sign and a small seal below it.

Tan Ya-pu, after spending eight months in a cell, walked down the corridor, past the prison guard whose bullet by a mere accident had missed his head.

In the empty house, on fragments of furniture, sat my step-mother. A few coins were still left in her purse—barely enough to carry them to Sian-Shih.

---

23. My Step-mother

Now I must tell you how my father, newly released, and my step-mother came to Sian-Shih.

The three-day feast of the moon is the first holiday of the fall, observed in August when the moon is full. In every kitchen the red-faced housewife bakes small moon-shaped cakes. They grind nut-meats and fold the paste into the cakes. People visit one another, bringing cakes of various funny shapes. All over the village, beginning in the early morning small boys accompanied by servants go carrying dishes full of these little cakes. Upon entering a house the boy bows, says his greeting, and presents the hostess with a dish of cakes. If there are no small boys in the family, the servant carries the dish and leaves it at its destination with a visiting card.

I was very impatient.

"Uncle, what is the news from Chengtu?"

"Good news. I received a letter. Your father is out of prison and we must look for a new house. Your father is coming back with your step-mother and there won't be enough room for all of us in this one."

"My father is free! Father is coming back! Father needs a new house." I was happy for the first time in months.

With a light step, almost skipping, I ran to the Tchens'.

The oldest Tchen was glad. "When your father comes back we will see your step-mother. Isn't that interesting?"

I grew subdued and dark and clenched my teeth: "Usually a step-mother is very strict with her step-sons. I am afraid her arrival will not interest me as much as you think."

But there were no words in the world that could disturb the clear, common sense of the older Tchen.

"Your step-mother is not that kind, I am sure, and your father is not a man who would let his wife mistreat his only son."

You could not contradict her, but it was hard for me to be quiet. And I lived like a blinking lamp, happy to see father, but afraid of my step-mother. But the happy feeling won.

The new house was found at last. We had a garden, the trees were lovely, and there were fish in the basin. The new house was more expensive than the old one. First of all, it was larger than the old house and also things in general had gone up in price. The house in Tan Tsia Chen held my babyhood, the first house in Sian-Shih saw my childhood, and this new one contained my thin, eager adolescence.

I was in school when father arrived in Sian-Shih. The director of the school gave me leave for a few days. On my way down I wanted to think about my father, but the thought of my step-mother would not leave my head. What if she should say to my father, "We are too poor to send Shih-hua to school. Send him to a store to work."

I stopped in front of the new house, choking with excitement, without strength to enter. But I could not continue to stand there, studying the cracks in the gate. In the passage I met a middle-aged nurse carrying my little sister, Shih-kuen whom I hadn't seen for a long time. She was very thin and was dressed in new clothes from head to foot. She looked contented. She screamed at the top of her voice, "My brother has come! My brother is here!"

For the first time I walked into the new house. I did not yet know the arrangement of the rooms. Bewildered, I looked around. The nurse and my sister led the procession.

My father was sitting at the window, reading, his back turned toward me. Next to him a strange woman was embroidering a child's slipper. "That is she," I decided. Father turned toward me without a smile. His face was much thinner and darker, and he had blue puffs under his eyes. He pointed to the woman and said, "Here is your step-mother." I bowed and greeted her.

She was small, smaller than my mother had been, very thin, flat-chested and sick-looking, almost like mother. She wore a black blouse and a black shirt. It looked very modest. Mother, too, had always been modestly dressed. Her feet were tiny, much smaller than mother's feet. Probably they had been bandaged when she was a child. Her face was not sleepy or fat; it was not dull. She had spirited eyes and an intelligent forehead. Is she as well-educated as my mother was, I wondered. She loves to talk, though. Mother had always been stingy with words. Her inflection was friendly and her smile attentive, but still I did not like her. She asked me if I had had my dinner—if I wouldn't like to have some food now, and whether it was difficult to study in school. Then, taking me by the elbow, she handed me a ten da yang bill. (It is customary for the step-mother to give presents to her step-children at the first meeting.) I took the money and rubbed it against my pocket.

She explained, "I did not know how much material you would need for a suit of clothes, or what kind of material you like best. You can choose some to suit your taste."

Like a turbulent river flowing into a quiet lake my exuberant uncle burst into the house. He cried, happy to see father, regarded him with eyes that were perhaps too brilliant, and greeted him in his own way: "Ya-pu, you are young. You do not understand what I, an old man, know. All that has happened to you is a well-deserved punishment for the betrayal of the Emperor. If you won't believe me now and pay attention to what I say, you will have worse things happen to you."

My father smiled: "We are brothers. We haven't seen each other for a long time. Let's drink and talk." And father led uncle into the main room toward the dinner table.

The days were strange. Every other house in the village knew exactly where the following day led. Every house had the coming days and months pre-arranged for different things—this month for planting tangerines, the next for sending the boy to school, marrying off a daughter, selling a house, and so on. Only our house did not know its next day.

I never talked to father. I was afraid to ask him a question, and he did not find it necessary to lead me into conversation. Perhaps he was afraid of spies. He wore a funny-shaped Japanese kimono instead of his jacket, and spent his days playing mah-jong with the neighbors. The bids were small and the losses not dangerous to our family purse. It was a convenient game—no conversation was necessary.

I was interested in father's orderly, Fan, who had remained loyal to him. In the dining room in the presence of guests Fan was the servant who did not dare to sit down, who rushed to my father at the slightest sign, and respectfully bent his head waiting for an order. The guests who dropped into the house did not notice Fan—he was a servant, an orderly . . . nothing. But at times, when there were no strangers in the house, Fan and my father would sit for a long time together, talking, discussing and reminiscing. The next morning Fan would come out of the house with a small parcel and a blanket, get into a boat, and pay the boatman to take him to the docks. It was Fan, my father's comrade, a member of the Kuomintang, going to inform the Center about the situation in Szechuan at the instruction of the restless Tan Ya-pu.

24. The Fugitive

IT WAS DECEMBER AND ALL THE LEAVES HAD FALLEN. THE trees on the mountain stretched out their bare branches against the cold sky. The Yangtze was again thin and blue. The cold made the people draw in their shoulders. The collectors of tangerine peels were in the streets, and this winter's fruit shone like bright spots in the hands of every person.

I was reading a book when a student came up to me and said: "Tan Shih-hua, a man wants to see you."

It was Fan. He took me outside the school and told me quietly this troubling news:

"Your father is in a bad predicament, but you are in a worse one. Police are coming here to arrest you. Go to the inspector and get leave. Don't tell him anything about your father."

I went to the inspector and after a short, but strong, argument got my leave, taking not a thing with me, not even a blanket. Fan and I ran down the slope to the river and hired a boat to take us to the village that lay half way between Teh chien and Sian-Shih. In the twilight, exposing my cheeks to the cold river air, I listened to Fan's whisper. He told me what had happened that morning.

Before the dawn had changed the light from blue to rose, an officer came to see my father and invited him to go to a tea-house to talk over an important matter. My father, who usually went to bed about eight or ten o'clock, was already up. As a rule the tea-houses were still closed at dawn, but this time one of them was open. My father went with the officer. How could he tell? Perhaps the man had some revolutionary communication. As they entered the tea-house my father saw that it was full of soldiers. It looked bad. He asked the officer to take the best place at the table. When that vain, unbending officer sat down, he took his seat at the opposite end of the table and asked what was the matter.

The officer said, "The daoyin of our county wants to see you and talk to you about the situation. He ordered me and my soldiers to accompany you."

The soldiers listened somberly to their conversation. Fan, who left the house immediately after my father, was now wandering around the tea-house. Nobody paid any attention to him.

My father answered, "I am a private citizen. I do not occupy any post at present. If the daoyin flatters me with his attention and expresses a desire to see me, you should no doubt have a letter from him to that effect. Will you please show it to me?"

"Yes, I have the letter," said the officer, "but I will not show it to you. What I have told you is sufficient."

Father continued, "I am a weak, unarmed man. I cannot do you any harm. I am in your hands. I'll just look at the letter and give it back to you right here."

The officer took a paper out of his pocket. The secret order of General Hu to arrest Tan Ya-pu, from the village Tan Tsia Chen, was in father's hands. The reason for the arrest was also given in the paper. Hu had intercepted a telegram from Sun Yat-sen to Tan Ia-pu, but could not decipher it. The paper went on to state that it would be desirable to execute Tan Ia-pu at the county seat to save the time it would take to transport him to Chengtu. In a stretch of a thousand li a thousand unforeseen things might happen. Everything in the document looked very bad for my father . . . except for a little detail: in the name the syllable Ya was misspelled.

Very quietly, almost laughing, my father handed back his

death warrant to the officer: "To my great regret, this order has to do with some other person of the same name. First of all, the order concerns a citizen of Tan Tsia Chen, and I live in Sian-Shih; and secondly, the name of this citizen Ia is not spelled the way I spell mine." He handed the officer his visiting card.

The bewildered officer held the order in one hand and my father's card in the other. His eyes kept shifting from one to another. The soldiers jumped from their seats and looked at the paper over his shoulders. Even they could see that the spelling of the two names was different and their somber disposition began to disappear. They began to whisper, nudging one another.

Before the officer could come to his senses, my father bowed to him politely and said with a clear smile on his face, "Will you permit me to invite you to my house? You must be tired after your journey. I hope you'll let me act as your host and then I myself will go with you to Teh chien to talk personally with the daoyin, because, of course, you are now in a strange position. I should think that a talk would clarify everything. If you don't mind, I should like to ask your 'brothers' to come to my house, too."

And my father pointed to his soldiers.

The officer looked at father, at his soldiers, at the card, and at the order; then again at the card, and again at the order, and frowned. Then his face cleared again. On one hand he wanted to be a good soldier, obeying the given order; on the other, he didn't want to act like a rude, ill-bred fellow. He ordered some of his soldiers to stay in the tea-house and the rest to follow my father, while he himself walked behind them. Fan followed them at a distance, saw them enter the house, but stayed outside the gate and wandered about, waiting to see what would happen.

At that time two tailors were working in our house. Father had arrived from Chengtu with no clothes. One of the tailors we had known for a long time—he was a great friend of my younger uncle. They often laughed and joked together. The other, a little younger, had been brought up by the old man.

My step-mother was not yet up. Father entered her room, and said aloud, "Hello, get up, quick!"

Then he whispered, "Danger! I am escaping."

All the money we had in the house at that moment amounted to three and one-half da yang. Father put them into his pocket, and ran out through the back door, which led to the garden. As he ran he said loudly enough to be heard all over the house, "Will you get a good breakfast for the guests? I must hurry to Teh chien to see the daoyin."

The back door closed after him just at the moment when the officer was asking the old tailor, "Is there another door to this house?"

"No, there is not," the old man answered quickly, and he fixed his eyes warningly at the younger tailor. The officer turned toward the latter and asked him the same question. The young tailor hesitated a moment, and said, "No." The officer, reassured, sat down, folding his hands over the hilt of his sabre which was placed between his knees. He could hear what was going on in the kitchen, while his soldiers remained on the street, guarding the entrance to the house.

My step-mother busied herself in the kitchen, ordering her servant around, giving instructions: "Hand me a pan; put some more wood in the stove; give me the water; where is the good tea? Good tea, I said, not this cheap stuff. . . ." Then, lowering her voice, but still talking loudly enough for the officer to hear her, she said anxiously to the servant:

"I really don't know how Lao-e will go to Teh chien. I am afraid I'll have to call a doctor. He has a terrible stomach ache. He could not sleep all night, and now it's getting worse."

The officer and his soldiers listened to the conversation sympathetically, and attributed my father's non-appearance to the necessity for remaining in the bathroom. Dishes were rattled and the servant rushed around setting tables with an increasing excitement and eagerness. My step-mother's audible distress over Lao-e's illness grew more and more anxious.

A half hour passed and father did not appear. The soldiers came to the officer and whispered to him excitedly. The officer, rattling his sabre, jumped up and called my step-mother. The bathroom was empty. He began to swear. Dragging the butts of their guns over the stone floor behind them, the soldiers rushed around searching closets and rooms. Amid a shower of curses they discovered the back door.

Screaming, the servants ran away. My step-mother was thrown on the floor. They beat her with the butts of their guns. The tailors were arrested and locked in a small room. The soldiers searched all the adjoining houses and arrested all the men in them. Finally it became apparent that father was not hiding in the house nor at one of his neighbor's. The furious soldiers broke down doors and tore the paper windows.

"He escaped, the scoundrel! Let's arrest everybody. Let the daoyin deal with them for his flight. He has a child in Teh chien —a son. Let's take the boy!"

When Fan, still safely wandering about, heard these words he rushed toward the docks just in time to jump into a boat leaving for Teh chien. In the meantime the soldiers scattered over the streets of the village leading toward the mountains. They ran past the small streets of Sian-Shih, past the tangerine orchards, and reached the rice fields. The road began to rise. They were near the woods beyond which lay the wilderness of the mountains. There, in front of the woods, my father's back was visible to them. My father saw the soldiers and rushed into the woods. Running and panting, they surrounded the woods so as not to let him escape. But my father was clever. He let all of them pass him and then jumped out of the woods, back to the road, and lay down on the very edge of the road in the border ditch of the reaped rice field. His body sank into a cold slime three feet deep. He had his head in a pile of rice straw. He lay close to the steep side of the ditch right under the road, like a taut string, freezing in the mud.

For four hours the soldiers searched the woods. Finally abandoning the hunt they came out into the road, passing within inches of the spot where father lay submerged in the freezing mud. Little lumps of earth, dislodged by their heavy feet, fell on his head. He heard their angry voices.

"Vanished right into the ground! It's impossible. He could not possibly have come through the woods before us, and if he had, we would have seen him in the rice fields. We must go to Teh chien and get hold of his pup. That will make him jump— even out of the ground!"

But soon the fierce, excited clamor died away in the distance and the tramp of feet could no longer be heard. Father lay quietly in the ditch until he was sure the searchers were a safe distance away. He was completely numb. He pulled himself with difficulty out of the icy marsh where he had been so long immersed and started painfully toward the woods. He made his way through the trees and came to the edge of a little rivulet thickly overgrown with bamboo. Struggling through the tangle of bamboo trunks, he emerged into a small clearing on the edge of a steep bank. Below him lay a house and yard, an unpretentious dwelling which might have belonged to either a fisherman or a wood-cutter. A woman was busy outside the house. My father jumped down the bank and into the garden. The woman screamed.

"I won't hurt you," shouted father, interrupting her cries. "I have been robbed by bandits. They are after me. Hide me! Quickly! And for Heaven's sake, stop that noise."

The woman ceased and stared at him suspiciously.

"What's your husband's name?" he asked.

"Chen."

Father searched desperately through his memory. "Isn't he a member of the Union of Go-Lao?"

She nodded. Relief and assurance came into father's voice. "Go get him. I am the da-ge."

She ran away without another word and quickly returned with two men. The older one was her husband. The younger, a glib, self-assured sort of fellow, was his nephew. Both were members of the Go-Lao, and they recognized father, although they looked with astonishment at the thick crust of slime with which he was coated from head to foot. By this time he was shaking with a chill and parched with fever. He ached in every limb, and his legs and feet were wounded and bleeding where he had torn them on the vicious bamboo stumps. The Chens listened attentively to his story, and when it was concluded took him into the house. The older man prepared medicine for him and bound his wounds. He gave him a fresh kimono, and led him to a little room at the back of the house so located that its existence was not apparent to the casual observer. The older Chen never went into it—it was used by his nephew. The nephew was ambitious. He wanted to become a great man, a colonel, and with this end in view had recently joined a group of bandits operating in the vicinity. For this calling he was well qualified, being quick, skillful and merciless. He knew that after a few successfully perpetrated robberies and kidnapings, accounts of his boldness and bravery would reach the government of Teh chien. Then a man would be sent to negotiate with him, and to suggest that he and his followers take service with the daoyin of Teh chien. He might be made the leader of a battalion or a regiment.

The hidden room was an essential part of his equipment. He could conceal his plunder there, or take sanctuary in it himself, if he were being pursued. In it he locked kidnaped merchants or officials, and there his tired comrades often slept. The youthful bandit was excited and pleased that Tan Ya-pu, a famous leader of men and an experienced commander, the renowned chief of police and brilliant president of the Union of Go-Lao, was now hiding in his secret chamber. The young bandit immediately offered my father a position of honor and importance with his group of raiders. Father declined, thanking him for the honor and expressing the hope that the time would come when he could call on the young Chen to help forward the revolution. For the present, he added, such an activity would not at all fall in with his plans. Moreover, the daoyin was persecuting him so persistently at the instigation of the government of the province, that any association with young Chen would only endanger the youthful leader unnecessarily.

Young Chen had all the qualifications of a successful bandit. In particular, he was an opportunist. Though my father had refused to join the robber band, Chen felt that his presence offered a chance for advancement which ought not to be neglected. He approached his uncle with the suggestion that they betray the fugitive to the daoyin. The older man revealed the plan to my father.

"My nephew," he said, "is treacherous, and I am powerless against him. The best thing for you to do is to go away as soon as you can."

My father had been at Chen's for two days, and he had begun to feel sufficiently recovered to travel again. His wounds were healing and the fever had subsided. The older Chen hired two peasants with a tzao. He arranged to meet them in the woods, and secretly conducted father to the rendezvous. My father pulled the curtains of the tzao together and directed the carriers to take him to a certain village. Before they reached it, however, he stopped the litter and paid off the peasants.

"I will walk the rest of the way," he said. He went into the woods and, peering from behind a tree, watched the peasants with the empty tzao until they were out of sight. Then he walked in the opposite direction. He was in a hurry to get over the county border. By taking paths that led through the woods, he avoided meeting people. At night his mattress was the frozen ground and his pillow the dry leaves. His objective was a town, 120 li away where the father of my dead mother lived. Three days later he entered my grandfather's house.

My grandfather welcomed him and gave him food and clothing—a peasant jacket of coarse blue linen, a pair of heavy trousers, faded and worn, and grass sandals to wear on his bare feet. My father tied the trousers around his ankles with wide tape, and bound his head with a black towel. For the time being the immaculate Tan Ya-pu of the police uniform and the negligent Tan Ya-pu who played mah-jong in a carelessly arranged kimono, vanished from the face of the earth. In their place was a nameless peasant in a remote, little village.

My grandfather sent for his nephew, a carpenter, who erected a false partition in the house, making a little closet about three feet wide. Two boards were installed, just wide enough to permit one to lie down on one's side. So skillfully was the work done that not even the sharpest eye could detect the presence of the hiding place. Here my father went into retreat and, like a woodchuck curled up in his hole, awaited a favorable opportunity to reappear in the world.

About a month and a half later, a new creature emerged to freedom and fresh air. He had long moustaches and a full beard. His hair came to his eyebrows. This man went to the village hall and registered himself under the name of Su. He said that he had wandered into the village looking for work in the fields because he was unable to earn his living as a carpenter. It was not necessary for my father to register—Chinese people may wander around the country without a passport—but he did it with the intention of obliterating every shadow of his old identity. My grandfather rented a plot of ground, gave him a mattock, a wheel-barrow and a shovel, and my father set to work to till the barren, stony soil.

25. From Place to Place

THE BOAT BROUGHT US TO THE VILLAGE BETWEEN TEH CHIEN and Sian-Shih. From here we had to walk a long distance to the center of the county, covering our tracks. The first night of our journey we spent in a filthy way-side tavern. The dirt and the stuffy air made me sick. I could not sleep. In the grey light of the dawn we hurried along across the fields to the house of one of my father's first cousins, not far from the next village. This aunt of mine (we call a first cousin an aunt) was a very rich woman and her house was a big establishment. I had seen her more than once at our table during holidays. She was always friendly and gay and I had no doubt that she would hide me from the soldiers of the daoyin. I had never been to her house before as my father did not want me to associate with her sons who were notorious hooligans. One of them was several classes ahead of me in school.

My unexpected arrival created a sensation. She stared at me, partly bewildered and partly glad to see me.

My aunt exclaimed, clapping her hands, "God's wind brought you in! Shih-hua!"

I was seated at the table, fed well and questioned about my father and about the school.

"Good, you'll stay with us awhile. My sons will be very glad to see you."

Fan now decided that I was safely established. As he was in a hurry to get back to Sian-Shih he said good-bye to his hostess, begging her several times to take good care of little Hua. Perhaps it was these parting words of Fan's that made her suspicious. She took me to her room and in a very business-like

[144]

way, acting as though she were one of the closest relatives and had already been taken into my secret, asked, "Now, what is the matter? Tell me all the details. Why did you come here?"

I could see that my aunt was troubled. I knew that she was my father's first cousin. How could I hide the facts from her? Perhaps I would have to stay a long time in the house. I told her the whole story.

After the sleepless night in the tavern I slept soundly. The next morning my aunt's husband, a thin old man with a beard that looked as though lime had been splashed on it, asked me in a very tender and compassionate tone, "Shih-hua, wouldn't you like to go and visit another aunt of yours? She lives not very far from here, just about forty li."

Why not? I said, "Yes, I'll go."

Encouraged by his success, the old man went on, "I know that some peasants are going there this morning. Why don't you go with them? You'll get lost if you go alone."

Suddenly everything became clear—they were trying to get rid of me. I felt sad and lonely. Fan was far away, I had no money to hire a tzao, and I knew that I could not walk forty li. Although twelve years old, I was as thin as a chick in a famine-stricken village. My lips began to tremble and I retired to a corner. My aunt softened: "Here, I'll find you a tzao tomorrow."

They did not say a word to me after that, neither that day nor the next morning. They simply called a tzao. With a deep bow I thanked my aunt for her hospitality. She pressed two da yang into my hand. I carefully moved her hand away. The money remained in it. Perhaps it was better for me to go. The farther I went from Teh chien the safer I would be.

The second aunt was even happier to see me than the first one. She and her husband came running out of the house to greet me. Their servants—a cook, a janitor and a gardener—stood silently at the door, staring at me.

While my aunt was occupying herself with me, her husband went to talk to the coolies. Their conversation lasted long. He looked back at me several times while listening to them. When he finally came back to me again, I could see from the hard expression in his eyes that he liked me considerably less than he had ten minutes ago. Without saying a word he passed by and went into the house. It was evident that the coolies had told him in complete detail of my flight. I informed my aunt immediately that I intended to stay only overnight and that I was going on the next morning to see my older uncle in Tan Tsia Chen.

The seat of the tzao, protected from the sun by a piece of burlap, swayed lightly on the shoulders of the coolies. The husky fellows would stop every twenty minutes under some big tree, take the filthy rags off their heads and dry themselves, brow and chest. They drank water, dipping it out with their hands or sucking it directly from a brook. They stopped at a little restaurant and ate rice and salted vegetables. Then they filled up their pipes, sat down and smoked for a long time. Then they straightened up, took up the poles and were ready again to move ahead, half-walking, half-running with long, measured strides, that enabled them to make about a hundred li a day.

My older uncle was not surprised to see me for he already knew what had happened. At last I had found a person whose eyes did not stare at me with fear, and who did not start planning to get rid of me. He took some old books and other rummage out of a dark closet and made a bed for me there. He asked his wife to prepare the best food for me, as though I were not just a nephew, but an equal of his—a possessor of learned degrees. I wandered about the house in which I had been born, looked into the prayer room, turned over the pages of the dusty family record, read the hieroglyphics of my ancestors'

[146]

names on the strips of wood hanging over the altar, and remembered my babyhood.

Then my uncle and I had a long and well-cooked dinner. My uncle drank wine—cup after cup—and got drunk. His voice rose to a high pitch.

"What is a revolution? Boy, what is this revolution of yours? What did your father find in the revolution? Your father is a foolish little rooster. I said to him so many times: don't betray the Emperor; things will get worse. Was I not right? Running away now, saving your head from the daoyin's soldiers. And you want me to have respect for your father? Well, he got what he wanted. Now the police are after him? Right! They want to execute him? Right! One should not make plots! But who is it, who wants to execute him? Yuan Shi-kai, the double traitor! He betrayed both the Emperor and the Republic. Tan Ya-pu, at least, was more honest: he betrayed only his Emperor. He should not have betrayed anybody at all. I said so! I told him so! . . ."

With tears in his eyes, shouting and cursing, my uncle went to his bedroom and dropped down on his bed. I crawled into my closet.

After a few days he said to me, "It is hard to hide you here. What will the villagers say if someone asks them, 'Who is the boy staying with Tan Sao-pu?' Of course they'll say, 'Tan Shih-hua, the son of the fugitive Tan Ya-pu.' We'll have to think of something better. It seems to me the best thing would be to send you to a monastery and change your name."

These words almost broke me. I had often wondered painfully what would happen to me next. I was trying to find a way to get back to school, but I had never thought of a monastery.

My uncle went somewhere and negotiated with some people. The cares and troubles of the last days made him walk faster than usual. Finally he ordered a splendid farewell dinner for me.

"Listen, nephew," he said, as we sat down at the dinner table, "today you are Tan Shih-hua for the last time. Say your beautiful name, which I gave you, and then forget it. Tomorrow you will be a poor orphan who was brought up by me, and your name will be Su-Shi. When I discover the whereabouts of your father I'll let him know your new name."

I did not like the name Su-Shi. I did not like, in general, what was in store for me. Enjoying the magnificent farewell dinner, my uncle drank warm wine out of a tea-pot and said, "Eat the meat, eat it. The rules of the monastery are strict. The people of the monastery are god-fearing people. They will not give you meat, butter or eggs. Shih-hua—I mean Su-Shi—eat all you can."

I would have been unable to eat had he said nothing. I fumbled feebly with my chopsticks in my plate, so as not to hurt his feelings.

"Don't be sad, Shih-hua. Everything will be all right. A monastery? It is not so bad. Remember that the first Emperor of the Ming dynasty was but a poor orphan and a monk. Nevertheless he chased the Tartars out of China and united the country under his strong hand. Don't forget, our ancestor who left Peking and retired to Szechuan was a general in the service of the Ming dynasty. Our other ancestors were writers, scientists, and people of the nobility. They all did a great deal of good. Who knows what your destiny will be?"

I did not answer. He went on with his consoling nonsense. The priggish stories about generals and emperors slid by my republican ear. With the end of my chopstick I wrote on the bottom of the cup, brown from the soya sauce: Su-Shi, Su-Shi. . . .

Suddenly my uncle became furious. He cut short his solemn speech and began to swear. He drank and swore, cursing my father and the revolution. The tears rolled down his nose and fell on his upper lip. He went on drinking till the glassy pupils of his eyes ceased to see. Then he made a few uncertain steps toward his room, fell on his bed and his loud breathing filled the room with the smell of wine and food.

26. The Monastery

THE ROAD WE WALKED ON WENT UP A WOODED MOUNTAIN, making sharp zig-zags. Pines, bamboo, cypress, locusts, oak, and arbor-vitae grew together on both sides of the road.

Ban-Pan was the name of the monastery. An empty cistern, shaped like a crescent, in front of the gates, was filled with fallen leaves. Three monks, the entire staff of the monastery, came out to greet us. My uncle introduced me to them. I looked up at their shaven heads and their husky figures. They were clad in blue robes with very wide sleeves. The youngest of them could not have been less than forty years old, more than three times as old as I was.

Pointing at the abbot, my uncle said, "Here is your *Si-Fu*." Si-Fu means teacher.

They took me from the bright, sun-lit court to a dark barn where two painted giants, the guardians of the temple, stood one on each side of the altar. The faces of the giants were brutal, and they held sharp, curved battle-axes in their hands. A whole præsidium of gods, with their master, the serene, large-bodied Buddha, sat along the wall. Incense burners, filled with ashes, and copper gongs stood in front of them.

I knelt. The two monks began to strike the resounding gongs. They lighted the candles and incense sticks. The abbot murmured a prayer. I had never heard words uttered with such rapidity. The persistent moan of the gongs, the smoke of incense sticks, the delirious mumbling of the abbot, and the furious wrath of the painted demons turned my brain. I did not know where I was, and was not sure I was anywhere at all.

The abbot told me to bow nine times to the ground. While I was making my bows, one of the two monks left the gongs, and

[149]

brought in a strange, long, blue garment which he held in his
outstretched hands. The abbot put this garment on my back.
It was the coarse blue linen robe of a Buddhist monk. It had
small, soft, round buttons. The monks were poor, their garments simple.

I buttoned up my new robe and bowed four times to the abbot
and once to each of the monks. Then a barber entered the room.
I learned later that at the suggestion of my uncle he had been
summoned by the monks beforehand. He dampened my hair
with warm water. My locks fell on the floor and about my
shoulders, under the sharp blade of his razor. Tan Shih-hua, a
high-school student, existed no longer—there was only a little
blue-headed Buddhist monk.

The monks, who were all illiterate, obsequiously begged my
uncle to give me a new name. (A monk has to change his worldly
name.) My uncle pretended to be thinking for a moment, and
then suggested that my name might be "Su". Su-Shi for everyday life, and Lao-Su for official occasions. There was no last
name. Monks are not supposed to have one. It took me a long
time to get used to the name "Su"; now it is my pen-name.

My uncle did not leave me all that first day. He walked
around and gave me instructions. The fact that I was a monk
seemed to amuse him.

"Listen, Shih-hua—Lao-Su: When you read the Buddhist
bible, don't mumble it, as the abbot does. Think over its teachings and try to understand them. The books of Buddhism have
a profound inner meaning."

That he was right I learned during the next few months. The
monks do not understand the bible; they only know how to
mutter its words. The Buddhist bible has two parts; one part contains the teachings, and the other the description of religious
rites. The monks know only the latter. But how was I to follow
my uncle's advice that I should think over its teachings, and try
to understand what I read? In that part of the bible dealing

with the rites, it was written that the blood which a woman loses while giving birth to a child is unclean. For that reason she is to be thrown into a bloody stream in the other world. But if her children read the bible her punishment will be less severe. I was trying to understand the teachings, but the harder I thought the more they bewildered me. I asked the abbot: "Who gave birth to Buddha?"

"A woman," he answered.

"And is Buddha's mother also swimming in the river of blood?"

The old man turned away: "Buddha is a different matter," said he, and ended our conversation.

The bible did not bring me peace, it made me angry. I read the stories about paradise and about hell and muttered prayers about the compensation for sins and virtues. Worthy people will be happy on this earth and their souls will be blessed in the other world. Why, then, if my mother is now in paradise, does she never come to tell me about her beautiful life? And if there is no paradise—why is it that in reward for her silent, endless work in life, my sweet, gentle, self-denying mother received so much suffering and an early death? Why does father, who consecrated his life for the good of the people, have to wander now like a homeless dog, while the scoundrel Hu sits safely in his palace, prosperous and rich?

My relations with the monks were not very friendly. I was made to do all kinds of errands for them. They themselves had long ago turned into lazy good-for-nothing hypocrites. They ate their food noisily, snored in their sleep, struck the gongs and muttered their prayers. When they bowed to the ground in front of the altar, they did it automatically, just as they counted their beads. Why did they do all this? They did not know.

The best room in the monastery belonged to the head of the village, whom the monks treated with a very special respect whenever he appeared. The very existence of the monastery depended upon the good will of this small, thin man with a few hairs on his upper lip, and with the shrewd eyes of a village ruler. If he had wished it, he could have forced the monks to begin wandering the next day from place to place. He happened to see me once.

"Who is that? Where is he from?" he asked the abbot.

"Tan Sian-shen brought him in."

"Is he well enough educated?"

"Tan Sian-shen taught him for a year."

"Well, then, he must know enough," said the old man. All the pupils of my uncle were well known in the village for their education.

The gates of the monastery were always closed. Pilgrims used to come up the hill-road to these gates. Poor coolies and peasants went to monasteries when their children were sick, or when they had had a nightmare. They also came to keep a vow that had been given before a crop had been sold, or a purchase made; or when they were childless and wanted children; or in the face of a drought or a meager crop. Their vows were simple: to light a candle, to burn two or three incense sticks, or a bunch of paper money in front of a god's statue, and to bow to him ten or a dozen times.

The pilgrims knocked at the gate with a copper knocker. The monk-gateman, who would be lying in his bed or sitting on the steps of the court counting his beads, jumped up and looked through a peephole. If he saw that the people were poor and that they came on foot, he opened the gate slowly, and in an ungracious manner admitted the long line through a half-open door. The pilgrims brought along bamboo baskets, in which they had imitation gold and silver nuggets that did not cost more than a cent each, candles, incense sticks, and also vegetables, eggs, and sometimes a roast. The monks, who did not eat meat nor eggs, sent it all to the kitchen—to be sold later to the well-to-do pilgrims.

[152]

The gateman did not spend much time or words on the poor people. He simply pointed at the house of the idols, not even bothering to call the abbot. The pilgrims walked carefully over the court, the stone surface of which was always very clean—the gateman and I swept it every day. They entered the house of the painted monsters. Throwing their heads back, they examined with fear the crooked faces and bulging eyes of the wooden guardians of the temple, enormous, dilapidated, clad in garments of soft, faded colors, covered with dust. They bowed to the ground in front of the clay gods, burnt their offerings, and whispered with embarrassment to the monk: "Ring to the gods, will you please, Ho-Shen?"

Ho-Shen was annoyed. Why trouble his gods for the sake of these bedraggled men, when all they had to offer were three eggs and a few leaves of salted cabbage? He pretended not to hear what they said.

"Ring to the gods, Ho-Shen, or they will not hear our prayers."

Then the monk picked up the gongs and struck them a few times, so indolently it seemed they would surely fall from his limp hands. He emptied their baskets in the kitchen and helped the pilgrims out of the gates, pushing them gently with his hand. Then he closed the gate, returned to his bed, and began counting his beads again.

Sometimes the knocks at the gate were loud, powerful, self-assured. Looking through the peephole, the gateman saw finely dressed people handing over their tired horses to the grooms. Or he saw heavy-bodied, rich men climbing out of their tzaos. Then—quicker than he could say the name of Buddha—the gateman swung the gate wide open to greet these desirable guests with bows, gentle smiles, and polite exclamations. The abbot hurried out of his cell, without being summoned. The backs of the monks became unusually flexible; their hands folded together again and again in the shape of a boat and money poured into this vessel: real money, not the imitation paper brought by the poor men.

The panting coolies, their brows and shoulders glistening with sweat, went to the kitchen to drink water and deliver the heavy baskets, filled with delicious dishes to be warmed up over the fire. They broke branches off the trees for crow's-nests to protect their heads against the ultra-violet rays of the mountain sun.

Gaily, imperatively, the prayer gongs rang in the hands of the monks. Even if the gods were old and deaf, the monks would have made them pay attention to the prayers of such pleasant pilgrims. One-two, the prayer was finished, and the monks, flattering and wiggling, invited the guests to the table to serve them tea, vegetables and fruit, to beg further donations for the monastery.

On such days I had no time to make observations, nor even to be annoyed. The abbot would be sending me every minute to bring hot water for the tea, or rice and fruit from the kitchen, or relish, sweets, and matches, or to the library for some books. At home it was different. There everyone worked for me—mother, my uncle, the servant, the oarsman in a boat, and the carriers of tzaos. But here, stretching out my tired legs in the evening, I came to the conclusion that a situation where the poor man has to serve the rich is not quite just.

Even without the pilgrims I had enough work. The monastery had to cultivate its grounds which had been cleared in the midst of thick woods. There the monks grew beans, corn, and wheat. They worked with mattocks. The fields covered about ten *mu,* and the monastery had no cattle nor ploughs with which to cultivate them. I was small, and not used to working with a mattock. My tender fingers knew only how to hold a brush and draw hieroglyphics. The iron beak of the mattock pulled me down and made my muscles ache. Its heavy handle covered my palm with callouses. My shirt would stick to my back like a wet bandage. I had not known before what hard labor the work of a peasant was; on the contrary I had thought it a most pleasant sight to watch the peasants' mattocks going up and down so rhythmically over the fields. Their work always touched me with its beauty. I could never understand my grandmother saying: "Shih-hua, don't touch this flower—a peasant had to work to grow it."

Next to the monastery was an oak-grove. In the fall, if you listened, you seemed to be in a hail-storm of falling acorns. The proprietor of the grove generously permitted the monks to use the acorns. He did not mind; they were cheap. The monks put a basket on my back and sent me to pick them. When the branch was pulled down a shower of ripe acorns fell on the grass. There were poisonous snakes in the grass sometimes, but I was not afraid of them. When I walked through the woods, I used to poke the ground in front of me with a cane, as shepherds do. I groped in the thick grass, gathering acorns—good and bad, old and new, ripe and rotten. The bending tired me. I came back bringing only a few acorns, most of them bad. Panting, I sat down on a step, while the abbot, dipping a handful of acorns out of the basket, so bad that a pig wouldn't eat them, called me all kinds of names. Later, I became accustomed to picking acorns. I learned how to do it. You had to set the basket on the ground under a covered branch, and then pull the branch like a dog's tail. All the acorns would shower straight into your basket.

At home in Sian-Shih I loved the jelly-like dish made from acorns. Mother used to grind them into a paste, squeeze the juice out of them through a piece of cloth, warm the paste to make it thicker, cut it into brick-shaped lumps and put these into frequently changed water which destroyed the bitter, astringent taste. In a few days we could eat the acorn-jelly with chicken or meat. This dish was served in the monastery also, but the cook did not keep the acorns in water long enough. It tasted very bad and made your tongue feel wooden. I had to learn to swallow it quickly, without touching it with my tongue. I used to swallow the acorn-jelly and philosophize: Why should a rich man eat good food without working? Why did a poor man have to work like a horse in order to get himself a bowl of stew which tasted like dish-water?

The Monastery Ban-Pan in the mountains of Sian-Shih was my first school of socialism. Thank you, uncle, for sending me to a poor monastery, for had it been a prosperous one, I should have remained what I had been before—a good-for-nothing, idle youngster.

The mountain air, combined with the physical work, strengthened me. In place of the aching knots on my arms, hard lumps of muscle grew. I began to forget school-subjects. The school, where I used to count the days between each vacation, seemed like a paradise now. The monks were not interested in me. I worked, and that was enough for them. My uncle did not pay for my keep there. I was merely their farm-hand and clerk. They treated me not badly, but indifferently. Had I suddenly become ill and died, it wouldn't have quickened their pace or caused them to raise their voices. As for me, I was not interested in them either. Ten, twenty questions and answers a day—that was all.

I never even thought of Tsai-in, but my anxiety for my father increased from day to day. As my muscles grew stronger, my nerves grew weaker. Never before had I believed in devils, but now I began to fear them. The wooden monsters of our altars were responsible for this. At night, especially, in the darkness of the temple, they did not resemble people but gigantic toads or insects. Every night the sleepy voice of the abbot would call me through the tense darkness of midnight. Behind the lower glass part of the window the darkness crawled like a black snake. I shoved my feet into my slippers and hurried through the abbot's room into the temple, full of shadows and rustlings. The small flame of the eternal lamp made the shadows of the monsters dance on the ceiling.

The large clay torsos of a clever god sitting on a lion, and of

a pensive one, riding an elephant, towered above the altar-table.
A rustle—small pieces of clay were dropping off. Lizards and
centipedes, resembling wheat-husks, crawled on the dusty
shoulders of the gods. The heads of the wooden guardians were
lost in the darkness. Who knew what they were doing up there?
Perhaps they were rolling their eyes or opening their toothy
mouths. Trying not to look at them, I picked up a bunch of
incense sticks, lighted them from the flame of the lamp, stuck
them into the ashes of an incense burner, and rushed back. My
fear increased. The movement of the air made the flame flicker;
the dance of the gods turned into a wild orgy. Something was
grabbing at my heels. . . . Pulling myself together, I walked
across the abbot's room to find him sitting on his bed, his legs
crossed under him, his hands folded together, long strings of
beads hanging down from his thumbs. His pupils did not gleam
in the dull cracks of his eyes—he was muttering his midnight
prayer.

Three times a month, every first, every fifteenth and every
last day, I had to go to a barn adjoining the temple. Two flat
copper bells hung there. I struck the large one first—eighteen
times, with long intervals. To the accompaniment of the moan of
the copper, I muttered special prayers. They were mixed in my
mind with the fragments of warm dreams. After striking the
large bell the proper number of times, I struck the small one,
in quick succession, saying with each sound of the bell one of the
various names of Buddha.

My older uncle came to see me. Speaking fast and softly, he
told me that father was out of danger. I could see that his eyes
were ready to cry with pity, and that only the presence of the
monks prevented the tears from rolling over his cheeks. He asked
me: "Do you like it here, Lao-Su?"

The monks stood there and did not go away. I answered, "Yes,
I like it very much."

But when we were walking alone in the woods around the monastery, I complained to him about my hard, lonely, and friendless life. My uncle answered, "Be patient."

Day after day the sun rose and then fell, like the beads in the hands of a monk. But my face was now tanned, my breathing even, and it meant nothing to me to carry a basket from the grove to the kitchen.

In the school my class-mates were passing into higher classes. They were learning new hieroglyphics, English words, theories of geometry, getting ahead of me. On the other side of the globe was the thunder and blood of the great European war. But the explosions of the shells were not heard in the quiet Ban-Pan. The fat Yuan Shi-kai was coining money with his portrait printed on it, recruiting soldiers so that he might declare himself Emperor. The quiet, large-browed Sun Yat-sen was collecting money from the Chinese abroad, travelling in Europe, observing the way the courts, parliaments, factories, and banks were conducted, planning his next revolution. His revolutionary followers, hiding in villages, were either teaching youngsters, playing mah-jong and cards, or biding their time until their hour came. Some, tired of waiting, became officers of the new regime. My father was growing wheat and giving half of the harvest to the land owner. He fertilized his garden beds of turnip, cucumber, and cabbage, working there especially hard because one does not have to pay rent for land that is under a garden.

Day after day, I rose at dawn. My broom would sweep dust, fragments of burned paper, peach-stones, and peels of tangerines from the court. The second monk would be cooking vegetables in mustard oil over an open fire. Then, eating, and afterward, lazy praying in front of the altar. Following the prayers, we would bow to the gods, folding our hands in the shape of a house. Then would follow basket, mattock, work, dinner. At eight in the evening, a few minutes of reading from the bible in tune to the monotonous ringing of locusts, after which we would all retire to our cells.

---

27. Father Is "Dead"

THE SUMMER OF 1915.

There was a knock at the gate. In the courtyard stood my younger uncle, looking like a pilgrim. A basket of incense sticks and other offerings hung on his arm, and, to the great joy of the monks, a tzao was standing behind the gates. Giving me a warning glance, he said to the abbot: "I want to take a walk in the mountains; could I have your boy for a guide?" and he handed his basket to the gateman.

To be sure the monk could not hear us we hurried up the path leading into the woods.

"Shih-hua, your father wants to see you. Your step-mother has just moved to his new place." He told me how my father was living now, and added, "We'll arrange it this way. I'll leave my basket here, and tomorrow a man will stop here and ask the monks to send it down with the boy. Take it straight to the village where your father is now living."

If he hadn't spoken to me, I would never have recognized my father in this middle-aged, coarse-looking peasant, with calloused, brown hands and a long black beard. For the first time his face lit up with a smile at the sight of me. He was amazed to see his son wind-burned, long-armed and tanned. My appearance was so unusual that my step-mother began to cry, hiding her face in a handkerchief. My father put a hand on her shoulder and said, "Don't cry. Everything is so much better now than it was six months ago."

Father's house had but three rooms. It stood alone in the field surrounded by a bamboo grove in which was an ancient well full of clear cold water. A large opening was cut out in a rock and steps led down to the water. From this well father carried buckets of water daily to sprinkle his garden and, in times of drought, his fields as well. Half a dozen hens and ducks pecked at the ground near the porch.

Father said, looking at my uncle, "As soon as the danger is over, we must send Hua back to school. If he goes on like this much longer he will forget all he has learned there."

My uncle frowned: "It is not yet time. I think that the daoyin might leave him alone if he were sure that you were dead. Don't you think it's about time for you to die?"

My father answered quietly: "I had thought of that. We must spread the rumor that I am dead. The question is, how to start it, and who would do it? If we had a good Go-Lao member around we could make him do it."

He thought for a long time, trying to remember names, consulting my uncle about them, rejecting most of them. Again he thought, and remembered new ones. He finally chose the name of a soldier, Fang.

"The talk of my death must not originate in our country. Tell Fang to go to Shanghai and begin spreading the rumor from there.".

When we parted father said to me, "You must obey the abbot and win his confidence. Then you will have more free time and we can see each other more often. It would be a good thing if I taught you a little; otherwise, you will grow up a complete ignoramus."

Again the days went by as monotonously as the sound of

the gongs at night. Day after day, week after week, month after month. I had been at the monastery a whole year. The monks were used to me now. My life was much freer and quieter. I was unusually fond of work. I would run voluntarily out to the woods to gather brush for the kitchen stove, and then, lifting the long tails of my robe, sped to my father. He would put paper, brushes, and ink before me, open a book and teach me subjects which I had already begun to forget.

Of course, Fan, who had saved me from the soldiers of the daoyin, would have been the best man to organize the death rumor of my father, but he was no longer in Szechuan. He was away somewhere fighting with one of the revolutionary groups against Yuan Shi-kai. But Comrade Fang was a very good executive. My younger uncle urged him to go. The discipline of Go-Lao was still strong, and Fang went down the great Yangtze into Shanghai with its roaring steamers, the whistles of factories, and the sirens of thousands of black, beetle-like cars.

In Shanghai there were many merchants from Szechuan, trading in cabbages. The merchants were glad to see their countryman, and, moreover, such an interesting one. He knew so many stories and so much gossip that they could have listened to him all day and night. They were most interested in his story about the famous Tan Ya-pu who had broken the necks of the Manchus in Teh chien and the adjoining districts.

"Tan Ya-pu," so ran Fang's story, "was already ill when he had to escape from the daoyin's soldiers. He was obliged to rest in the freezing cold of the rice fields and the woods. The sharp bamboo stumps tore his clothes. Exhausted, he reached the river. Some way or other, with his last few cents, he went down the Yangtze to Shanghai, and from there he fled to Canton. But when he reached Canton and was safe, his strength gave out and he died."

The gossip ran from mouth to mouth. In a few weeks, there were several people who said that Tan Ya-pu had died in their arms. These eye-witnesses remembered the expression of his face, his last words, and the place where he was temporarily buried until his relatives should arrive to carry his remains back to his native Szechuan. My father was well pleased with his invention. Not only his comrades, but his worst enemies, officials, landlords, and merchants were shocked. Tan Ya-pu, who had overthrown the Manchus, dead? Their famous countryman dead?

The meetings of card players in clubs and temples were replaced by meetings of mourners. My father's name and title were written in beautiful hieroglyphics on a large tablet buried under wreaths and flowers. There were touching funeral orations. The former members of the Kuomintang, who had betrayed the revolution and sold out for the title of official and for a quiet, undisturbed life, addressed the crowd in lofty words. They enumerated the merits of the deceased, bringing tears to the eyes of listeners. Their own voices would tremble as if they had really lost a dearly prized friend.

The officials, whose eyes also glistened with moisture, said that the personality of my father was truly unique and wonderful, and that even if it was true that at times he was too daring and dangerous to society, nobody would ever be able to withhold from the luminous name of Tan Ya-pu the glory of the fact that it was he who had liberated Teh chien from the rule of the Manchus, and held the power in his own strong hands, never taking a cent for himself, and never spilling a drop of his citizen's blood. The intellectuals of the town, wearing the insignia of mourning, arranged the wake-dinners and invited my younger uncle to tell them about the heroic deeds of his great brother. My uncle went. Why not? It was all for the best. The only thing he had to be wary of was to be sad enough in appearance and not to forget the original story. Even the daoyin who, six months ago, was sending his soldiers to capture Tan for execution, dropped a tear in his soup. With the "death" of my father, the government lost interest in me.

The bronze knocker at the monastery gate sounded three times. My older uncle, gay and red-cheeked from the cold winter air which persisted in the mountains, appeared in the doorway and called:

"Shih-hua, Tan Shih-hua!"

The monks were bewildered to see me run out to the sound of this name which they had never heard before.

"Put your clothes on, nephew. We are going to Teh chien. You must continue your schooling."

The monks were amazed. What? Lao-Su is not Lao-Su at all, but Tan Shih-hua! He is no orphan, but a nephew of the esteemed Tan Sao-pu! He is not an errand-boy in a monastery, but a man who is soon to be graduated from the high school in Teh chien!

The embarrassed abbot humbly said to my uncle: "We had our doubts about Lao-Su for a long time. He was such an extraordinary boy! Ask him if we didn't treat him well."

I could see regret in the eyes of the monks. A cheap and skillful farm-hand was leaving their monastery. Such a good clerk, too.

My uncle and I went to see my "dead" father first. I had to say good-bye to him. From now on our meetings would not be so easy to arrange. My father wiped his soil-covered hand on the bottom of his shirt and said: "Now you are really a 'Su'." "Su" means "ressurrection".

I was surprised at my father's gentleness. His closeness to the earth seemed to have made him more approachable.

In Tan Tsia Chen I took off the wide-sleeved robe of the monks. My uncle dressed me in the very last word in mourning clothes. I wore a black paper skull-cap with a white button and white slippers. I was to go back to Sian-Shih garbed in these sad garments and to continue wearing them for three years.

The school-inspector, who had not wanted to let me go two years ago, was now the head of the school. He met me almost crying with joy.

"Why did you run away two years ago? If you had told me your troubles then I could have helped you!"

I bowed politely. I knew that the day after my flight he had received orders to turn me over to the police.

In passing I saw the Tchen sisters in Sian-Shih. How they had grown since I had seen them last—Tsai-in, especially. She had the carriage of a grown-up person. It embarrassed me to think that I could still sit down next to her, put my head in her lap, and listen to her recite poems over my up-turned face.

The sisters were glad to see me. They asked in unison: "Shih-hua, is it really true that your father is dead? Where were you, then, all these two years?"

"Yes, my father died. I spent two years in a monastery."

They would not believe me until I began reading prayers the way monks do in a temple. The giggling of the sisters stopped. They stared at me in amazement and then burst out into hilarious laughter:

"Ho-Shen! Ho-Shen! Shih-hua is a Ho-Shen!" and the word Ho-Shen remained as my nickname.

For several days I attended school as a listener, trying to remember the forgotten subjects. I passed the examinations after New Year's and joined the life of the students again. I had to catch up on what I had missed during my two years' absence. My former comrades, now in different classes, surrounded me in a dense crowd. They asked me where I had been, cursed the daoyin, and the government, regretted my father's death, wanted to know all the details, and told me about the war in Europe, and what low scoundrels the Germans were.

I was overwhelmed by the news; I sat and repeated sad, restrained words about my father's death. Together with my comrades I cursed the government and hated the Germans.

28. An Execution

THE DAYS OF POLITICAL SLUMBER WERE OVER. YUAN SHI-KAI declared himself Emperor. His former stableman, now General Tsao Kun, was moving his troops toward Szechuan to aid the governor of the province against the army of Tsai Sun-pu, a follower of Sun Yat-sen, who was threatening the province from the South.

The feet of marching soldiers echoed over the roads to Szechuan. Travelling salesmen came home with tales of the coming war, the battles that had already taken place, and districts that had been demolished. It was still fairly quiet around our town. Here the war was not between the armies, but between the police and the gangs of bandits which had increased considerably during the last few years of war and revolution. The gangs consisted of people like the nephew of the peasant Chen who lived in the bamboo forest, or of professional soldiers who were left with nothing to do when the war ended, or of former members of Go-Lao, or wandering farm-hands who could not find employment, and poor peasants put off their land for failure to pay their landlords. There was no lack of ammunition. The defeated armies from the North had left enough rifles in the district. Small bands of discontents would form into a larger group. They would kidnap the rich, the high officials and tax-collectors, take them into the woods and demand a ransom. The rich country people began to move into the towns where they felt safer under the protection of its walls and the police force.

In answer to the kidnappings and robberies, detachments of the daoyin's soldiers searched the woods and villages, sometimes catching the bandits. The walls of each village were plastered with white squares of paper offering rich rewards for

[165]

the capture of a brigand alive, or for his head. Executions of bandits in town followed one another rapidly. Our cook, returning from town, told thrilling stories about the bandits—how brave or cowardly they were at the execution.

One morning the messenger boy who went to town every day for the school mail brought back the news that in a few days fifty bandits would be executed.

"Fifty bandits; fifty of them! It is long since the citizens have had such satisfaction." The messenger boy was choking with excitement. A rumble of voices went through the school. The leader of the gang, a notorious bandit, aroused most interest, for according to rumors he had murdered the father of one of the school-boys. We sat in groups on our beds, leaving cards and coins alone, and told each other stories, imagined and true, about bandits. We recalled the poses and gestures of the hero-bandits we had seen at the theater; sang their songs and recited their speeches. Those of the students who were better informed told us that on the eve of their execution the prisoners condemned to die were given a good dinner and were allowed to drink as much brandy as they wanted. The class-mates of the boy whose father had been murdered were vengefully triumphant. A few others remarked: "But are the daoyin and his soldiers any better than the bandits?"

The date of the execution was set for Saturday. Saturday was composition day. When you had finished your composition and had given it to the teacher you were free till next Monday. The entire school was seized with an extraordinary zeal. Slow brains seemed to acquire wings, fingers moved faster than thought. In an hour and a half all the compositions were written and a crowd of boys in black jackets ran down toward the river.

An empty lot under the peaked town wall, back of the docks, was the site chosen for the execution. The wall and its peaks were black with people. The second stories of the houses on the other side of the wall were crowded like a theater. A three-fold circle of people, looking over the shoulders and bayonets of a chain of policemen, stood around the lot. At first there was no one on the lot but two dogs and a busy pig. Then came the first detachment of soldiers. The anguished copper shriek of four trumpeters deafened our ears. The advance detachment of soldiers marched in time to the beat of the sad sound, their rifles resting on their shoulders. The bandits followed them walking slowly, in hand-shackles and chains. Their hands were chained together behind their backs and a bamboo rod placed in them. A small plaque was attached to the top end of the rod which rose above the head. On this plaque was written the name of the bandit's village and a description of his crime. The procession was long, the audience silent. The fetters clinked their iron teeth. Some of the prisoners walked with hunched shoulders, some threw back their heads and smiled defiantly, others scowled at the public like wolves. The eyes of some were closed and the blood seemed to have left their cheeks. There were a few who looked as if the nearness of death had already transformed them into corpses; they had no strength to walk and were almost carried by the policemen. Small clouds of dust rose behind their dragging feet. We counted those who passed—there were only forty-nine. The fiftieth had passed away in prison, dreading death.

Back of the last prisoner were the troops. Four carriers bore the blue tzao of the police inspector. He was followed by the executioner, a tall man who looked straight ahead. He carried solemnly in his outstretched hand, as a priest carries a cross, a large sharp sword in a leather scabbard. The sword was pointing down and a large red bow was tied around its handle. The executioner was dressed in the usual police uniform.

Frightened, I crumpled my neighbor's sleeve in my hand, afraid to look at the bandits over the heads of the human circle. I swayed on my feet, and my head spun, but I was ashamed to expose my weakness before my comrades.

The procession approached the empty square. The soldiers

broke the ring of people and formed a half-circle. The criminals were stood up in front of them in two lines, facing the river. The policeman made them kneel. Two or three of the bandits cried out loud, pleading sadly: "Kill us! Kill us! In a few years we will come back as young as we are now. Kill us!" They were quoting the words of a Buddhist exorcism. Some of them stretched themselves out flat on the ground, almost senseless, pressing their wet, open lips against the dirty sand. Behind the two lines of criminals was a red square on which the gang-leader knelt. With the permission of the daoyin his relatives had spread a red, woolen rug on the ground in order that his blood might not fall on the naked earth. After the execution they would wrap the bleeding body in this rug and carry it away.

Back of the red rug, closer to the wall, a table had been placed. The police inspector sat at the table, the commander of the detachment and the executioner sat next to him.

We could see near the river a pile of freshly cut and crudely painted timber. Those were the coffins—forty-nine of them. They were badly made; the boards were full of cracks.

The hoof-shaped crowd of spectators became a solid, homogeneous mass. Over the heads of the kneeling people on the lot towered the policemen. The preparations were short. A policeman pulled the bamboo rod out of the hands of the gang-leader and placed it on the table in front of the inspector. The inspector turned his head toward the executioner. With sure, quick steps the executioner walked to the gang-leader from behind. The sword glistened in the air. The head, like a watermelon which had been dropped, crashed down, and two streams of blood spurted upwards from the neck—just for one second. Then the blood streamed down slowly. The executioner gave the kneeling, headless body a push. Someone screamed in the crowd. Others sprang back. Children began to cry.

The bandits did not see the death of their leader, but from the craning necks of the spectators they knew it had taken place.

A policeman walked along the first line of kneeling men. He pulled out the plaques from their chained hands and counted them. Then the inspector took the bunch of rods with the plaques attached to them from the policemen and counted them again, placing each one separately on the table. The counting finished, he gave a signal to the commander. A short piercing whistle followed. A detachment of soldiers marched back of the first line of criminals and halted, one standing behind each criminal. Twenty-four soldiers back of twenty-four doomed people. At the second whistle of the commander, the rifles were shouldered, their muzzles level with the heads in front of them. A short, sharp report sounded, as if a large board had been broken in two. It looked as though somebody had kicked the kneeling men from behind. Smoke from the rifles, clouds of dust from the falling bodies rose over the square.

Stepping over the corpses the soldiers stood back of the second line and after another whistle, the rifles went up again and the firing followed. Then, suddenly and hurriedly, almost on a run, the hoof-like line of soldiers closed tightly around the corpses. The inspector, the commander, and a policeman walked along the piles of human flesh and rags, examining the bodies to make sure that they were all dead. They removed the chains from the feet and the hands of the executed. The chains clinked gaily.

Again there was a bird-like whistle. The bugler sounded the command. The circle of soldiers fell into formation and marched away. Then the public pressed in a tight ring around the executed and the weeping of relatives filled the silence. You could hear the coffins scratch the sand as they were pulled toward the bodies. The relatives of the gang-leader wrapped him in the rug, tying his head in a separate bundle. The scuffling feet of the people soon rubbed the bloodstains out of the ground.

Like an army of ants the crowd began to crawl away. The grey, dusty surface of the lot became more and more visible as the streams of people grew thicker in the adjoining streets.

They walked away sullenly, pitying the dead.

"Perhaps they were unjustly condemned. Perhaps they became bandits because they had nothing to eat and nobody to help them. There are so many hungry people everywhere. What difference does it make where one dies? In a hut of starvation or in a public square by a bullet?"

All that night I could not sleep. Visions of the dead bodies and the red blood streaming over the headless man on the red rug haunted me. When I lifted my head over the blanket I saw the frightened faces of other pupils floating above their beds.

My school life went on monotonously day after day. A crop of thick black hair now covered my shaven monk's head.

We were terribly poor. In order to pay for my board at school, my younger uncle took my father's winter coat—a sheep-skin covered with silk, the price of which was about 20 da yang—and went to see some of our relatives with the hope of selling or pawning it. The richest of them, a prosperous merchant, a land owner, notorious all over the country as the worst usurer, whose real name was Tschan, but who was better known as "Dog's Head", offered to take it and sell it to his friend who needed a winter coat and who would pay . . . well, not twenty but fourteen da yang.

We needed money badly—my uncle decided to let the coat go. Dog's Head took the coat and gave him three da yang, saying that he would pay the rest of the money on the following day. The next day he promised to pay "tomorrow" again. Weeks went by without any results. Whenever I went to see him, hoping to get some of my money, because the cook in the school made my life miserable demanding my board money and threatening to give me no food, Dog's Head would say meekly and politely: "My dear nephew, I am very sorry, but my friend has no money at present. Be patient. Tomorrow I'll ask him to hurry up."

Finally the cook carried out his threat. I was given no dinner. I decided to get my money. I followed Dog's Head wherever he went. He would pay me a few tung tze at a time. These, strung together on a wire in heavy bunches of copper tsan, enabled me to extract from the cook my bowl of supper rice. I had to use all my ingenuity in this terrific sport of getting my own money out of this fat pig. Altogether I managed to get seven da yang, exactly one half of the sum he owed me.

The school year ended—the boys went home and the corridors were empty and silent. Giving up the hope of getting my money to pay my debt to the cook, I bought my passage home with the last few tung tze, left all my clothes and books with the cook, and went to Sian-Shih.

A few days later the fat figure of Dog's Head appeared in our house, his face red and his eyes anxious. Handing me the bundle of my things which I had left in the school he said affectionately: "Here, my dear nephew, is your luggage. I hope you'll forgive your old cousin for being so slow with the money. I tried my best to get it from that friend of mine, but I could not, and so I brought you my own money to pay the debt."

I stood in front of him, holding my bundle in complete bewilderment. Something must have happened. It was obvious that he knew something which I, wearing my white mourning in a forsaken village of Sian-Shih, did not know.

A couple of days later terrible news startled the citizens of Teh chien like the crack of a whip: "Tan Ya-pu is alive! Tan Ya-pu is coming to Teh chien with his troops!"

II

1. Almost Governor

THE THREE MONTHS' REIGN OF YUAN SHI-KAI HAD SUDDENLY come to an end. The revolutionists organized their guerilla troops and began moving northward. Their army grew larger and larger, increasing its number continuously by crowds of hungry peasants anxious to avenge the Northerners for the destruction of their villages and the rape of their wives and daughters. They called themselves Ho Kuo Chun "the Army for the Defense of the Republic". It consisted no longer of regiments, but divisions. A commander of each division had two assistants—a chief of the staff and a secretary. The secretary of the division advancing toward Teh chien was my father.

His arrival explained to me the model behavior of Dog's Head. All our relatives—the richer they were, the quicker the reaction—came to see us, bringing with them presents of welcome: silk materials, money, fruit, jars of jam.

The fat figure of Dog's Head appeared again in our house, accompanied by coolies carrying heavy bundles—pillows, blankets, and a new fur-lined silk winter coat. In addition he took out of his purse twenty new silver da yang. But father, informed of his previous conduct, did not come out to greet him. My younger uncle, tall and somber, came out in his stead. Without ceremony he said looking straight into Dog's Head's eyes: "Take your people and things and go home. Two years ago when we needed your help you were not to be found anywhere. Now we don't need it any more. We can get along without you."

The coolies giggled. Dog's Head lost face. The entire town would talk of how Tan Ya-pu had put him out of his house.

The relatives who had been so anxious to get rid of me in the days of my misery now greeted my father ecstatically.

Weeks of tolerant liberalism followed the five years of reaction. Members of the Kuomintang were again on the up-grade. The President of China, General Li Yuan-hun, proved to be a liberal and appointed General Fang Tseng-Yuen governor of the provinces of Hu-Bei and Hunan. The little Tai—the former head of the Police Department in Chengtu—was his secretary. He recommended my father to the general as the best candidate for the office of governor in the province of An-Hui.

In order to carry this recommendation through, my father would have had to go to Peking, taking along about five thousand tung tze. He would have had to go around seeing the notables, ministers, members of Parliament, take them to dinners and present them with precious gifts. Then he would finally return to the province, having in his pocket, instead of money, the President's order, appointing Tan Ya-pu to a high and lucrative office with unlimited possibilities.

Father had neither money nor the desire to become a governor. Nevertheless the rumor of his candidacy for the post spread around and caused an extraordinary outburst of respect and affection from our villagers and relatives. At the same time they were being very cautious; today you were a governor and tomorrow you might have to hide in the woods like a wild animal. They all were in a hurry to be of service to father, in order to be able later on to ask favors in return. Each tried to make his service cost him as little as possible.

The rich Si, the owner of several inns, a comrade of father and a member of Go-Lao, brought him a beautiful horse. Si knew perfectly well that father never rode horses. My father thanked him, but declined to accept the present. Si went home with his horse and the reputation of being a generous man, without losing a tung tze. But he obviously looked seriously toward a lucrative position under the new governor. A few days later, when my father was away, Si sent a messenger to our house with an invitation for me to come and visit him. I had never seen the man before, so why should I go and visit him? My comrade Fang agreed with me. I politely declined the invitation. The messenger went away, but soon came back inviting both of us to come.

"All right, Shih-hua!" shouted Fang. "Let's go and see our horse."

Fang was an officer, father's aide-de-camp. He was gay and talkative, and when he spoke he made everybody laugh. He loved to flirt, and was often beaten up by the enraged husbands or brothers of his sweethearts. Under the hail of the most ferocious blows from fists, pokers or sticks, he would simply say: "The muscles of a boxer are softer than wool, but stronger than steel." At times he would return the blows. Then the attacker would fly across the floor screaming. People would say to him: "You have killed the man!" To which he would answer complacently, "I could have, had I wanted to. That's why I am a boxer—to know where death is hiding in the human body."

"Where is it hiding, Fang?" I would ask.

"It is a secret of boxers and their trainers. But it is not a joke. When I finished my training I swore that I would never kill a man without reason."

"Dress up, Shih-hua, quick!" said Fang. "Otherwise Si will

drink up all the brandy before my lips have a chance to touch it."

The room in Si's house was crowded with wealthy villagers. Si hurried forward eagerly, smiling and bowing. I was introduced to his guests and they all looked at me with great admiration as though I were a bowl full of the best shark-fins.

Si exclaimed: "I am so very happy to have the son of my best friend, the great Tan Ya-pu (an admiring whisper went over the room at the mention of the name) visit me. I beg the first-born of such a distinguished person to take the place of honor at my table, the place which he deserves to occupy in view of the great deeds of his father."

The noise of moving chairs sounded to me like a cannon salute. The soft hand of Si pushed me gently toward the place of honor at the head of the table, the place which is usually occupied by the grey-bearded, the most learned, the fattest.

All this ceremony embarrassed me greatly. I gave Fang a desperate glance, but he was enjoying it. Noticing my glance, he folded his hands as if holding a butterfly, and shook them obsequiously under his chin, bowing low like the rest of the guests. No examination had ever made me feel worse than this dinner. To work with a brush under the gaze of a nasty inspector was nothing at all in comparison with this task of working with a pair of chopsticks, filling my mouth with pinches of food from various dishes placed in front of me by the host. Twenty pairs of eyes belonging to the richest people of our village seemed to hang heavily on the ends of my chopsticks, making them drip the gravy and stain the table cloth.

Si fed me dish after dish, his tongue not ceasing for a moment:

"Although I am only a friend of your father's, Shih-hua, I feel as if I were one of your uncles. I have really more right to be called a relative of yours than some of your disgusting cousins, who permit themselves to make money out of their poor

[178]

kinsmen. If I had only known that you needed money when you were in school you would not have had to worry."

A rumble of approval rose toward the ceiling, mixing itself with the steam of new dishes.

"I know very well that your family is still in need. The prices of everything are up. The salary of your uncle is small and you have so many relatives who are anxious to get what they can out of such a noble family as yours. Your expenses are great. Remember, Shih-hua, if you ever need money, come to me. I'll divide my last morsel of food with you."

The fat heads nodded approvingly at this altruistic speech. Through the noise of their voices I heard the words of Fang: "Hear! It's the saddle for your horse."

My mouth was working hard, pinches of food went into it, words of gratitude came out. We had about twenty different courses. I was tired of saying polite words. I sat and blinked. A deadly weight pressed down on my heart and on my stomach.

"When you come home and have a few minutes' time, write to your father and tell him about the reception I gave you. And here, take this, please." He handed me a fresh ten da yang bill.

The sight of money put me, as usual, in a state of defense. Forgetting all the rules of etiquette, I shook my head and pushed the bill away.

"Thanks ever so much. You are very kind, but I do not need money at present. Believe me, please, that I'll come to you, as you were so kind to suggest, if I need it. Thank you."

Si insisted and the guests pretended not to notice our duel. Fang was scratching something on a piece of paper. I continued to resist. Glancing down, I noticed the paper on my lap; Fang had thrown it there. On it he had written crookedly: "Take it. I'll explain later."

I was all alone in my fight. Everybody was against me, even Fang. My resistance changed into anger—I pushed away the bill determinedly, and said: "I beg you to excuse me, but under no circumstances will I accept this money. I do not accept money without permission from my father."

The end of my sentence was covered by Fang's words: "Tan Ya-pu is right, forbidding children to accept money. The grown up should take the money instead of children. Let me have it, please," and, taking the bill out of the fat fingers of Si, he folded it carefully and put it into his pocket.

Complete silence reigned in the dining room—all heads turned toward the officer with the black jacket into whose pocket the bill had disappeared. Fang's voice went on: "The General-Inspector, Lao-feng, and the esteemed Lao-tai offered the position of governor to the father of Shih-hua, but alas, our beloved Tan Ya-pu has not money enough to transform that offer into reality. I grieved over that fact. But when I see now how much money our brother Si has, and how generous he is, I suggest that all the distinguished people gathered in this room ask the General-Inspector to offer the post to our brother Si."

An undefinable noise, which sounded much like laughter, greeted Fang's words. Si shuddered.

"The post of governor! My silly brain never dared dream of such a thing. All I wish to do in my life is to help the children of the da-ge to get their education."

Fang's answer sounded a bit too gay. It was almost improper. He said: "All right, if you wish to help the children of Tan Ya-pu, go ahead and help them, but see that you help them in any circumstance." He emphasized the word "any".

Si lifted his heavy body. "Of course I'll help them in any circumstance." He was annoyed. He put his fat fingers into a dish of gravy accidentally, and spilled it all over the table.

The dethroned Manchu Emperor of China, Hsuan tung, was still living in the golden-roofed palace at Peking. In the summer of 1917, General Chang Hsun, a monarchist, declared the fourteen-year-old boy Hsuan tung restored to the throne. Li Yuan hun had to flee to a European concession, without having completed his presidential career. The post of governor of the province of An-Hui became a myth, a dream, a legend.

Si immediately came to our house. He met Fang in the court and Fang bowed to him politely and ironically. Without answering his bow, but walking at a safe distance, Si passed him by and asked me if comrade Fan were in the house. Fan was another assistant of my father, the same man who had saved me once from the daoyin's soldiers.

Si entered the house and soon came back looking almost pleased.

Fang rushed to Fan's room: "What did he have to say, that fat bag?"

"Nothing at all," answered Fan. "He just borrowed seven da yang from me."

"I'm surprised," said Fang, "that he didn't claim we owe him three more."

---

2. The Matchmaking

THE EVEN FLOW OF MY SCHOOL DAYS WAS MIXED WITH THE days of my meetings with Tchen Tsai-in in the village. She grew up to be a lively, humorous and gentle girl. My step-mother was very fond of her and even the somber eyes of my father would soften when he looked at her busy little figure. She used to help my step-mother with her embroidery. When I came back from school she hardly ever left our house. We grew strongly attached to each other. I was fifteen and she was thirteen years old. Our former boisterous mischievousness was replaced by silent and tender attention. Perhaps it was love that was beginning to grow. That word never occurred to me at the time. In any case a strong friendship was maturing between us.

We would sit for hours opposite each other without so much as touching finger-tips. She played the flute and sang softly— old, exquisite songs. I would draw polite verses with my brush on a piece of paper. There was not a word about Tsai-in in these verses. They were about clouds, pine-trees in the evening, heroic girls of ancient times, or boats racing along the river. I would rapidly turn, in my memory, the pages of the volumes of ancient poems, and columns full of delicate moods and emotions would cover the sheets.

Tsai-in would sing and I, biting the end of my brush, would try to think of what her singing was like—the song of a thrush, the ringing of those tiny crickets which people often keep in small boxes under their pillow so that sleep may come pleasantly to the sound of their song.

When my schoolmates pronounced the word "love", with an obscene wink, I shuddered. The physiological aspect of love did not interest me. Perhaps I was not strong enough for it. I knew all about it from comrades who succeeded in instructing me through their stories and through books containing verses about the various concubines of the Emperors and the contemporary singers in the tea-houses of Shanghai. But I would not join the boys when they went to that part of town where the restaurants and the houses were from which came sounds of women's laughter and song. The youngsters were met at the entrance by a couple of strong male servants who bowed politely. Should a visitor get rough, he could easily be kicked out into the street by these husky fellows. In the house the boys would sit in a room opposite a door through which beautifully groomed girls passed, one after another. The youngsters would watch them hungrily and then tell the old lady (*amah*) which of the girls they wanted. Then they would listen to the chatter of their girls with the indifferent air of experienced lovers, caress their

[182]

bracelets casually, and calculate how much the night would cost them.

In my head I had arranged in an orderly row, like books on a shelf, all possible information concerning men and women. It began with the Middle Ages, when the brothels were government institutions, and continued to the present time, when the bald-headed old amahs were buying lovely girls in famine-stricken villages to send them down the river into the brothels of Hankow, Shanghai and Nanking.

My father and his division came back from their wanderings in the late fall of 1917. He was tired and irritable. The revolution was wavering. There could not be a revolution in Szechuan alone if the other provinces were unresponsive.

Again the go-between, sweet as honey, appeared in our house. She and my step-mother would spend hours whispering to each other. Finally she went to my father's room. I was glad to see the go-between in our house. I did not quite know what she came for, but I had a feeling that I was going to get a most unexpected and joyful present. The go-between did not stay long in my father's room. When she came out the sweet smile was gone from her lips. My step-mother, whose eyes were red, called me and said: "The go-between has asked your father's permission to arrange the engagement between you and Tsai-in. Your father said, 'Although I do not interfere with family affairs and do not know whether this marriage is necessary or possible, I personally do not approve of it. I know the father of this young girl too well. He is an official whose name is stained with the worst vices: bribery, flattery, soulless egotism, cruelty. In my opinion posterity repeats the image of the fathers. Such a marriage might weaken the will of the son of a revolutionist.' "

It would have been better had my father beaten my hand a hundred times with a bamboo ruler, or killed me as he once killed the frightened hen that jumped on his table, than to hear him speak thus about Tsai-in. I felt as if he had split me in two with his straight, heavy sword. The two halves were aching and would not grow together again. My step-mother saw my angry, suffering face, my trembling fingers, the teeth biting at my lips.

"Shih-hua, go immediately to your father and tell him that you do not agree with him."

I made a step forward, but stopped. Go to my father? Look straight into his merciless eyes and tell him that I did not agree? Demand Tsai-in for myself? Set my will against his? I could not do that. Father meant more to me than all the brides of the universe, more than my school, more than the memory of my mother. I could do anything but go against my father.

I stood by the window, trying to justify him. He had had more experience. He knew better than I what was right and what wasn't. How did I know whether I loved Tsai-in or not? Perhaps it was all in my imagination. Perhaps we were only friends after all. It was really true—her father was a scoundrel. I ended my reflections by saying sadly, and somewhat arrogantly: "Let it be as my father wishes."

The refusal of my father broke me down more than my illness had. From that day I forgot the path to the house of the family Tchen. Tsai-in still came daily to see us, always vivacious and lovely. I made up my mind never to mention to her what had happened. If only the go-between would not tell, and so start gossip crawling over the streets of Sian-Shih. But the go-between kept quiet—my father's refusal was her professional failure. Why tell people of her failures? It might spoil her reputation.

Another girl's voice joined the voice of Tsai-in. It was my little sister Kuen. She was big now and a friend of Tsai-in. She went to school and brought home "eggs" of praise. She was nine years old—or perhaps she was only eight.

Tsai-in would play her bamboo flute and look into my eyes. Had it been the older Tchen sister she would have taken me by the shoulder long ago and said, "Shih-hua, tell me what is the matter? You are not like yourself."

Tsai-in did not suspect anything. Perhaps the years spent in the monastery had taught me how to keep secrets behind the helpless light in my eyes.

---

3. The Engagement

M Y FATHER WAS AWAY ON HIS LONG TRIPS AND CAMPAIGNS. I grew completely estranged from my family. Somewhere in the house, without coming in touch with me, my sister was growing up.

My step-mother would lower her eyes every time she saw me. She felt guilty for my father who had forbidden my marriage to Tsai-in. At the same time her only thought was to marry me as soon as she could and to the best possible advantage.

The engagements of my comrades, fifteen-year-old boys, were being announced and celebrated one after another. Some of them—those who had money, for the most part—would give up forever the study of tiresome geometry, geography, the English language, and ancient verse, and go with their young wives to the country where they would learn how to run big estates. Some would stay in town, trying to make their way in the world working in their uncles' offices. Every such engagement was an insult to my step-mother. At night she would cry. During the day time she would run to our relatives, complaining of our poverty and our misfortune. She was ready to humiliate herself before the go-between, who occasionally came to our house to find out if there was a chance to engage me to some girl in

Sian-Shih or in a nearby village. My step-mother's answer was tearful and pathetic: "We are poor. We are ready to marry Shih-hua to any girl who would consent to marry him. You should ask the parents of the girls, and not our needy family, which hasn't enough money for three meals a day. Ask them if they would care to have us as relatives."

Something was going on behind my back. I noticed the quick whisper of the go-between with her husband, whenever they met me on holidays in the streets of Sian-Shih. There was something unpleasant in the jokes and remarks of my friends at the celebrations of their engagements.

The days of the New Year vacation flew by as casually as cards dealt by a skillful player. I tried to stay in the house as little as possible. It was crowded with relatives all the time and I sickened at the sight of their faces, which broadened with smiles whenever they looked at me. Their hands, which at the time of my flight had shoved an obsequious da yang or two into mine were now trying to pat my back condescendingly. I bowed politely and would not talk. They would make fun of me. Who gave them the right to ridicule me? Let them gossip with my step-mother, let them drink their endless cups of tea, and tell each other about the illnesses of their children and last year's price of tangerines. I could always go off to my schoolmates and play chess, recite poems, or talk about France and the university.

I came home about dinner-time. The fine odor of pungent dishes, unusual for our house, surprised me. Why a special dinner tonight? Why so many people in the house? Besides the relatives who were there that morning many neighbors had come and some guests from the country. Why did they all stare at me? I had nothing to do with the celebration. It was neither my birthday nor the day of my graduation. I was astonished by the fact that the guests greeted me somewhat solemnly and that the relatives did not joke as usual, but smiled significantly. I

passed quickly into the reception room. The guests were standing around their tables. They would not sit down, but all looked
at one corner of the room. There stood a special table. At first
glance one would think that a pile of burning coal had been
scattered on it—it was so red. The relatives kept looking first
at me, then at the table, then at me again. I had to find out what
it was all about. I walked straight to the table. Notebooks in
glossy red bindings, books tied cross-wise with red ribbons,
sticks of black chalk showing black ends from their leather
coverings, brushes with red handles and red eggs were piled up
on the table. It was clear. These presents were spread out for
me. I had been engaged.

These small red things were sent to me by the parents of
some unknown girl in return for gifts that had evidently been
presented to them by my step-mother. When had she had time
to send all the things demanded by etiquette—silk gowns, pieces
of silk material, small packages of sticky sweets, and a pair of
pink-colored geese in a bamboo basket, the symbol of our future matrimonial faithfulness? (According to Chinese belief,
there is no couple more faithful to each other than geese, neither
on earth, nor in the water, nor in the air.)

The red color of the presents made the blood rush to my
head. Another moment and I would have burst out crying and
thrown the things at my pathetic step-mother. But it was not in
vain that since my babyhood I had been taught good manners
by my uncle, my grandmother, my teachers, and my mother,
whose last words were: "Never fight, Shih-hua." On the surface
I was as silent as a black Japanese grenade, but like a grenade
I was ready to explode. My aunts giggled. One of them said
sympathetically: "See, Shih-hua, you are a grown-up man, and
you need a fiancée."

This was more than I could stand.

"It seems that this fiancée was needed more by my step-
mother."

She was in the crowd of guests, busily giving orders to the

servants. I heard how her whispers were suddenly choked by
my outburst. She bit her lips and lowered her eyes; she was
embarrassed but did not lose her head. She did not have to retreat—the victory was hers. Plenty of fifteen-year-old boys cry
in anger on the day of their engagement.

The chairs rumbled around the tables. Steam curled above
the porcelain bowls. Behind my chair I stood like an automaton.
The delicacies spread out in front of me on the table seemed
more revolting than the rotten rice in the school. To sit down
next to those people who a minute ago had thrown me at the
burning furnace of these red presents! To listen to them chew
their food and make their silly jokes! To offer them more and
more dishes and smile into their mocking eyes!

"I don't want to! I won't do it!"

For a second time my step-mother asked me to sit down. Suddenly I sprang back and ran out of the room. I walked along the
street, burning with anger. Oh, if only somebody would insult
me so I could strike him in return and hit again and again till
the blood streamed and he cried out in pain.

How dared they, all these aunts and my step-mother, this
strange woman brought by my father from Chengtu, how dared
they decide what I should do! I was big enough to make decisions for myself. When father forbade my marriage it was
one thing, but when my step-mother behind my back made me
an object of all this humiliating ridicule . . . Who was this
girl? What girl were they going to place next me at the dinner
table and put into my bed on the night of the wedding? Perhaps she was ugly? Illiterate? Stupid? Slovenly? I did not
know who she was, nor from what village she came.

I went to my schoolmate. He watched very quietly as I paced
his room in excitement. Then he arranged the chess men on
the board.

"I was engaged today," I shouted to him the terrible words.

He was not perturbed: "Yes," he said. "The name of your
fiancée is Yuan. Sit down and play."

But I could not sit down yet.

Two different thoughts tore at my brain. One thought was—
I don't want a wife. The second was—what about my step-
mother? She was doing what she considered a very important
and necessary thing. She had arranged this engagement purely
out of her love for me. She had no children of her own and that
was why she was deciding things for us. But this feeling of
sympathy was immediately destroyed by the first thought: I do
not want a wife.

"Listen," I said to my comrade, "I am not going to marry."

"Nonsense," he answered quietly. "You will marry. You
cannot break an engagement. If you break the engagement you'll
ruin your family. The parents of your Yuan will start a case
against the go-between. The go-between will blame your step-
mother, and then she'll never stop paying the court. And you
would be fortunate if the case ended with only a fine. The judges
may be afraid your step-mother might run away—they know
that all Tans are good at running away—and they might put
her in prison for the duration of the trial. Stop pacing the
room, Shih-hua, let's play chess. It is not becoming to a chess
champion to be so shamefacedly upset over such an unimportant
and inevitable thing."

I stopped in front of the chess board, took a man in my hand
and made my first move. It was fortunate that Tsai-in was not
in Sian-Shih at that time. She was visiting some of her friends.

Vacation was over and I went back to school. In my absence
a magnificent wedding stirred up the quiet Sian-Shih. The older
sister Tchen was married to one of the richest land owners of
the province. After the wedding the entire family Tchen, and
Tsai-in with them, of course, went to visit the newly married
couple in the castle on their large country estate.

Thus ended my friendship with the sisters Tchen. I often
thought of Tsai-in, but I never tried to find out what happened
to her.

Where was I to go after I had finished school?

I did not want to go to England. English people were too haughty. Moreover they did not ask me to come there. I would not go to Japan, either. The people of that country were too cruel to China. The hieroglyphics of their "21 demands" were drawn on every cheap fan so that the people of China would not forget them. America? But only the pupils of American schools and then mostly Christians were being sent to America.

France—a country of revolutions, a republic, the native land of Jean-Jacques Rousseau. Moreover France liked us.

"Long live cheap Chinese labor!" The working people of France were in the trenches. The contractors in Shanghai were hiring strong people for work at French ports and in French factories. They paid their passage and the salary they offered was not bad. The comrade who explained the situation to me was all excited and his only worry was how to get to Shanghai.

He was a husky, strongly built fellow who looked forward to working for eight hours a day and studying for six. He was sure he could make it. It was really good for one to mix physical and mental labor. And so we organized a group, talked over all the possible ways of getting money together and at night we dreamed about France, shining France. She was teaching us, paying us real money, and our strong arms were willing to lift any load in order to buy those necessary six hours of study.

(Two years after these dreams, the gay, intelligent, amiable France turned out to be a base miser, with greasy, greedy fingers, and a mouth screwed into a nasty, mocking smile.)

My comrade went to France. I failed in my efforts, but with every letter, I saw his ardor fade. The loads he had to carry were too heavy. No time was left for study. At the end of the day his legs and arms shook with fatigue. The "not a bad salary", which in Szechuan seemed enormous, enabled him to buy less food than a tzao carrier could buy in Sian-Shih with a day's earnings.

While the war was going on the labor of Chinese students

was needed in France. But with the war ended French stevedores returned to the ports. "Down with cheap Chinese labor!" The Chinese walked from their work to their shacks through a line of people who watched them with hungry, angry eyes. One after another Chinese students lost their jobs. Their passage to France was paid for, but the ticket back cost hundreds of da yang. Instead of studying, the students stood in front of grocery stores, looking at the food displayed in the windows.

The student-coolies stretched out their hands on the streets, but the people passed them by. They fainted on the streets of Marseilles and Lyons, and the indifferent gendarmes lifted them like sick dogs and put them into ambulances. In the hospitals doctors would not believe in their illness—the temperature was normal, the pulse was normal. Hunger was not scarlet fever, nor typhus. The French Government was not obliged to cure people suffering from hunger.

With their last copper coin they would buy a sheet of paper and a stamp. Months would pass before the letter would reach their home district. And then a letter would come from China. It often happened that they were not accepted at the given address:

"So and so does not live here any more."

"Where does he live?"

"Nowhere. He's in the cemetery. He hanged himself two weeks ago."

My gay comrade died in France. At the autopsy the surgeon found an undigested potato in his stomach. He had eaten nothing but potatoes without salt for weeks.

But all that happened later, much later.

4. The Fourth of May

THE DAYS WERE GETTING HOTTER AND HOTTER. THE BLUE Yangtze grew muddy, the new spring foliage darkened the mountains. People's clothes were lighter, the brims of their hats larger. Paper fans began to quiver again in the hands of peddlers. The same insulting, unforgettable twenty-one demands of the Japanese were still drawn on the fans.

Only a month was left before my graduation. We were having our examination period. And suddenly, like a black Japanese bomb, the Fourth of May exploded over our heads.

Busy with our noisy studying we did not see the teachers running hurriedly to the office of the director. The servants who carried tea to the conference whispered in our inattentive ears: "A letter. . . . Important. From Peking. They don't know whether or not to show it to the students."

Finally, however, the director, accompanied by the inspector and the secretary, were seen walking through the court of the school. The secretary pasted a long letter on the black announcement board. A thick crowd of students, panting with excitement, gathered quickly around the board. Our best orator, who had a ringing voice and clear enunciation, read every sentence of that remarkable letter which began the epoch of the so-called "Chinese Renaissance". The letter was from a student organization in Peking to all the schools of China. I do not recall now the exact wording of the letter, although I read it again and again, but I remember very well its content and the order.

The revolution of 1911 overthrew the cursed Manchu dynasty and established a republic in China but did not bring peace. The evil-minded, greedy, selfish and ambitious people grabbed power in the provinces and the capital. Instead of taking care of the country they waged war among themselves for the possession of the riches in the cities and villages. They sold, wholesale and retail, Chinese resources to the eternal enemies of the "Middle Country"—the foreigners. Yuan Shi-kai, the usurper of the power, who declared himself Emperor, almost accepted the shameful demands of Japan, which would have put China in the position of Korea. The profiteers and liars, replacing one another as rulers of China, would borrow money from foreigners and pay it back in Chinese land, Chinese custom-house concessions, Chinese factories, mines, iron, tea, or animal skins. The rulers of China joined the Allies in the war against Germany and banished the Germans from a part of Chinese territory occupied by them. They had a right to expect that at the end of the war they would be rewarded for their services and be helped in their efforts to improve their miserable existence. But it turned out that the Allies of China were also profiting by the weakness of China and instead of rewarding her for services they were going to give the land, taken from the Germans, to China's other enemy—Japan. In addition to Taiwang Island, Korea, and Laotun Peninsula, which Japan had already taken away from China, it was now proposed to take possession of Tzintao and the Shantung Peninsula. Instead of putting Japan in her place, the Chinese Premier was ready to give her that land in return for a substantial loan. The minister of foreign affairs, Tsao Tun-lin, notorious for his dishonesty, was conducting negotiations with Japan through Hsan Tsun-sian, Chinese ambassador to Japan.

On the fourth of May the students of National University of Peking learned that the decisive negotiations, concerning the price for which the land was going to be sold, were taking place in the palace of Tsao Tun-lin.

The auditoriums, laboratories, and dormitories grew suddenly empty and an unusual meeting of students took place.

Indignant speeches flared up. The demonstration, absorbing on its way students of other schools and universities, moved rapidly toward the house of the greatest scoundrel and profiteer of China, Tsao Tun-lin. No guard could keep out these representatives of the people from that conference of traitors. Tsao Tun-lin, who knew the arrangement of the palace rooms better than his guest, managed to escape through a back door. Hsan Tsun-sian was seized by the students and given the punishment he deserved. Half-conscious and bleeding he was carried away to a hospital by the servants of his host.

Instead of supporting the students and the intelligentsia and punishing the traitors and their accomplices who had escaped the anger of the people, the government of China took the side of the scoundrels.

"We," read the letter, "the students of all universities and all high schools of Peking hereby assembled:

1. Declare a strike in protest against the action of the government and summon all schools and universities of China to join us;

2. Organizing a Union of students of the universities and high schools of all China to join our Union;

3. Summon the people of China, the intelligentsia, the land owners, tradesmen, industrialists and merchants to boycott Japan:

All goods carrying Japanese trademarks must be destroyed;

All Chinese investments must be withdrawn from Japanese banks;

Merchants, manufacturers and citizens must not accept Japanese money as payment;

Chinese employees working for Japanese must leave their jobs. The funds necessary to the all-students' unions shall be made up of the dues paid by members of the organization and contributions made by citizens.

We must unite all! Join the union! Appoint a delegate to supervise the execution of the boycott."

The proclamation was signed by the student Teh chienians who were studying in Peking University.

The letter upset us completely: Boycott. . . . Union. . . . Constitution. . . . Organization. . . . Collections. . . . All these were strange words. The weight of important political action was laid upon our narrow boyish shoulders. The buzzing of our voices around the blackboard was incessant. Groups of students yelled and shouted in our li tang, usually so solemnly silent. Where were our books? They lay scattered about and the hot summer dust began to settle on their open pages. We felt like insurgents. Anxious Huan, my closest friend, was squinting and frowning:

"Shih-hua, we received the letter, but what about the two other schools? And the school for girls? What if they haven't received the letter and we are unable to persuade them to join us?"

I remembered my father, dark and unshaven and busy before the overthrow of the Manchus, and it made me feel happy.

That night we could not sleep. Our meeting rumbled loudly in the light of oil lamps, and the timid sparrow-like twitter of the younger boys mingled with the harsh breaking voices of the sixteen-year-olds. The meeting passed dimly like a cloud of rain. The letter mentioned the constitution of the organization. We had none and we knew nothing about constitutions. We spent much time saying disconnected and incoherent phrases. Finally we decided to appoint a committee—a president, a secretary, a treasurer, and two delegates to represent our organization in the two other schools. I was appointed the secretary.

We had to collect our fund. We resolved that each pupil should contribute one da yang.

Somebody's voice shouted from behind the crowd, "The teachers have read the letter and say that they will contribute part of their salary."

The meeting burst into applause.

"We must go tomorrow to see the merchants and ask them for a contribution."

"Will they contribute?"

"They will."

"My father will contribute."

"So will mine."

"And mine."

From that night on I had not a single thought for the hateful wedding which had been set for next fall.

The general meeting of students of all the schools of the town took place in our school—our li tang was the largest. On the day of the meeting the li tang resounded with people as never before. Eight hundred students were packed into the room. Noise, exciting speeches. One student after another came up on the platform. When had they learned to speak? When had they found these ardent gestures—these boys who only yesterday were engaged in childish scuffles. Where did they learn to make those exalted, convincing speeches, to which teachers, directors, and the representatives of merchants now listened so attentively, nodding their heavy heads in time to the angry shouts of their sons and pupils?

The three boys' high schools dedicated themselves, down to the last person, to the anti-Japanese boycott.

The girls joined the boys. Two girls' schools agreed to go in with us but the school administration did not permit them to take part in our meetings. They did not even send their delegates. But a letter from them, written in accurate hieroglyphics, was read out by the chairman.

Every word of every orator fell into the crackling fire of applause. The treasurer reported the rapid growth of Union funds. I, the secretary, waving over my head a blueprint map of the town, announced how we were going to carry out the boycott.

"All Japanese merchandise must be destroyed," I shouted.

"Not a single Japanese object must be hidden. For this, you must elect people whose hands are clean. The Peking comrades summon us to join the strike!"

"The strike!"

One after another the orators rose up praising the strike.

Then Huan spoke: "The strike—it is all very well. It is right. But we are not studying anyway. We are almost through with our examinations, and our summer vacations begin the day after tomorrow."

The meeting was in sad bewilderment. How could we strike if we weren't studying at present anyway? The director saved the situation.

"Let us leave everything as it is, but we'll inform Peking that we have joined the strike."

That solved the problem. Our vacation was solemnly transformed into a strike.

The town was divided into three districts, according to the number and situation of the three schools. Each school had to clean every store and storehouse in its district of Japanese merchandise. Twelve representatives of each school spent their days walking from one store to another inspecting the goods. Coolies, carrying baskets, followed them. The school delegates walked solemnly with an air of importance and without a smile. They were joyously greeted by the clerks of tobacco shops and by the agents of Shanghai manufacturers. These people were ready to support the student movement with all their money. The owners of small stores, trading in local merchandise, the fruit sellers, the vegetable men, the wood sellers, and the sellers of other local products, smiled at the procession. But the owners of dry-good stores, haberdasheries and crockery stores scowled. They thought at first that everything would go smoothly. The boys might shout awhile, perhaps take ten or twenty da yang contribution, and that would be the end of it all.

But things went differently. For instance: a delegate entered a store. A thermos bottle and an ashtray were displayed in the window. Japanese hieroglyphics were clearly written on the bottom of the pieces. The delegate raised the fragile objects and threw them on the pavement. He turned the store inside out while the owner trembled with rage.

Coolies standing behind the delegate began to giggle, winking at the store-keeper. The store-keeper tried to hide a shelf of saucers behind his back. He had paid so much for it! He was ready to put it away in his cellar. Would the delegate give him permission to send it back to Japan and have his money refunded. It was he who was losing money. . . . The delegate pushed him aside and with one motion of his hand swept the blueish porcelain to the floor.

The store-keeper wiped the cold sweat off his brow and asked the delegate to step with him into an adjoining room. The delegate, who thought it was a storeroom, followed him.

"Take it. It's for you personally. But please leave my store alone. Take it." He shoved twenty da yang into the hand of the delegate.

The delegate turned pale, sprang back and shouted all over the store: "If you don't want me to drag you out to the public square where we are going to burn the Japanese goods, put your dirty money back into your pocket."

Larger objects which could not have been destroyed on the spot were gaily loaded on the backs of the coolies and carried to a temple of which the school boys had taken possession. There they were very carefully guarded and, when enough things had been amassed, were carried to a distant square. Sad store-keepers and bald-headed old women cried at the delegates as they passed:

"Crazy lunatics! To burn such good, expensive things—all for nothing."

Crowds of people surrounded the fire. Celluloid combs flared up with a white sizzle. The rubber goods burned with an awful

[198]

stench that mixed with the smoke of soap, bolts of Japanese silk, and toys. Flasks and bottles of perfume exploded in the blaze. People watched the burning objects with greedy eyes, hoping to save something from the flames, but a guard of school-boys stood threateningly around the fire to see that vengeance was carried out.

Those were amazing days. In Hankow, Changshi, Foochow, Shanghai, in every city in which university or high-school students were present, packages of matches and tooth powder, clocks, silk umbrellas were cast on the flames. Mirrors cracked, piles of wrapping paper and boxes of patent medicine glowed in the vengeful fires, as the members of school committees stood around shedding tears of anger.

The heads of our organization were flooded with work. The indignant shouts of merchants waving bunches of bills and receipts went on for hours in our committee room. They were complaining about our delegates who, confusing Chinese trademarks with Japanese, had destroyed their Chinese merchandise. We tried to pacify the merchants.

"We'll take measures. We'll point it out to our delegates. We are sorry but we have had so little experience. Mistakes are possible."

But some of the merchants, too, were behaving outrageously. Instead of setting out all of their Japanese goods in front of their stores, they tried to hide them. They scraped off Japanese trademarks and replaced them with American and Chinese. And so the destruction of merchandise unintentionally turned into a war against the merchants.

"Come with me," cried a merchant hoarsely. "Come with me. They are rummaging in my store now, and I'll prove to you that they are taking the merchandise unjustly. I contributed fifty da yang to your fund. You demand too much. You will not ruin Japan this way, you will ruin Chinese trade. You are too young."

I went with the merchant to his store. The store looked as if a general had just passed through it with his troops. Perspiring from his effort, a delegate was turning over, with the help of a coolie, a bolt of gingham. The material had an English trademark but a coolie had explained to the delegate that the marks were too fresh and that if you looked carefully against the light you might see traces of the old trademark.

"Look," and the merchant pushed the English trademark into my face, "these are English goods and they want to burn them for Japanese."

The coolie fingered the material. Shaking his head doubtfully, he remarked, "This isn't English. Only Japan can manufacture such bad material."

The saliva began to pour out of the merchant's mouth. He threw himself at the coolie.

"Get out, you filthy scoundrel! Who permitted you to come here?"

The delegate explained to me his doubts about the mark. I noticed the merchant's son, my schoolmate, standing behind the counter. The boy was silent, but he was pale and obviously excited.

I said, turning toward the merchant, "You insist that this is an English trademark, but we think that previously the material had a Japanese trademark." I looked at his son. He nodded his confirmation.

"Look around," I ordered. "Perhaps we'll find Japanese labels somewhere here." I walked toward the cashier's desk. The Japanese labels were in it. We put them against the glossy squares on the material—they matched perfectly. The merchant laughed.

"That proves nothing."

But his voice did.

"Are all the goods you have out here?"

"This is all."

"You do not keep your merchandise anywhere else?"

And as the merchant did not answer, I asked his son directly, "Is there any more?"

The boy's eyes moved from the figure of his father to a closed door.

"Go behind that door and look."

"A-a-a-a!" An animal-like sound cut the air. The merchant had noticed his son's signal. "Ah, you scoundrel—you are against your own father!"

The son turned pale, hesitated, looked at his father, then at me and cried suddenly: "I am not against my father but against the Japs and the traitors."

The merchant was astonished, outraged at his answer.

"We'll talk it over at home."

He was better off than the others. He at least had someone on whom to vent his anger.

Gradually we matured, became more intelligent and skillful. Our original senseless ardor was replaced by organized work. But it was more and more difficult for the committee to collect funds and extract money from the hostile merchants. Even the agents of Shanghai manufacturers now only smiled encouragingly. They would not open their purses.

In my secretarial desk I had four reports about delegates who had accepted bribes. The reports were written in heavy hieroglyphics as though they had been made with the branch of a tree on sand. Probably some half-literate coolie had written them.

That summer the students of the high schools did not go home for their vacations. The vacation of 1919 proved to be a strike indeed.

5. Surrender

My wedding was set for the fall. Two months before it was to take place, while I was still madly rushing along the burning-hot streets of the town, which occasionally was drenched by a sudden rain, my step-mother summoned my father from his division.

I returned to the country. From the fresh air of political work I plunged up to my neck into the foul washtub of village gossip. Then began the long tortuous conversations with my father. I expressed to him sharply and angrily all my grievances. Father was annoyed. He could not treat me with casual superiority now. We looked straight into each other's eyes, and our eyes were stubborn.

All this bother was disagreeable to my father. His heart was not with us but with his insurgent division. At times he tried to be gentle, but he was no good at it. At times he tried to frown, but he felt that he was wrong. From day to day he mumbled and grumbled over me, trying to tie together those loose ends—my step-mother's will and my refusal. Then he would remain silent for a long time. He would raise his eyebrows, wrinkle his forehead, bite his lips and begin talking about the university. In that we also could not agree. I loved literature and was attracted by the new literary movement being advocated in distant Peking by Professors Hu-shih and Chen Tu-su. They taught that the new Chinese literature and Chinese newspapers should be written in the popular language and not in the ancient literary language of China which was known to nobody except the educated mandarins.

My dream was to go to Peking myself, to work on a newspaper and to study our own and foreign novels, short stories,

[202]

poetry. Father regarded me because of this as a good-for-nothing loafer. He felt I should become an engineer.

"If I were a mechanic it would have been much easier for me to work for the revolution. I am a lawyer. I know how to write orders, how to interpret laws, how to command. But as soon as the reaction kicks me out into the woods, I am hardly able to support myself. All my two hands can do is to hold a mattock. That is the common misfortune of all revolutionaries of the epoch that overthrew the Emperors. How to speak eloquently and to throw bombs—that was all we knew. But that isn't enough."

Perhaps father was right, but I wanted to go to Peking.

"Peking is a backward city. The people are fat, dull Northerners. Too much office-politics and too much temptation for a provincial youngster. It's the headquarters of scoundrels, bribers and boot-lickers who are ready to sell themselves at a moment's notice."

I tried to convey to him all the attractiveness of a literary career. I did it simply and without ardor, because by his expression I could see that he did not understand me. Then again we would grow silent and retire to our own rooms. The next day we would meet again, frowning and obstinate.

More than a month passed this way without our dispute making much progress. I became more and more irritable. My nerves, upset by the summer's political work, were giving me trouble. I lost sleep and my appetite.

Father got sick with a leg infection. He could walk only with my or my step-mother's help. Generally he would sit in an armchair, stretching out his leg like a log, or he would lie down on a sofa. The doctor who came to see him again and again shook his head and spoke of amputation.

The clenched teeth of my father supplied the persuasive force which his speech lacked. I grew sorry for this man whose leg was in constant, unrelenting pain. I began to feel almost that I was wrong. How did I dare to keep him away from his division by my stubbornness and silly nonsense, and force him to talk to me all this time? The pity, the same pity which more than once was to defeat me in the presence of another's weakness or helplessness, decided our argument. I could not stand the suffering eyes of my father, although I knew that he was suffering not from my step-mother's act but from his infection.

"Let's have the wedding, Fu-tsin. Tell step-mother that I agree."

She rushed to me, moved to tears by my noble decision, but I did not let her open her mouth to thank me. I turned my back on her and went out.

Immediately the whole house was filled with whispers, shouts, commands, bargainings. My step-mother was surrounded by a crowd of aunts and other women hired for washing, cleaning and cooking. My younger uncle, the treasurer, went from relative to relative arranging loans, borrowing money, of which we had to have plenty—at the very least 2000 da yang. I did not take part in anything. I would not come near my younger cousins who were making lists of guests and writing invitations on red cards. How heavy were those packs of cards! I could not lift them with one hand. A hired man sat all day long writing addresses and hieroglyphics.

The house was all decked out for the occasion. The walls inside were white-washed and looked whiter than bean milk. The corner posts and the bottom part of the outside walls were blackened, the upper part and window frames painted red. All black and red, our house looked like the face of a brave theatrical hero. New paper, which sang under the force of the wind, was stretched taut over the lattice of the windows to replace the old, dusty, faded rags.

One could hear drum-like beating in our court all week. It was the women beating the dust out of winter coats, blankets, mattresses and robes. They spread them out and hung them on thin bamboo reeds, which are used in China instead of clotheslines. Quiet little pools of water filled the court. The clean furniture glistened as it dried in the sun. The taking of the furniture out of the house created disorder. Greater disorder was created by the arrival of guests who came at the rate of five to ten a day.

I walked about, keeping near the walls, trying to slide by the people who were bumping into each other like fish in a small aquarium. Our house soon was too small to hold them all. We rented an inn to accommodate the overflow. My uncle went to our neighbors and the priests of the village temples, hiring more buildings to use as dining rooms during the days of the wedding.

Vases of fresh flowers were placed on tables and shelves. Red and green lanterns of different shapes decorated with hicroglyphics and pictures hung under the ceiling. The lanterns would ring slightly whenever the flying bugs dashed into them. Each lantern had a wick which was to be lighted on the night of the celebration.

Much time was spent in arranging a room for me and my future wife. A large bed was constructed and covered with new sheets and a soft comforter with a square piece of slippery pink silk in the middle. Fresh pillows were placed at the head, embroidered with the figure of a baby sitting on half of a pomegranate. Wardrobes, tables and the rest of my fiancée's dowry were placed in the same room in an orderly fashion. I could not help scowling scornfully when I looked at these dark wooden objects. I knew that all this cheaply made trash would warp, crack and fall to pieces in a month. After the furniture was all arranged and the room tidied the relatives were brought in to look at it. They winked slyly, nudging each other. Then the doors of the room were locked until the day of the wedding.

The relatives discovered a fearful defect in our house—the absence of *shen-kan*—the shrine on which hang the tablets bearing the names of the ancestors. At first they only exchanged glances, then they whispered and finally began to honk like geese: "You can't have a wedding without shen-kan. The marriage will be unlucky and no good will come of it. The spirits of the ancestors will get angry at such disrespect and will make it disagreeable, not only for you but for us also. The shrine is absolutely necessary."

My step-mother resisted. She knew that father would not build the shrine. The relatives saw her embarrassment and took the whole thing on themselves. They called on a carpenter, a wood-carver, and a painter. A long black-and-gold shrine was soon ranged along the wall of the prayer room. They paid for it and told my step-mother that they were making it a present to our family. When one says in China, "I make it a present", it means "Get *your* present ready." It was our turn now to reimburse our relatives for the cost of the shrine. I believe we still owe it to them.

A red silk curtain divided our li tang, hiding the shrine from the entrance. A large carpet was spread on the floor. The nearest relatives came to the house on the eve of the wedding to spend the night with us. They took rustling red rosettes out of a basket and pinned them to their dressy ma-gua, so that the people would recognize them the next day as the hosts of the wedding.

The chef, engaged for the occasion, arrived and took command of the kitchens, not only in our house, with scores of hired cooks, dish-washers and other help, but also of the sub-kitchens in the neighboring houses. The same night my family gave me my last bachelor party. My unmarried comrades dined and drank with me. Some of them were fifteen, some fourteen, and some thirteen years old.

I sat in a place of honor but could not say a thing. I was sick, my nerves quivered, a sharp pain shot through my body, flaring up now in my eyes, now in my shoulder, now in my fingers. People around me were joking, making speeches. But the jokes fell flat. The boys felt that a hospital would have been a more suitable place for me than a wedding party. Moreover they knew that I was being married against my will. Nevertheless they got up, one after another, and lifting their cups of warm wine, recited poems and wished me luck and happiness. Had I liked my future bride or had she been beautiful, my guests would have been making jokes about her all evening.

But this party was more like a funeral. At every mention of my fiancée I would scowl. The boys tried not to mention even the word "bride". The party did not last long. The house, preoccupied by its cares and worries, was not interested in it, and my sick father needed rest. When the last bowing boy had disappeared behind the gates, my uncle said, "Shih-hua, run to the inn, see if all the guests have had tea and if there are enough pillows. I am afraid we'll have to borrow some more and take them over." Like an obedient automaton I ran to the inn. It was autumn, but the weather was still warm. The fresh evening air blew over my perspiring back.

That night I did my best to sleep. There weren't enough beds to accommodate all the guests and some of them had to sleep together. I lay on the floor, on a thin mattress, next to my cousin. The mattress was narrow and hard. I woke up every minute and listened to my heart beating madly. All night long I kept on moistening my parched lips.

6. The Wedding

THE AUTUMN DAWN WAS LATE AND SLOW TO BREAK. THE HOUSE began to stir reluctantly like an awakening animal. I was aware of people talking drowsily in the dim light. I heard a dull, snorting, barking noise at the gate. I went out. Eight coolies were carefully setting a wedding tzao down, all covered with rustling starched silk flowers among which, here and there, were bunches of fresh blooms. Their insistent fragrance in the morning dew cut a perfumed passage through the sweating coolies. On one side an orchestra of twenty men were busying themselves with barrel-shaped drums and horns. They had spent all night coming over from Teh chien on a boat and were now waiting for someone to guide them to the village of my future bride. My older uncle was standing at the gate. He looked lovingly at the tzao.

"Sixty da yang we paid for it," he said, stroking the hanging clusters of flowers. He lifted the outside embroidered curtain, then the second curtain which had no decorations, and examined the soft-cushioned interior lined with red silk. The sight of the tzao threw my uncle into an exalted mood.

"Ah, Shih-hua, nowhere in China can you find more sumptuous tzaos than these of Szechuan. In other provinces people have to get along with dead silk flowers. In our province, where millions and millions of flowers grow, we are able to cover our tzaos with pounds and pounds of living blooms." Once started my uncle never could stop talking. He went on telling me the story of Szechuan tzaos in the days of his beloved Emperors.

The arrival of the go-between and her husband was greeted with welcoming sounds by the musicians. The stiff silk of her jacket glistened and rustled. A gorgeous red silk flower was pinned in her hair at the back of her head. Gold bracelets tinkled on her plump wrists and the jewels in her rings gleamed like her eyes. She had made good on this marriage. Now that she had come, the musicians could start.

The players hoisted their drums on their backs. The coolies lowered their shoulders under the poles of the tzaos. Lifting the curtain, the go-between climbed into the second one, less decorated than the other. Along the narrow streets the tzaos,

[208]

swinging on the shoulders of the carriers, descended to the docks. The distance to my fiancée's village was forty li, about twenty miles. They were going to the village by boat, but were coming back on foot in about six or eight hours.

At eight o'clock we had our breakfast. I sat at the table, my hands folded, my head lowered. The only sound was our kuei-tze striking against the porcelain of the bowls. My uncle said, "Eat, Shih-hua, eat. Get all your strength. It will be a strenuous day."

My head was dizzy and I could hardly restrain myself from showing my disgust. Everything seemed revolting to me: the food, the steam over the tea-cups, the whispering ushers and my busy step-mother. My shoulders could hardly bear the touch of my new grey silk ma-gua. It seemed to be made of sheet metal.

After the breakfast guests began to arrive. As they approached the gate a hornist played a welcome, giving a signal to one of the ushers. Looking important and carefully dressed, the relatives crossed our threshold. A man with a red rosette held the door open for them. The intervals between the arrival of new guests grew shorter and shorter. The screams of the trumpets followed one another quickly and the exhausted hornist gave up his place to a fresh player.

My father reclined on a sofa in the reception room behind a silk curtain. The guests walked up to him, bowed their heads and wished him good fortune.

Father, leaning on his elbow and trying not to move his leg, answered, "Please pardon me. I cannot receive you standing."

Then the guests walked to my older uncle and said the same thing. Then they said it to my younger uncle, my step-mother and my uncles' wives. That done, they scattered themselves all over the house and transformed it into a kind of club. Books were laid out on the tables, tea was served, the dice of mah-jong rattled and cards were shuffled in every room. People who had not seen one another for many years now met and exchanged the rotting grains of gossip and news. One or two ushers were present in each room. The guests would come up to them and whisper:

"Who is the man at the door?"

"Could we see the room of the bride and the bride-groom?"

"Where is the dowry?"

"How do I get to the toilet?"

Our house—rooms and courts—was filled to the brim with a sticky mass of silk taffeta robes and glossy coiffures. Soon the place could hold no more guests. The late ones entered the house only to bow to my father. They were then directed to the neighboring houses. Gradually the entire block around our house was occupied by guests who had come to my wedding. Anyone who wished to utter the proper formula of congratulation and bring a present could come to the wedding feast and have a seat at the dinner table. Ushers took the presents from the hands of the guests and piled them in a room located near the gate. Some guests brought money, baskets of fruit or pieces of red silk. Most of them, however, gave red *dan-tao* which were nothing more than strips of silk material with congratulations and good wishes written on them. On some of these dan-tao the hieroglyphics were sewn or embroidered. These could be removed and the material used for some household purpose. The value of a present was usually higher than the cost of the dinner. These presents were a kind of payment for the food and drinks.

Coolies, who had no money, gave their services. During the days preceding the wedding they had carried heavy furniture from room to room, moved wardrobes and tables. Now, all dressed up, they mingled with the guests.

I wandered about the house trying to hide in some corner where I wouldn't have to answer questions or talk with the relatives. In one of the back rooms I had a glimpse of my small sister, Shih-kuen. Playing chess with her little thin-voiced girl friends, she was deciding a serious move and paid no attention to me or the guests.

About a hundred relatives—cousins, aunts, their brothers and sisters, nephews and nieces, and scores of other relatives five or ten times removed—were there. People of the village whom father had happened to visit, or to whom he had given presents, all the members of the local Kuomintang and of the Kuomintang of nearby villages, brothers of the old Go-Lao who came to congratulate their da-ge on the wedding of his first-born, were also present. The owners of big estates, teachers, store-keepers and soft-spoken, cautious officials—all came to my wedding. At two o'clock the number of guests had reached sixteen hundred.

Suddenly the boys who were playing on the street next to our house rushed into our court screaming: *"Lai-la! Lai-la!* She is coming! She is coming!" And in great excitement they grabbed the servants by the coat-tails and pulled them toward the gate.

Four hornists thundered their welcome. The ushers rushed to the gate. Forming a double line from the gate to the entrance of the house, all the way to the li tang they made a narrow passageway through the curious guests. I was hurriedly led into the reception room for it was not becoming for a bridegroom to stand in the court at this solemn moment of the ceremony.

A rumble of drums and the gay melody of an orchestra surrounded a tightly closed tzao covered with flowers. The ordinary tzaos of the go-between and the relatives of my fiancée swung on the shoulders of the carriers and formed the tail end of the procession.

Special ushers chosen for this task helped the respectable fat women out of their stuffy tzaos. The women were perspiring from the heat. The silk of their trousers glistened as they walked, balancing themselves awkwardly on their small, hoof-like feet.

The orchestra lined up along the passage formed by the ushers from the gate to the reception room. Eight coolies, shining with fatigue but happy at the thought that the long journey was ended, walked through the opening carrying their tzao.

A stuffy smell of sweat and fading flowers clung about them.

Blind, unaware, choked by the heavy air, weak from sickness, I made two steps toward the tzao. The orchestra went wild. The drummers tried to break their drums. Then all sound was drowned out by the machine-gun rattle of rockets that exploded above us in fiery garlands.

Two women with rosettes lifted the first fancy curtain. Then they raised the second and brought out a human being from the soft interior. A figure dressed in a red silk dress reaching down to the ankles appeared before me. It was covered with a thick red veil and wore red stockings and red slippers.

This red thing was my wife.

She stood next me on the rug facing the shrine. Three times we bowed low to the lacquered strips of wood bearing the names of my ancestors. Then the women with rosettes took her to a special room where they changed her garment to a regular dress made of soft red silk. They let her have a moment of rest after the long journey in the stuffy flower box, wiped her perspiring face, powdered her forehead, nose and chin, put rouge on her cheeks and temples, and blackened her eyelashes and eyebrows.

While she was being made up, the oldest in our family, the grey-whiskered, shaking brother of my grandfather, was invited to come to the prayer room. I continued to stand in my place. The worst part was yet to come. My wife came in and stood next to me. Her face was round and fat. The ceremony of bowing began. We bowed to the old man, to the old woman, and to all the oldest members of families that had come from distant villages, in the strict order of seniority. They returned our bows and presented us with gifts—a ring, a pair of earrings, a bracelet. I could hardly refrain from shrieking—so painful was it to go on making bows, eighty, a hundred, a hundred and forty times. Steel would have snapped under such a strain.

My older uncle stood behind me and tried to encourage me.

"Just a few more, be patient. This is nothing—in our time we did not nod, we had to kneel and bow to the ground."

[212]

I knew it. Every youth in China knows it. For that reason even people who are in love with each other are afraid of the wedding. One must be a very good sportsman to go through the exhausting test of this Chinese ceremony.

The gallery of older relatives came to an end at last. At each bow a hot wave of blood rushed to my head. My bride had more endurance. She bent and unbent as though made of rubber. Her complacent expression remained on her fat face.

After the older relatives came the turn of the younger ones. Now we, my wife and I, stood like the elders, and all the youngsters, our first cousins and those twice and three or four times removed, came up and bowed to us silently, for youngsters are forbidden to talk at a wedding. They are such undisciplined creatures, they might say some unlucky word, such as "coffin" or "death". At a wedding or on New Year's day or on a day of birth such words must not be said. They bring bad luck. I heard no bad words at my wedding but, judging by the "happiness" of my marriage, someone must have been saying them all through it.

My wife and I gave them presents. We did not actually hand them presents, we only talked about them. They got their presents later, after the ceremony was over.

The bowing finished, my wife retired to her room and sat there not saying a word. The guests crowded at the door watching her as if she were a bird in a zoo. They made jokes and personal remarks:

"Her legs are too fat."

"Don't you think she uses too much rouge?"

"You can see by her eyes she has a bad temper."

She sat quietly, not taking their jokes to heart. All over China a newly married girl is always teased this way.

Then we had dinner. Tables were in every room, in every court, and in the temples. Bowl after bowl of different foods was set out. The steam of a hundred dishes rose and vanished in the clear autumn air of Sian-Shih. My bride sat at the dinner table as she had sat in her room, her hands folded on her knees. She touched no food. Next to her sat the two maids she had brought from her house. They heaped her plates with food and took them back untouched. They arranged the crumpled folds of her blouse and the net over her hair.

All the guests were chewing loudly and hitting their kuei-tzes against the porcelain bowls. One could hear them sucking their soup and belching.

For me the wedding dinner was merely a long journey. I travelled from table to table, a servant in front of me carrying a tray with eight cups of wine on it. The eight people sitting at each square table would take a cup, wish me joy, and drink. Then, with a smile, they would show me their empty cups, and I would bow to them. I was always walking and bowing, walking and bowing.

The dinner lasted interminably. The sun was going down. I could hardly move my feet—sick, green in the face, and exhausted, I thought of the bandits as they were carried to the place of execution. The sun had disappeared behind the mountains when the dinner ended and the guests began to get up from the tables, bowing their thanks.

The guests and some of the relatives left, some of them to go back to their villages that same night. Only the nearest relatives, the teachers and their families, stayed on. Supper was easier to bear. There were only ten tables—eighty people. This time I sat at the table, and it was my wife's turn to walk around with cups of wine and to bow. The people at the tables, gay with drinking, laughed at her every step. The youngsters, pointing at older men, would ask her: "Who's that? What's his name?" And as she did not know the names of all those present, she would get them confused and the people would laugh, shaking the tables with their fat bellies.

The yellow light of kerosene lamps marked the coming of night. My older uncle had already finished reciting poetry and had begun cursing the revolutionists who had betrayed their

Emperor. Someone left the table hurriedly, knocking over a chair. Somebody else began to sing an aria in a high voice. When I got up from my place fat shiny heads turned their drunken, glistening eyes on me and the remarks usual at a wedding fell from their lips.

My father had already gone to bed. My younger uncle had fallen asleep on a chair, exhausted.

I looked at the spots of gravy on a porcelain plate. The spots began to move, taking on the shapes of animals, people's faces, trees, flocks of sheep. I was feverish, hot perspiration covered my face. I heard a final shaft of wit.

"Look, his face has changed—he can't wait."

Supporting one another, gay and drunken, uncles and aunts began to leave the room. A number of people snored, leaning on the tables.

I went to our bedroom. A strange woman, who today had been declared my wife, was preparing herself for the night. She yawned widely and frequently. I sat on the bed, my back turned to her. I pulled off my clothes and got under the blankets. My body was cold. I could sense, through fatigue and numbness, my wife near me on the other side of the bed. She stretched herself out and fell asleep without saying a word.

---

7. The Honeymoon

IN THE MORNING I COULD HARDLY GET OUT OF BED. THE doors and the windows of my room danced before my eyes. There was a chill in my blood. As I rinsed my face with cold water, I pressed my cool wet hands against my ears. What a wonderful thing is silence! How tired my eardrums were of the sound of shuffling feet, the rustle of silk robes, the endless mumbling of congratulations, the roaring ovens in the kitchen and the sizzling pans. My uncle came and hurried me. Two couples—I and my wife, the go-between and her husband—were to go to my wife's village and pay her father a visit.

There again there was a li tang, but not as richly decorated as ours, and there were guests, but not quite so many. Again we had to go through the painful exercise of bowing three times to the elders, receiving their gifts and submitting to the dutiful salutations of the younger people.

Then the dinner followed, interminable, drunken and rich, noisy with speeches and congratulations. Tan Guan-in, feeling gayer than she had last night, sat next to me. It was her name now: Tan—my family name, Guan—her last name, In—her first name, the name of a many-petalled flower, something like a chrysanthemum, which grows wild in our meadows.

The day before the people of our house had gazed at her as at a strange bird that had flown in unexpectedly. Today, her kin and country-people stared at me just as absorbedly, with just the same mockery. They held out their wine cups to me but because of my apathy and lack of appetite they probably exchanged opinions later in the back courts of the house, calling me a green lad, a dry stick, a leg of a mosquito.

On the way back I lost the last of my strength. I tried to snuggle into a corner of the boat and take a nap, but every bone in my body ached and every square inch of my neck was sore as though it had been scalded. Noticing that I wanted to lean against something and thinking perhaps I was drunk, my wife tried to shove her knees, tightly covered with red silk trousers, under my drooping head. But even in my delirious and half-conscious state, I drew my face away from her thigh and leaned my head against the side of the boat. I hated this woman as a chain-gang prisoner hates the log chained to his ankle.

One more day was crushed into powder. I passed the following night in horrible dreams, screaming, jumping out of bed, shivering with chills, or dripping with hot perspiration. In the morning I refused to get up and my father sent me to Teh chien.

I lay in bed in the house of my comrade Huan. It was a nice house, situated in a quiet place and very quiet itself. Had it not been for a baby mouse that occasionally ran across the room, pricking the floor with its needle-like nails, one might have heard nothing but one's own heart-beats.

A few of my comrades were always with me. By the expression on their faces I could see that they were worried. They sat for hours by my bedside, and when I felt better, they told me school news about the boycott and the universities. They gave me tea. I watched their robes move as they arranged my blankets carefully.

With an effort I swallowed bitter black medicine. My body was tucked comfortably into a darkish cover. The back of my head was warmed by a soft pillow. My ears were packed in blessed silence. Above me were the quiet parallels of the ceiling boards along which a few bugs slowly crawled. Sometimes I turned on my side and looked for a long time at the boards of the floor. They were laid just as accurately as the boards of the ceiling. The solitude and silence had a soothing effect on my nerves. I was now able to think of my step-mother without gnashing my teeth. I could even serenely imagine my Guan-in.

Huan replaced me at the school. As I was the secretary of the student organization, he had more work than usual and came home late.

I was slow in convalescing. It was still impossible for me to take on the affairs of the organization and so I turned to reading the newspapers.

"The Party of the Poor," said the newspapers, "has won in Russia." It had thrown out the rich and the nobles, it had ransacked villages, executed thousands of people, robbed the landlords of their land and divided it among the peasants. Above the dispatches were the names of the news agencies: "Reuter", "Go-Wen", "Toho". I knew these agencies. A few years ago they had been thundering daily for us to crush the German bandits and join the ranks of the noble Allies.

Although I was afraid of executions and hated robbers, I held no ill feelings against this "Party of the Poor". The property of the landlords had been divided among the peasants? Well, perhaps it was not so bad. Had I not seen my father, digging the soil with a mattock when he was in hiding, turn into a peasant? I myself had labored long enough at the monastery to know the hardships of peasant work. It was then that I had wondered why a peasant-tenant should give half of the product of his labor to the idle landlords. I felt almost happy because the land had been taken away from them in that distant northern country. But what was this "Party of the Poor"?

If someone had told me at that time that the Party of the Poor was a workers' party, I wouldn't have understood. Our province had no factories. Farm-hands wandering with a scythe and a pitchfork from village to village, coolies towing boats, carrying loads at docks, pulling at oars or running under the weight of the poles of tzaos, were all half-peasants. All they dreamed of was to save a little money and go back to the soil or to open a small store in town.

The Party of the Poor was called "Go-ti-Pai", which means "the most extreme movement". And the word extreme had a tinge of lawlessness. It almost meant banditry. But I knew where this word had originated. It came from Japan. And I knew from the newspapers that Japan had brought her troops into Siberia and wished to work out in the Far East the same program she had drawn up for our Manchuria. Of course, the Japanese would give the Party of the Poor a scornful and insulting name.

The Party of the Poor, I figured out, was probably a peasant party, perhaps following the teachings of Kropotkin. We had heard already about the Russian anarchist Kropotkin from students of the university who came occasionally to Teh chien. The real leader, Lenin, was not yet known to us.

I sat in my bed rustling newspapers and trying to guess from the meager and hostile lines of the dispatches what the revolution in this cruel northern nation meant. A people who, at the time of my birth, had marked the Chinese in Manchuria with hand-shackles and numbered plaques, and who, two years before that, at the time of the Boxer Rebellion, had marched over villages and city streets, through quiet temples and ornate palaces full of rare and exquisite objects, swinging their bayonets and the butts of their rifles. Now they had divided the land.

I remembered the Taipings who seventy years ago started a peasant revolt in the South, cut their braids off, banished opium and wine, replaced Buddha with Christ and created their capital at Nanking. Then they had ended their march to the north toward Manchu Peking. They settled down, relaxed, and were soon demolished by Manchu troops under the command of three thousand British soldiers.

While the Taipings were advancing as conquerors and liberators, they spared the lives and property of peaceful citizens. But when the troops of their enemies started to press them from the north, and treason to gnaw at their strength from inside, the Taipings began to confiscate food and take away property from the rich, and to search for traitors and secret enemies.

Three million people were destroyed by the Manchus and the English, pacifying the Taipings. The dark villages of southern China directed their deep hatred against the Taipings and revolutionary organizations. Decades passed before the somber peasant was able to distinguish behind the shoulders of those unhappy rebels the features of the real enemies of China—the Manchu magnates and the correct and cruel Europeans.

In strange and mysterious O-go (the Chinese name for Russia) the Party of the Poor was dividing the land among the peasants. In our own Szechuan, government troops were carrying

[219]

on their manoeuvres against guerilla armies mustered by the Kuomintang and Sun Yat-sen against Peking. My aging father was still pulling the tow-line of a revolutionary with the same panting stubbornness with which a boatman pulls a heavy barge against the current—a very heavy barge loaded with thick-headed merchants and stern, suspicious peasants.

Little by little I was getting stronger. My legs could now support my body, my brain began to work. My hands ceased twitching and my lips no longer quivered. Anger against my step-mother and my wife settled down at the bottom of my heart like slime in a pond.

The winter passed from the year 1919 to the year 1920. I left the apartment of Huan and moved into the school dormitory in order to be closer to the library where I could read ancient Chinese literature. My decision to go to Peking and study literature was definitely set.

---

8. My Wife

IN A CHINESE FAMILY GIRLS ARE CHEAP, BOYS EXPENSIVE. Chinese society rests on the males. They have to look after the memory of the ancestors. A girl's place is in the kitchen and the nursery. She is noticed only when she becomes the mother of a son. And if she fails to give birth to a child her coffin is not allowed to stand in the li tang of the house in which she has lived all her married life. There is a saying: "Ignorance is an ornament to a woman." (However, my little sister went to school. How did it happen? My father was so indifferent to her fate and to mine. To this day I cannot understand by whose grace she was sent to school, whether by my younger uncle's or my step-mother's.)

But my wife was an honest-to-goodness illiterate. A year younger than I, she was completely alien to me. Usually in China a husband does not speak to his wife for a year or two after the wedding and turns his face away when he meets her. I acted exactly that way to my wife. When I came back to Sian-Shih during holidays I would enter the house and, according to an established order, I would first bow to my father, my step-mother, my uncles and aunts, say polite words to them, ask them about their health and answer their questions about Teh chien. Only after that might I go to my wife. But I did not go to her. I would keep up the conversation with the older people or go to my father's room, take a brush and help him verify the lists of people in his detachment, look over his bills, add the figures. Without interrupting his work he would usually say, "Well, in about three months from now you'll be going to Shanghai to study engineering, won't you?"

I would remain silent. He would repeat the question. Then I'd say, "I am interested in literature."

Father would hunch his shoulders over his work. He did not like my answer. But that did not matter much, the next day he would repeat all he had said about engineers and would be telling me again how necessary it was for China to build factories, run steamers, construct locomotives, and dig coal. And while he talked the lovely, singing rhythms of the exquisite lines of Tan's verse would be ringing in my head.

I would see my wife only when it was unavoidable, at dinner and supper. I would nod with restraint in her direction without saying a word and then not give her another glance. At night I would lie on the very edge of our wide bed, squeamishly shrinking away from her.

She remained silent. A Chinese girl is not supposed to annoy her husband with sobs or complain that he does not love her, nor should she cling to him or invite him to her bed. Over-sensuality on the part of a wife is considered lawful grounds for divorce. Even should a girl fall in love with her husband whom she sees for the first time when she comes out of her tzao all dressed up in red, she must not tell him of her feelings. In case she comes from an illiterate village she simply would not know how to tell him of her love, because it must be told in precise and exquisite words, chosen for lovers by the high masters of phrase in all dynasties. And how could a simple village girl whose vocabulary consisted of words like "cow" "store" or "cooked beans" know about the beauty of Tan's verse?

My wife's face remained complacent. It is not for a Chinese girl to cry over the fact that her husband does not love her. But the eyes and the nose of my step-mother irritated me. They were constantly moist and red. She seemed to be grieving for me. Often she would turn her face away, lifting a tiny handkerchief to her nostrils. My wife undoubtedly was complaining to her.

The house became disgusting and alien to me. I was constantly annoyed by hearing through the paper partition women sobbing and whispering, "We must have a grandson. . . . We have no grandson. . . . What about a grandson?" It was my step-mother whispering to my wife and my father, for she saw that I was not becoming attached to my wife. The marriage to her was no good at all. I would not sleep with my wife; how could there be a child?

I have observed three different attitudes toward marriage among the married youth of China. Preceding the epoch of the renaissance, i. e. up until 1919, marriage was a family duty. Young people went into marriage with their heads down, accepting it as one accepts the inevitable, an illness, a tax, or the death of an old man. Things went differently after the renaissance. There were people who accepted marriage but accepted it angrily, and regarded their wives as a curse, a shameful sore.

[222]

The sore ached and one was ashamed of it, but still it could not be cut out. Some of these people would try to drown their discontent and disgust in study. The others would fall into decadence and degeneration. Their lives became a round of drink, theatrical performances, and song. They would seek educated women in public houses, exquisite women who knew how to recite verse and carry on philosophical conversations. Asked about their wives, they would answer with a joke or snap, "Why talk about her? She's somewhere in the village, the illiterate beast."

The third category would not be bound by the marriage. They would try to find a way to get rid of their wives. They divorced them if it was possible to get them to agree to a divorce. (Divorce by mutual agreement was allowed by the Chinese court.) Failing this, they would scrape together enough money to run away. Their families would curse them because they had to go through a divorce trial which meant paying the family of the deserted wife. This was a painful process, often carried on through several generations. And if young men found it impossible to get a divorce and failed to run away, they would hang themselves with a piece of string in a toilet. Suicides' bodies, swollen and brown, often would be discovered, washed up by streams after the July cloudbursts.

I belonged to the second group. The presence of my wife tortured me like an abscess, like constantly dripping water. Besides, women in general held little attraction for me.

This wordless, completely alien, unbeautiful body, shoved into my bed with the sole purpose that a perpetuator of the family Tan should whine in our house, irritated me. Love, of which I had read in scores of books, seemed to me the silly fancy of consoling verse-makers. I began to believe that there was no love in the world. It was just a lie, like the story of paradise and hell I had read in the Buddhist bible in the monastery. There was no such thing as love, only a small paper bag into which silkworms were put—a female and a male—and then the paper bag was sealed and the necessary number of eggs were automatically obtained. There was only a marriage bed into which a dull and frightened girl and a protesting boy had been shoved together. After that, children to nurse, children conceived unwillingly and in disgust.

It was only after I came to the university that I became convinced, watching the free romances between boy and girl students, that the so-called love could be real. I observed how they were attracted to one another, and how they glowed when they met—as though electric lights had been turned on suddenly behind their faces. But even in the university love passed me by. There were girl students. I knew that they liked me. They smiled at me, and when I happened to pass by, they would turn around and look at me. There were sisters of my comrades who would go walking with me and who, taking my hand in their helpless fingers, would ask me to recite poetry. I knew that they liked me, but I did not need them.

Now the university, too, is behind me, and it seems to me that I have never loved a woman, and no woman ever loved me. I don't know whether or not Tchen Tsai-in loved me. But at times it seems to me that father was wrong when he forbade my marriage to her. I have observed many marriages and in all of them without exception I noticed one thing—a wife always accepts the beliefs of her husband. Tsai-in would not have turned me into a reactionary. I would have made her a member of the Kuomintang, a radical, a sympathizer with Soviet Russia.

The black months went on crawling by after my wedding. The atmosphere which clings around the place of a crime was in the house, a state of anguish pervaded it as though someone had died. I became accustomed, without constant indignation, to pay no attention to my wife or to my step-mother's sobbing. My father's talk about Shanghai and the technical college went in one ear and out the other. Once my step-mother came to me, trembling, full of words of regret and repentance.

"I did not know it would turn out this way. Forgive me, Shih-hua."

She sat down on the floor. How hollow-chested, how thin and pathetic she was! Words fell from her lips faster than the tears flowed out of her eyes. I was shocked. I touched her arm. I felt pity for her and for myself and even for the slow-moving girl, who had been pushed into our house against her will and made my wife. I tried to quiet my step-mother.

"Stop crying. Why make yourself suffer like this? Everything will be all right."

She bowed to me. Moved and humbled, sobbing and sniffling, she went to her room.

That same night as I sat down at the table next to the empty chair of my father, I engaged in conversation with my wife for the first time.

"Where did my father go?"

She was astonished.

"I don't know for sure, but I think he went to Ti-bao."

My step-mother's face lighted up with the same expression of delight one sees on the face of a woman who has given birth to a long-expected child.

I began to address my wife daily with three or four such phrases.

"Did my comrade come to see me? What is the matter with uncle? Why didn't my sister go to school?"

That was all. I tried to ask these miserly questions when my step-mother was present.

Guan-in was obviously attracted to me. She was not satisfied with being only my wife, she wanted to be a mother. What is marriage good for without that?

The laws of physiology are stronger than hate, more binding than spite. The common bed did its part. But there was no tenderness. And when the next morning my wife began saying sweet words to me and wanted to help me dress, I pushed away her outstretched hand which held my slippers. As before, I pulled on my clothes and walked out of the room, giving her just as much attention as was necessary to hurt and humiliate her, to kill the smile on her lips and put out the light in her eyes. I was fulfilling my duties as a lover with clenched teeth, without remembering. I noticed that my spitefulness was infecting my wife. But I did not care.

She asked my permission to go and see her parents. She came back feeling happier, but soon grew quiet again. She would be silent until I threw her a question—as a bone is thrown to a dog. Her visits to her parents became more and more frequent. I did not object. I was glad to see less of this unwanted woman and her disagreeable face; to hear less of that crude village speech to which I was condemned to listen all my life.

The burning summer of 1920 was softened by mountain winds. General Sung Ke-wu was capturing the last remnants of Ho Kuo Chun. Troubled people came to see father, warning him to flee.

It did not take him long to get ready. The last moment before he left, when the coolies were already waiting for him, coughing at the gate, he called me.

"There is no use in your staying here long. Go to Shanghai and study engineering."

I did not answer.

"You may take a hundred da yang from your step-mother. A hundred is not much but unfortunately we spent the rest of the money on your wedding."

I was silent.

"A hundred will be enough to take you to Shanghai and keep you there for a month. During that time your step-mother and your uncle will get some more money and send it to you. I think about four hundred da yang a year will be sufficient. Telegraph home as soon as you get there."

I could not very well remain silent any longer.

"All right, I'll telegraph you. Don't worry. Good luck. Take care of yourself."

Two months after my father's departure I packed my suitcases. Coolies lifted them on their backs and carried them to the boat which was taking me to Chungking where I would get a steamer. My step-mother, my wife, my sister, and my aunts walked with me to the docks. My step-mother, stroking my sleeve, asked for the last time: "And where are you going, Shih-hua?"

I looked at the women, smiled, bowed to them and wished them the best of luck. The waves rippled, the shore moved away. The women, getting smaller and smaller, began to ascend the slope of the hill without having received an answer to their question.

In Chungking my companions and the ticket for the steamer sailing from Chungking to Ichang were waiting for me. I had decided where I was going long before with my comrades. Seventeen years ago my father had gone to Japan without saying a word to anybody. Today, without saying a word to anybody, I was going to Peking.

9. River and Rails

THERE WERE FOUR OF US: I, HUAN, COMRADE MING AND MY cousin Tan Shan-su. Tan Shan-su was a great fellow. He had character. He had refused to marry the girl chosen for him by his family. She had died recently and he had married a girl student of his own choice.

A few of our friends saw us off. They tied a package of

tangerines to my fingers, and asked me to write them about Peking, about the students and the anti-Japanese boycott and to send them the university programs as soon as possible. Our steamer was anchored in the middle of the river. A boatman took us to the gangplank, which was already surrounded by dozens of boats. The handkerchiefs of our friends fluttered on the shore. The striped American flag with stars gathered in one corner of it waved to them from the mast. The steamer belonged to the American line owned by Robert Dollar. War was going on in Szechuan then and all Chinese steamships had been either seized by the generals and used for carrying their troops and cannon, or were navigated only in the lower Yangtze.

Robert Dollar was no fool. As soon as the monopoly of passenger traffic was his, he immediately raised the price of the tickets. Formerly the price of a third-class ticket from Chung-king to Ichang—a day and a half trip—was ten da yang; going up the river, twenty da yang. Now it was forty instead of ten, but as there was no alternative, I paid the forty out of my hundred. Heavy silver coins weighed my pockets down. Paper money was not convenient for travelling purposes—its value varied in different provinces. Silver da yang with the profile of Yuan Shi-Kai on them were the only money retaining the same value all over China.

Mandarins and manufacturers travelled first class. Dog's Head and his partners travelled this way. But there was a class superior to first class—on the top decks of some of the steamers were special cabins for foreigners. Even Dog's Head would not have been allowed to go there, no matter how much money they were willing to pay. These special cabins for foreigners were only on the big boats sailing down from Ichang. Our boat was a small shallow one which travelled only over the upper Yangtze.

The third class was in the steerage. There the people were lying around in disorder, on and under their belongings. Walking across this section you would inevitably step on someone's foot. The human skeleton was not made for the contortions which the passengers on the Dollar steamer had to perform. Heads of snoring people were hanging down over their suit-cases, their mouths turned upwards. A smell of musty blankets and unwashed clothing pervaded the place. People delayed going to the toilet until they could endure it no longer. They cleared their throats and then took a long time looking around for a crack in the floor where they could spit.

An inspector, a foreigner, wearing the cap of an official, came down for our tickets, walking over people's blankets and bodies. He kicked away their feet and swore at the passengers although they had not been guilty of one disrespectful word. Two clerks in white jackets followed him and gave orders to open all bag-gage. With swift hands, they turned over the carefully packed bundles and bags. The fingers of one of them dug under my books. What were they looking for? Opium, arms? In any case they were not looking for contraband—they were not customs officials.

At twilight our steamer stopped opposite the city of Yan-Sian. The long city spread out along the river underneath a black mountain. We could see a large grey spot above the city, pressed from all sides by the darkness of an enormous garden. It was the pedagogical school. The masts of many barges rose like a great comb between us and the shore. The oil tanks of the Asia Oil Company and The Standard Oil Company looked like the round concrete tombs of some rich tribal cemetery. Our anchor plunged into the water opposite The Standard Oil Company. Like iron filings pulled by a magnet, rowboats were drawn to our steamer. Soon it was surrounded by a ring of boat-lanterns and peddlers shouting furiously. They were selling beer from some boats. After a passenger had swallowed his beer, they deftly caught the glass thrown back at them.

A stuffy steam rose over charcoal stoves on which greasy meat-cakes and noodles were being cooked. The hungry passengers bought eggs, sausage, and cold jellied soup. Floating restaurant boats with semi-circular awnings, lighted with kerosene lamps,

bobbed against the side of our craft, inviting the merchants, tired
from the day's journey and accustomed to a good supper, to
come in. Boats with gambling tables were loud with the shouts
of winners, the click of dice, and the ring of copper coins flung
from one gambler to another. The air in the steerage was hot and
still. The boats outside on the river were opened to the fresh
river wind.

The gambling boats were followed by floating brothels rocking on the water. Women with powdered faces, gold earrings
and bracelets looked over their sides. From under the awning
came the barely audible sounds of ku-tzin. A high falsetto sang
softly. The barkers shouted, praising the virtues of their women.
Passengers on the steamer took a long look at the women,
fingered the money in their pockets, obviously figuring out the
cost. They signalled, and the floating brothel, with a strong swing
of the stern oar, began pushing its way through the crowd of
other barges toward the gangway. With careful hands on the
fat bottoms of their customers the barkers helped them into
their boats. Those who were not rich enough watched and
envied. The lucky ones! They will spend their night in the fresh
air. They will sleep with women who, from the deck of the
steamer, in the evening light, seem to be first-rate beauties.

We stayed there all night, surrounded by the lanterns of the
moving boats, for we could not travel in the dark. The great
rapids and the quiet shallows of the Yangtze were too dangerous.

We reached Ichang about dinner-time. There we changed our
steamer for a bigger one bound for Hankow. There were many
steamers at Ichang. We took a Chinese one. After one night in
the steerage we decided to have a good time. We bought second
class tickets, paying eight da yang for a journey of a day and a
half. Now we were travelling like millionaires. The second class
had its own deck on which we could sit in a Shanghai wicker
chair. We could walk along it and talk excitedly about Peking,
and tease the shy daughters of merchants who were on their way

from one city to another. Book-sellers walked back and forth on the deck. They offered the bored passengers story books and the fat Shanghai editions of novels. If a passenger looked exceedingly bored, they extracted from underneath their pile of books, pornographic pictures of actresses and courtesans.

In Hankow our travel over water ended and the journey by rail began. Fifteen minutes on the docks of Hankow nearly ruined me. The rumble of trucks and derricks, the dust from falling bags, the sad howl of the load-carriers, the terrible wagons with bloated wheels, wagons without horses which I had never seen before except in pictures, men harnessed to light carriages running and ringing shrill bells. But most of all the terrible dust which got into your nostrils, your throat, your eyes and ears, and settled down between your fingers, drying up your skin!

Hotel agents, swinging lanterns bearing the names of their establishments, insolently grabbed us by the elbows and shouted their invitations into our ears. In comparison with all this fury and movement, the noise of the docks in Teh chien was like the breath of a sleeping baby. And as for Sian-Shih? It probably did not exist at all.

I was deafened by the noise of the trucks. My eyes could not endure the sight of derricks moving up and down. I was ready to rush back up the Yangtze, notwithstanding the steerage and the swearing officials, if only I might get into the quiet room of our house in Sian-Shih and hear once more its distant gongs sound in the middle of the night.

My cousin was laughing: "Look out, Shih-hua. This is not a village."

It was not his first visit to Hankow. He pushed aside the hotel agents, skillfully crossed the street, unafraid of the automobiles, and led us to a house he knew.

Clever fellow, Shan-su. I liked him. His confident voice restored my equilibrium. I was ashamed of myself for being ready to give up before reaching Peking. When I had managed to resist the will of my father, how could I let the rumbling of Hankow and the dust of the port break me down?

The railroad station smelled of coal. The enormous engine frightened me. I was afraid the rumbling steam might explode it. I was bewildered by the rails. According to the pictures I had seen, it seemed that the ties should be made of iron and the rails much thicker. In reality the rails were nothing but a thin strip of steel. It seemed to me that they could not possibly resist the weight of that many-wheeled cauldron. I jumped down on the ties and tried to break off the edge of a rail. It would not break. I felt better.

Third class had only benches—two seats on each bench. It was filled with soldiers. They piled up their things on luggage nets along the walls and stood their rifles close by. The soldiers were sprawled all over the bench—already asleep. We had to ask them to move a bit. In answer they cursed, moved unwillingly and looked with interest at our suitcases, as though weighing their contents.

It was a thirty-six hour journey to Peking and there was no use trying to sleep. Soldiers kept walking back and forth and getting off in numbers at stations. There were now only three of us as Tan Shan-su had remained in Hankow. He was on his way South.

I tried to listen to the conversation around me but could not understand a word of it. The northern tongue was foreign to my Szechuan ear.

In the morning I saw a new country. Fields divided the horizon. A few, a very few trees grew along the canals and over the mounds of village graves. How expensive wood must be in this country! The tree I saw most often was a telegraph pole blossoming with porcelain flowers. We began to get hungry. Our throats were dry. At every station we rushed to a window looking for the peddlers who sold water. There was none. There was no boiling water at the stations either. What an outrage—

the railroad was in French hands. Not until I was almost ready to scream with thirst did I decide to go to the dining car. Two of us went. We jumped carefully over the noisy buffers from one car to another. We passed through the second class. It was also thick with people, and there were also two seats on a bench, but the air was clean, people looked respectable, their skullcaps were glossy and the juice of the fruit they were eating lacquered their lips.

In first class we walked along the corridor looking into the compartments. Here, on soft divans covered with plaids, were important-looking officials and boisterous groups of toothy Japanese. There were also some foreigners in light-colored suits.

"Yan-Gui-tze," I said to my comrade.

"Yan-Gui-tze," he echoed.

Yan means foreign, and it also means a "ram" and the expression Yan-Gui-tze reminded us of bulging grey eyes. The Europeans have eyes like a ram. I felt like laughing—the eyes of the Chinese are black.

At the entrance to the dining car we were stopped by a waiter dressed in a white robe with green trimmings. He looked us over and for some reason examined the bottoms of our robes.

"What do you want?"

"We want dinner."

"You can't have it."

"Why not? The restaurant is for everybody."

"I tell you, you can't." He jumped aside with a bow to admit a foreigner who was smoking a cigar. "And besides the dinner costs two da yang."

"For both?"

The waiter smiled contemptuously and closed the door.

Angry and embarrassed we went back to third class. A tradesman who was returning to Peking from a trip to his own village where he had gone to attend the funeral of his grandmother, explained to us sympathetically, "They won't let you come in without a ma-gua. And besides it's very expensive. You can feed yourself for a week for two da yang if you buy food from the peddlers at the stations."

We surrendered and at the very next station bought a fried duck, red with pepper, and some pears, hard as stones. We ate the duck tearing it apart with our fingers and threw the bones out of the window.

We flashed by fields, roofs of pagodas, barges on the canals, smoke-stacks. We saw painted wooden generals erected on the tops of town walls. Across the generals were displayed large advertisements: "The best cigarettes."

---

10. Peking

I DON'T THINK THERE IS A SINGLE SPOT IN CHINA WHERE customs officials do not inspect people's baggage and collect duty on it. It is easy to understand, because the customs houses are in the hands of foreign nations and the money they collect goes into the amortization of loans which they have given to our premiers, presidents, and military parties. Foreigners, followed by coolies carrying their suitcases, passed by the tables undisturbed, as they had pass cards.

Why bother to inspect a student's belongings wrapped in a cotton blanket? Tying our things up, the three provincials, I, Huan, and Ming, passed under an arch out through the thickness of the Peking wall, and out into a public square.

In Hankow I had happened to hear a telephone bell ring. I did not talk over the telephone, I merely heard its piercing bird-like ring. Here on the square a thousand telephones seemed to be ringing. These were the rickshaws. In China these little carriages are called *yan-che* which means a foreign carriage. (The word rickshaw I learned later from my Russian professor.) They were introduced into China about thirty years ago and today they provide a living for nearly a hundred thousand coolies. They are found mainly in the cities situated on the sea shore or on level ground. In Teh chien and Sian-Shih we did not have these yan-ches, for no man could have pulled a carriage over the stone steps, the mountain paths and the sloping roads of Szechuan.

Fifteen yan-ches rushed toward us, the men shouting "Take me! Take me!" They lifted the poles of their carriages over our heads and tore at us from all sides as though we were the remains of a beefsteak and they a pack of starving dogs. But we were not sure it was proper for us to travel in a yan-che. We examined the swollen rubber tires of the thin-spoked wheels critically and then walked to the very end of the square where the *lo-ches* were standing. A lo-che is a springless wagon with large iron wheels and a semi-circular cloth top. It is the most ancient vehicle in China. Lo means mule, che means wagon. It is also called a *tzao-che*. We crawled into its stuffy box. From there we looked at Peking through its cross-like windows, shaking in time with the rapid stride of the horses until we were dizzy and began to hiccough.

The streets were full of people harnessed to light carriages. Their heavy passengers sat so still they seemed to be strapped in position. From time to time they pressed with their toes the button of a signal bell attached to the floor of the carriage. Landlords, money-changers, owners of antique shops with their wives and daughters, passed by us in glass carriages pulled by leisurely horses. The west wind called by the Europeans the typhoon drove yellowish dust into our faces. It gritted in our teeth, dried up our nostrils, formed small black crumbs in the corners of our eyes. Our handkerchiefs which we, choking from the impure air, kept pressing against our nostrils, had long ago

[235]

turned into black kitchen rags. This dust was the first thing I noticed in Peking. Another thing was the Manchu women. Tall, wearing long robes, they had their eye-lids and temples rouged. High chignons above their heads resembled the letter T. Such coiffures I had seen only in the theater. In Peking you saw them on the streets. Peddlers paraded the streets or squatted at corners, playing instruments, striking gongs, beating drums and singing their wares in a tongue unknown to me.

Our lo-che turned off the street where little chains of electric lights flared up without the help of a match in shop windows and buildings, and carried us between the windowless walls of the alleys. We had ceased to wonder a long time ago where the fellow was going.

Our journey ended in front of a small hotel. Evidently our driver had business connections with the hotel and was going to be paid a commission for bringing us there. The rooms were poorly furnished and had no beds. Here for the first time I saw a *kan*, a built-in sleeping platform. There was nothing underneath it. In summer time, as it was then, the opening to this empty space was boarded up. In winter a charcoal stove was set there and the warm air coming from it enveloped the sleeper and served as an extra cover.

The proprietor informed us he would charge eighty cents a day for board and room. Eighty cents a day just for room and board! And what about clothes, textbooks, carfare? Our conference was short. We decided to write to our fellow countrymen in Peking as quickly as possible, and ask them to get us out of this cursed place, where they robbed new-comers from the provinces. The mail was very efficient. A day later we met some of our countrymen. They scolded us and gave us advice.

"The best thing to do is to get into a college dormitory. There you pay sixteen da yang a year for a bed in a double room. But you can't get any room in the university dormitory at present. You'll have to rent a furnished room. There you'll have to pay ten or twenty da yang a month for your board and a place on a kan."

Ten da yang was not so bad, although the room was a bit far from the university.

The problem of living quarters separated me from my companions. The most difficult thing now was to decide what to study. With university programs and lecture-schedules spread around me I tried to decide what to do. My father was right in giving preference to the study of a definite profession. But chemists and agriculturists had to pay a special fee for the use of laboratories, and the necessary books were very expensive. Literature was much cheaper. But what if I flunked my examinations? I must be sure of something. I wrote another application —this time to the medical college. I had to fill out the longest questionnaire. After moving his nose from one side to the other over my graduation papers, the clerk handed them back to me, saying: "You are not old enough. Come back next year."

From the west side of Peking where I lived, I hurried over every day to the north section of the city, to the large university courts.

I changed my last three da yang bill. I spent a da yang and a half on a telegram home asking for assistance. The newspapers were full of bad news. Letters and money from Szechuan to Peking moved slowly and with uncertainty. Huan, whom I met in the university, took me by the hand and said: "How lucky we were. We got here in time. Now the war has cut off all communication between the South and the West."

Such "luck" offered me little consolation. My money was melting away. Days of unpleasant conversations with my countrymen, who themselves had very little in their pockets, followed.

It was the middle of the summer. Rain water was rushing through the alleys of Peking. The yan-ches carried their passengers, breaking streams of water with their stomachs. Then the rain rolled off the streets and evaporated and the sun heated dusty Peking to such an extent that it might have been put on an anvil and hammered.

I was saving in every way I could. I would hurry in the morning, without food, ten li to the library and walk back around noon time on the shady side of the street. I knew the first man I would see in my house would be a servant with my bill which was growing larger every day. He would come to my room and begin to tell me that it was time to pay because the hotel had to meet its taxes and because the price of food was going up. I had spent a lot of time explaining to him that I would surely pay, that my parents had already sent me money from home, but that it had not yet reached me on account of the war. But my voice sounded unconvincing. How could I be sure that my family had really sent me money? Perhaps my father, outraged by my disobedience, had forbidden my relatives to have anything to do with me.

I would ask the servant to bring me my dinner. Half an hour would pass, an hour—still no dinner. My brain, lacking nourishment, could not function. I would go to the proprietor, smile, bow, beg him to give me some dinner, express a hope that the money would arrive the next day. I would stand before him for a long time, flourish compliments and talk smilingly until he grew tired of the performance and ordered the servant to bring me my dinner.

Some left-overs would be brought to me, but my appetite would be gone. The food was unpleasant and pressed like a heavy stone against my liver. But far more sickening was the memory of my humiliating conduct before the proprietor and the realization that it would have to be repeated.

The time of the examinations came. All of them were to be written examinations. It was so in the time of the mandarins and their cages and it is so in the newest Chinese universities.

[238]

The first three days were the most important: mathematics, Chinese and one foreign language, usually English. English was the most popular in Chinese high schools. On the fourth and fifth day we had history, geology, zoölogy, botany, mineralogy, chemistry, physics—all the natural sciences. Then we had a month's rest, if one could so call a state of anxiety and hunger.

We had to wait a whole month for the results, during which time the tension of my nerves never relaxed. It was not hard to fail and there were two thousand applicants for three hundred openings. Other institutions of higher learning admitted even fewer.

The good news came all at once. Money from Szechuan and a notice from the university. I had passed! I was a student! I was in a hurry to get out of my furnished room and move to the university dormitory. But what gave me most joy was the fact that my decision to go to Peking had not spoiled my relations with my father.

11. Living

A STUDENT'S CERTIFICATE IN MY POCKET, MONEY IN MY purse and daily dinners in my stomach—what more could a provincial desire? To celebrate the great event I bought myself a dressy silk robe and a pair of round eye-glasses. I did not need them for reading, my eyes were good, but glasses made one look learned. They were, however, a terrible nuisance. The dust settled on them and they had to be wiped frequently. They pressed against the bridge of my nose and pulled at my ears. But appearance was more important.

A bunch of keys tinkled in my pocket—the flat keys of my suitcase and of my room; silver coins were slipped into a knitted money-bag; under a handkerchief in my trouser pocket was a pen knife. I used it to pare the dusty Peking apples more often than to sharpen pencils. A small notebook and a fountain pen. The fountain pen was not very good and I was afraid that it might leak in my pocket. I kept a small pack of visiting cards behind the sweat band of my straw hat—they would not get crumpled there, though I ran the risk of getting them wet with perspiration. Whenever I met a new person, I removed my hat and politely presented my card. The only thing that I did not have in my pocket was a celluloid cigarette holder. I had weak lungs and did not smoke.

With my countrymen I wandered along the quiet alleys and through the mad business streets of Peking—streets echoing with bells and shouting and a-gleam with golden signs. Streets where the penetrating noise of tamborines burst from the doors of smelly theaters; streets with stores dressed up and lacquered like brides on their wedding day, from which slow-moving Pekingese emerged, pushing aside the thick cotton-padded curtains which hung before each entrance. We called the Pekingese northern clods. They impressed us as being naïve and without temperament.

I used to pass by a door with a sign "Photography" over it. On each side of this door was a life-size portrait in a glass case. On the left was a portrait of a celebrated beauty from a famous brothel; on the right a portrait of a general, a ruler of Peking, wearing helmet and choking in a high, gilded collar. Walking along this street past the two glass windows, during my stay in Peking, I observed with satisfaction how short-lived were the generals in their solid glass case. Su Shih-chan was replaced by Li Uan-hun, Li Uan-hun by Tuan Tse-hsui, Tuan Tse-hsui by

Feng U-sian, Feng U-sian by Chang Tso-lin. The presidents
changed but the photographer's studio prospered and the same
beauty went on holding the same handkerchief in her beautiful
white hand.

I wandered with my friends in Central Park, which had been
the Imperial Park. The black foliage of arbor-vitae hung motionless above the benches. We laughed importantly and joked in a
business-like manner. We shot bold glances at passers-by—at
the shy daughters of merchants, fat and rosy-cheeked, who wore
blue trousers and gold bracelets; at the plain-looking, bobbed-
haired girl students in short, foreign-style skirts, and at the
prostitutes with their exquisite stone-like faces and perfect
bangs. These latter went past us without looking. Neither our
robes nor eye-glasses could hide from their experienced eye the
thinness of our pocket-books.

I loved Central Park with its professors hurrying along on
its paths to conferences, with its fresh air, protected from the
dusty filth of the streets by walls and arbor-vitae. I loved its
restaurants, where the cups tinkled and where I could sit an
infinite number of hours at a table, playing one of my favorite
games—*ui-ti,* a game that is played on a board divided into
three hundred and sixty squares.

"Hey! Szechuan Lao-tu! (the old man from Szechuan)" my
countrymen would hail me from another table. We sat and drank
tea. Those who had lived long in Peking told me of the arguments that used to take place between the students and theater
goers. Some of them had admired the actor Mei Lan-fang who
used to play young women's parts with a skill unsurpassed by
any beautiful girl. Mei Lan-fang, whose wardrobe was valued
at 40,000 da yang and who was paid 2000 da yang a performance.
The other group of students admired the famous actress, Lu
Si-guei. The Mei Lan-fangists insisted irritatingly that a woman
on the stage was a disgrace, that Lu Si-guei was nothing but a
courtesan, and that a woman could never be better at acting

[241]

than a man. The adherents of Lu Si-guei called their opponents conservatives and went in mobs to attend the performance of their favorite.

My friends told me about the stormy year of 1919, how theater-going, verse-reading, and gay student parties had all come to an end. The students rushed into political circles and meetings. They picketed, boycotted, broke into the houses of the hated nobles and made the government with its police, its troops and its prisons listen to them. These moods still predominated. Sitting in Central Park I felt excitedly that all the students were revolutionaries and that I was one too. I felt proud, my glasses gleamed. (Those eye-glasses didn't last long. Someone stole them from me in the dormitory and I did not buy another pair.)

The clear autumn sun rose over Peking. The dust settled, the plum-trees growing in front of foreign hotels dropped their leaves. The chill morning brought to mind thoughts of padded robes. In the courts men made black eggs from the coal dust. They were preparing the winter fuel of Peking.

The National University had five dormitories with a hundred little cells in each. Four of them were for male students and the other for the girls. Li, who was studying chemistry, and I lived in one of these wind-blown cells. The doors of each cell— there were two students in each—gave on a paved court shaded from the sun by gigantic branches which were now bare. Every morning we were awakened at six o'clock by the bell of the gateman. It was still dark and our skin, warm from sleep, was covered with goose flesh—the iron stoves went out during the night. The stoker was coming, rattling his coal pail and leaning on his poker.

I put on my trousers and my sweat-shirt over the shirt and under-trousers in which I slept. Then my socks and shoes. Before the bathroom a long line waited. We dipped out hot water with an iron dipper from a large steaming cauldron. A washbasin was set on a high stool in front of the window of each. White drops dripped from tooth-brushes to the stone floor. The appetite, stimulated by movement, began to express itself. It took another minute to put on a robe and an overcoat and run to breakfast.

Many small lunchrooms were scattered around the university. I bought a cup of bean milk for four tung tze. For ten tung tze I got two doughnuts to go with my milk or a couple of soft *mantos*, pale steam-scalded rolls, five tung tze each. From the lunchroom I went to the university. For a tung tze I bought a small university paper from the gateman. Then I ran into the reading room to read it and also to read the large general newspaper, for which you paid two tung tze and which boys had been selling on the streets since six o'clock.

Twelve o'clock was dinner-time. Students from the same province ate together. I patronized a lunchroom, the manager of which came from Szechuan. There the *man-tzes*, the southern savages, as the Pekingese jokingly called us, gathered.

This restaurant was famous for its meat rolled in pancakes, red boiled cabbage and bean jelly. I usually ate ten tung tze worth of soup and then some meat and vegetables. Those who had won at cards the night before or had received money from home ordered a better dish—chicken soup with a slice of sea-cucumber floating in it. And those who were hard up ate beef broth and a cup of rice. We did not pay for rice—rice in China is served free, as bread is in America. Three times a year on important holidays I gave the waiter a da yang or two as a tip. The waiter would thank me, half-kneeling.

After dinner we went to the dormitory to rinse our mouths. Then we sprawled on our beds and talked over university news. The university bell announced the end of dinner-time. Again study followed, after which at six o'clock we ate our supper. This would cost about twenty-five tung tze, and we ate the same things, excepting the soup.

After supper we would go and visit friends, to chat and joke, to play chess or the ku-tzin. At ten o'clock Peking went to bed. One after another the switches clicked in the rooms. Exactly at midnight the gateman turned off the main switch, plunging those who were still reading into darkness.

One sunny November morning a white envelope was handed to me from the black window of the sentry box. The hieroglyphics of the address had been written, as it seemed to me, by my uncle's hand.

I had a daughter. About this and also about other house news, about money, about my father still hiding in the old castle, my step-mother wrote to me. My wife herself could not write.

The letter brought back the memory of my wife and my hatred of her. But the hatred gave place to a kind of calm.

"A daughter? Fine. Am I glad? Perhaps I am. I don't know. Probably I am. In any case I am glad because my step-mother is glad; she wanted this child."

The daughter was an item with which I had balanced accounts with my step-mother. Now she could demand nothing more of me.

12. The Russian Section

THE BOOKS MOST POPULAR WITH THE YOUTH OF CHINA AT that time were the autobiography of Kropotkin and "Moral Tales" by Tolstoy. I swallowed the pages of Kropotkin's book dreaming of labor equality among people. I devoured the two freshly printed popular pamphlets entitled "The Russian City" and "The Socialism Advanced by Comrade Kropotkin Now a

Reality in Russia". The "Moral Tales" of Tolstoy had just been translated into Chinese and it seemed clear to me that there was no higher political teaching in the world than Anarchism. Bolshevism was Anarchism and Tolstoy was the most revolutionary writer in Russia. The figure of an ancient sage, Lao-Tse, whose teachings, under the name of Taoism, were the religion of the entire intelligentsia of the old China, rose over the shoulders of Kropotkin and Tolstoy. It seemed to me that Lao-Tse was likewise an anarchist. Kropotkin called for the equality of people but wasn't it Lao-Tse who had written: "Why should there be divisions in the world, even the division into the wise and the stupid? The fact that there are wise people in the world in itself creates an injustice. The wise men must be destroyed because they bend the will of the rest. If the wise did not die, life in the world would be turned into stone."

Tolstoy said: "Don't oppose evil. You can't destroy evil by evil. Do not judge. Don't fight. Don't raise either your hand or your voice against anybody. Keep away from temptation. Perfect yourself."

And thus Lao-Tse: "The heart is at peace when there are no objects of desire around it. Every beautiful woman arousing lust is guilty of the troubles in the human heart. The serenity of the heart is the crown of creation."

This anarchism of folded hands was deep in the Chinese peasantry. Pay taxes as quickly as you can; pay your debts in due time; don't get into an argument with the police; do not try to get away from your village. It was on this slack leash that history held the Chinese peasant. And this was why he despised every restless man who, in order to break away from the boredom of everyday life, joined gangs of brigands, the army, or even went travelling. How difficult it is to get this peasant angry and set him against the smooth rich man from whom he has rented his land for decades.

The theory of Anarchism happened to get into my hands right after I read Tolstoy and Kropotkin. The impression was overwhelming. During the years of cultural rebirth Anarchism was the religion of the new Chinese intelligentsia. Even the president of our university was an anarchist. At public meetings the platforms were held by anarchist orators. Speeches and pamphlets were brimming with arrogant protests and calls for action. But when a forceful demand would come from the audience: "What's your program? Announce your constitution! Where is the organization? Where should we meet?"—it would embarrass the orator, but only for a minute.

"We have no party—we are against the idea. A party means violence. We have no constitution—we are against it—a constitution means fetters. We represent a free association of free protestants."

The word "Russia" fell more and more frequently from the students' lips. Newspapers wrote about the intervention, about the Japanese, the Americans, the Czechs, the French, the Italians, the English, who were trying to break down the doors of the new state, which in spite of hunger and misery had succeeded in expelling the foreign troops from its land. Newspapers wrote about trains filled with the defeated defenders of the old Russia, freezing on their way through Siberia. And sometimes the better-informed students would point out to me the fluffy-bearded people in long grey coats, who stood around the largest hotel in Peking, and say: "Russian generals kicked out by the Bolsheviks."

The philological faculty of the university had Chinese, English, French, German and Japanese sections. I could have chosen the Chinese section where I would have studied the classics and the ancient poets who wrote in the popular language. I could have taken the English section for I was familiar with the language, having studied it diligently in high school. Equipped with this language, I could later get a job in a customs house, or on a railroad, or in a post office, in a bank, or I could go to

America and become a translator at the Embassy. But I did not want to be in this section.

Among the announcements which hung on the board of the philological faculty one read as follows: "The Section of Russian Literature at the Philological Faculty. Applications still being received. Students who signed for the section but are not familiar with the Russian language and Russian grammar are obliged to take a two-year preliminary course in these subjects."

Young people from different provinces of China were standing on their toes reading this vertical strip of paper. A hot argument took place.

"A difficult language."

"The Russian section is interesting."

"Russian literature is revolutionary."

"They have such a revolutionary writer as Leo Tolstoy."

"When we know Russian literature we'll understand Russian socialism."

"Kropotkin is a Russian."

"The translations of Tolstoy's writings sell."

But the future consuls talked with caution—the revolutionaries might not approve of their intention and slap them in the face with a book. About fifty signed up. When the crowd gathered at the first meeting of the section, the youths gazed in wonder at one another. What had brought them together? Who? Two people: Kropotkin and Tolstoy.

The university worked with irregularity. The more experienced students sensed the coming of events. The government's appropriation for the university was one million da yang a year. But the money slipped past the university straight into the pockets of the government officials in the Ministry of Education. The president went to the Minister several times and extorted a thousand or two. The university professors had not received their salary for half a year. For a long time they had been eating and living in their apartments by the good grace of their landlords and the nearby grocers who extended them credit from month to month. The New Year, when people pay their debts, was near but the money due them disappeared into the deep pockets of officials and the barrels of the generals' cannon.

The students grew more and more depressed—again, thanks to the fighting army, they received neither letters nor money. The students grew poor. The owners of the lunchrooms began to talk rudely to them, and the hungry eyes of the young people flared with anger at the sight of police pickets with bayonets. The pickets were especially thick around the gates of the Foreign Settlement where the recently overthrown Ministers were hiding from persecution. Victorious U Pei-fu sent out selected soldiers in white spats and arm-bands to catch the Ministers. But the soldiers stood there in vain. All the Ministers were safely transferred to Tientsin—from the Settlement to the station was only a short walk. The soldiers walked back and forth peeping through the gates but not daring to enter. Entrance to the diplomatic quarter was forbidden an armed Chinese.

The alien square with its grey walls is cut into the flesh of China and separated from the city by empty lots, which protect the Settlement from an unexpected attack. Noiseless automobiles, shining like my mother's coffin, scooted in and out through the gates of the Settlement. The streets in the Settlement were mirrored with asphalt and the cars hissed over them as though they were passing over paper covered with honey.

I did not like to walk through the Settlement. The long and empty streets, the steel gates thrown open, the sentries in different uniforms, the empty walls surrounding the various embassies. The entrances were far apart, each one guarded. A chain of waiting yan-ches stood along the sidewalk. There were German, Belgian, French, and Dutch Embassies. At the very end of the Settlement, near the gates opening on the old driveway to the Imperial Palace, stood the American Embassy. It had a tall steel radio tower, so tall you ran a risk of breaking your neck looking at it. Across the street was the large but now quiet building of the Russian Embassy. Once in awhile one could see a man in a white linen uniform walking among the trees of the Russian park. One of those who had been kicked out of the country, by the peasant revolution.

"All to the meeting!"

Along a canal, full of rotten slippery tubs and the dead bodies of cats, past trees so ancient that they were nothing more than dusty bark, through spacious courts of former princes, into the meeting room of the university. The stairs shook under our feet.

Heads and newspapers.

A telegram addressed to the Chinese people had arrived from Moscow:

"The new Russian government proposes to sign a treaty with China—a treaty between equals. It recognizes that the Tsarist policy was dishonest and based on violence. The two peoples, like two comrades, must extend their hands to each other."

It was signed by Karakhan. The name sounded Mongolian.

One orator after another sprang to the platform. Joyfully waving their hands they tossed their inspiriting phrases into the crowd. The audience applauded. I applauded. The message had been sent to the people. We, the students, were the people. We would order the Ministers out, we would speak with the Republic, we would help China expel the guards of those nations whose flags were lazily flapping over the Embassies. The meeting roared. Policemen walked along the street, peeping through the gates, listening to the distant rumble of voices and picking up the excited remarks of the students as they came out. The policemen did not dare to come in. The government was still too weak to raise its voice. The enemies of the new-comer, U Pei-fu, were not yet sufficiently subdued.

13. Politics

T HE CLUB OF "STUDY AND WORK".

It was both a mutual aid society and a productive guild. It had about thirty charter members each of whom contributed from thirty to fifty da yang. Of course the money was not paid in all at once. Some paid two and some five da yang a month, according to their financial status. This money enabled the club to open a dining room, a drygoods and stationery store. There were no profits. The members had the advantage of reduced prices. Service in the dining room and in the store was conducted by the members. While one-half of the members were at the university attending their courses, the other half took charge of the tables and the counters.

Both boy and girl students were members of the club. Not, however, the well brought up young ladies who wore high heeled slippers and rolled their hair like the horns of a ram on their temples, nor the ones learning to sing hymns in Christian colleges and to play tennis with sportsmen from the Y.M.C.A. No, the girl radicals of the club bobbed their hair, hunched their backs over books, shouted from meeting platforms and lived with students without marriage, openly, changing their "friends" without much thought. The Peking philistines snorted and choked with indignation. They made their daughters cross the street at the sight of the dishevelled head of a girl student.

A daughter of a member of Parliament, an important, solid and notable man, joined the club. Her father put her out of the house, calling her a slut. She would leave one student for another, lightly, with amazing indifference. Her "friends" were jealous.

[250]

"Why did you go with him? Why did you sleep with him?"

"Oh, don't be worried. Nothing happened. As a matter of fact, I am unwell right now."

Many young men in the club broke off their previous marriages and married girl students. Those who were better off celebrated their marriages in the new manner. They hired a large room in a restaurant and ordered a big dinner. Their friends came with presents and sealed their marriage with speeches and wishes of good luck. Those who were not rich simply sent red cards to their acquaintances informing them of a new marriage. Such cards relieved the groom of the necessity of buying a dinner, and the friends of bringing presents.

The club did not exist very long, only six months. The store went bankrupt—the merchants refused to extend credit and the members' dues were slow to come in. Students would come and eat (you could not very well refuse your fellow-student) but would not pay (you could not very well go to court about it), and disappeared (you couldn't ask the police to find them).

The club had ceased to exist in my time but the spirit of the club was still fresh in student groups.

A peaceful meeting. Craning our necks, we listened to a man standing behind the professor's table. The tangled pompadour of his slightly curled hair fell on a gentle forehead. Gentle, slightly puffed eyes. A large moustache curtained his mouth. This was Professor Li Tao-hsao. His speech was long-drawn-out. He gesticulated as though he were pushing apart brush that impeded his progress. He proposed that we organize a group to study Marxism. A leaflet with a picture of Marx passed through our hands. We looked at his shaggy face and tried to pronounce his name. "Marx", heard for the first time, was difficult for a Chinese ear to catch.

Li Tao-hsao read us the Communist Manifesto. We listened, excited by the statement that revolution was inevitable. But we were a little astonished to learn that coolies, rickshaw men and boatmen were going to be the heroes of this revolution. Li Tao-hsao told us about factories and factory workers. The idea of factories had never entered my head, for Peking, as far as factories were concerned, was as empty as Sian-Shih. No smoke stacks rose over this city.

"Workers of the World, Unite!"

That's fine, but what to do before they have united?

If only we could invent a single word—a wonderful, sincere word, and shout it across the world! Then people would repent eagerly and take each other by the hand to march with the light step of friendship all over the globe. But how to find such a word? We rushed to the lectures on Esperanto, the international language which was to make brothers of all people.

The Peking police held a different view. An officer all dressed in black, a nickeled sword at his side, came to a lecture on Esperanto, accompanied by two policemen. He put his hand behind his back and listened politely. When the bewildered instructor stopped talking, he came up to the students and asked them, "What kind of propaganda are you carrying on here?"

The students glanced at one another and smiled.

"This is not propaganda. We are studying a language which is understood by the whole world. Won't you listen to it, officer, and take part in our study?"

"A language which is understood all over the world?" But he listened, convinced that a police officer should surely understand what is understood by the entire world. He sat there until his suppressed yawns almost broke the muscles of his jaw. Boredom and lack of understanding were written all over his face. He collected his guards and walked out, his white-gloved hands behind his back.

The odor of our political occupations bothered the noses of the police. Figures in black trousers and caps with white bands appeared more and more frequently among the light ankle-long robes of the students. They were policemen—it meant that the power of U Pei-fu was growing. At first they stood around the outside door. Then they grew bolder and walked inside to the announcement board. Evidently they had been previously informed. Swiftly the eyes of the policeman went over the black columns of hieroglyphics. Finally he put his finger on the announcement of the next session for the study of Marxism.

"Where is this organization of yours which occupies itself with the study of Marxism. Take me to your lecture room."

Some of the students sprang back without answering, but one confident joker remained. He understood that the situation would have to be clarified at once to avoid future trouble.

He looked surprised.

"Marxism? The study of Marxism? But what is Marxism?"

The policeman got angry.

"You know that better than we do. Don't pretend to be a fool."

"Marxism, did you say? Where did you find that strange word?"

The finger of the policeman again pointed at the paper.

The student followed his finger.

"But look, officer, what it says. Read carefully. It says: a society for the study of Maxism. We study Maxism. But you want Marxism. There's nothing like that here."

What saved us was the absence of the letter "r" from the Chinese alphabet. The secretary had actually written Maxism instead of Marxism.

There were twenty in the society. Twice a week, without ever skipping a lecture, we listened to Li Tao-hsao. Anarchism shrank in our heads to a little bunch of rags under the blows of the heavy paragraphs of Marx. As yet there were no books on Marxism in Chinese. We read them in English and Japanese. Our society grew larger. Besides Marx, we read Rousseau's "Social Contract"; we read Bertrand Russell and John Dewey (both of these gave lectures in Peking and their names filled the newspaper pages for weeks) and the books with titles like "The New Society" and "Contemporary Socialism".

Soon we were not satisfied with theory alone. We wanted to put theory into practise. If the revolution was to be accomplished by coolies, how would they be able to accomplish it? Surely not by sitting endlessly near their yan-ches and playing dice, by bending under yokes with heavy baskets, by bawling the same unintelligible songs which they did not understand, or by sweeping the university courts. They were not even able to sign their own names.

We organized a little circle for the purpose of propaganda. We called it "The Group for Popular Education". In order to keep the police from getting too interested in the activities of the circle it was organized under the auspices of the university. In reality the work of the circle was under the control of the society for the study of Marxism.

Revolution was in the air. It blew about us like a light wind— a wind like warm wine, that made people feel drunk.

The president gave us a little separate house. We put in benches, brought a few large round spittoons from the university storeroom, stabilized the shaking tables, and our club for propaganda was ready. After six o'clock, when the auditorium grew empty, the sound of the university bell gathered into this room the university furnace men, the janitors and the yan-ches from the nearby tea-house where they usually spent their evenings after taking home the prosperous professors and students. The room was filled to capacity. The listeners sat without ribaldry, restrained and serious. Fat lips sucked at pipes. A choking smoke rose and enveloped the room.

A student, whose turn it was to lecture, began. We took up simple questions. What is the state? What is Japan? What place does China occupy on the globe? Where do diseases come from?

They listened. It was difficult but they wanted to understand. From time to time they cleared their throats but they never spat on the floor. They got up and used the spittoon. That also was the result of our teaching. We told them about tuberculosis and now they were protecting their lungs and the floor of the club room.

After the lectures they would sit a long time whispering but saying nothing out loud. We waited for questions. Days and weeks passed before they got used to us, before they began to ask questions or even argue a point with the lecturers.

Rumors about the students' club spread from one coolie to another, and new faces began to appear. At first they would stand at the entrance, just looking. Then the subject would arouse their interest and they would tiptoe awkwardly into the room and find themselves a place.

My turn came to speak. I stood behind the table and began my lecture. I was a good secretary but a bad chairman, a good debater but a bad lecturer. I was accustomed to speak to an audience but this time I found it difficult. I felt as though a pillow had been pressed against my face. I chose the simplest words, used the most understandable sentences, and still I saw that the eyes of my listeners remained unresponsive. They puffed faster at their pipes. They were bored, but out of politeness they would not betray their boredom by a yawn or a remark. In the middle of the lecture I suddenly knew what was the matter: I was using the Szechuan dialect and they were Pekingese. I should have had an interpreter. I brought my lecture to an end hurriedly. When we were assigning dates to the speakers later that same evening, I chose the most advanced date for myself, hoping in the meantime to improve my pronunciation and make it more like the Peking dialect.

Later on waiters and other restaurant workers began to appear. Some printers wandered in, two well-dressed workers from a power station and finally even several railroad workers. Even though it did not live very long—this small circle for popular education, later suppressed by the police and left to die by the subsiding of the students' movement—I know that the first revolutionary coolies and the first organizers of trade-unions were born in the smoke-filled silence of our little house.

In the midst of our propaganda work our circle for the study of Marxism outgrew itself. At the initiative of Li Tao-hsao a Union of Socialist Youth was created. This was the high tide of student life in China. In the spring of 1921 the future Communists, the men of the following years, were being built. In February 1921 the melting point was reached. The patience of our professors came to an end. They went on strike. The gas lamps in laboratories grew cold, dust covered the yellow lacquered tables and the desks of the professors, the bell which used to mark the beginning and end of lectures turned green. It was cold in our dormitories. The university had no money with which to pay its professors or to buy coal.

Textbooks printed by the university were appraised now in American cents instead of Chinese tung tze as they used to be. It was easy to understand why. The value of Chinese tung tze was decreasing from day to day. Nevertheless, the new prices fell as a heavy tax on the students' pockets. More than once in their conversations they mentioned bitterly the name of the president.

Through the long-drawn-out lectures of Li Tao-hsao, through the smoke-filled hours of the propaganda circle, through the bursting green of the spring trees, we reached the first summer heat.

The Students' Union issued an order to all universities of Peking: "The strike of the instructors makes it useless for students to remain in Peking. All students must return home to their towns."

I obeyed. I packed my books, leaflets, my pictures of Peking, my new silk robe, and the newspapers describing the beating of the professors by the police in front of the Ministry of Education.

14. The Two Fathers

MY STEP-MOTHER MET ME IN OUR HALF-EMPTY HOUSE. Father was still in hiding under an assumed name. My little sister was visiting relatives, my uncle was away on a trip, my wife and child were staying with her family.

My step-mother lowered her voice and told me guiltily about the little girl. My wife did not like her—the child was not a boy. She did not even want to nurse her and they had had to hire a nurse. Unfortunately the nurse had turned out to be a filthy woman. Now the child was all covered with ring-worms and sores.

The old hatred of my wife twisted my face. I listened impatiently to the words of my step-mother and waited for the coolie who had been sent to my wife's family. I heard steps in the court: at last!

A strange, slovenly woman, with disgustingly large breasts protruding from her robe, brought in a child dressed in a clean shirt. The woman—this was the highly praised nurse—wanted to give the little girl to me. But I would not take her into my arms. Children are such small slippery things. We—the child and I—stared at each other.

My wife was standing in the door bowing and smiling.

Without restraining my anger, without even greeting her, I turned to my step-mother and pointed at the dirty spots behind the baby's ears. My step-mother paused a moment in reproach and then said to my wife, "Is the child dirty again?"

My wife did not answer. Her face fell. She had grown thinner since last year. Without looking at the child or at me or my step-mother, she went to her room.

I passed woods and wood-cutters in the olive orchards and

bamboo growths along the river. My father was hidden far away in a fortified castle protected by hillocks and walls. A path to the gates went over a stone ridge. One man could have successfully defended the castle. People had to walk in single file over the ridge. Bullets could pick them all off easily.

My father's room was small. He wore a white peasant blouse with buttons down the side.

I said: "Hello, father."

He answered: "Hello, father. You are also a father now, Shih-hua."

I looked at him bewildered. He was smiling, almost joking. I knew from his letters that he had forgiven me Peking, but still I expected to be rebuked. No. Nothing. He asked me how difficult the examinations were. How did I like to live in the university, was it warm in the dormitory, how big was the library, how learned the professors?

"About the professors I don't know. They are out on strike."

He answered slowly, and I listened to his words as one listens to a teacher.

"Although you have a strike at present, see to it, Shih-hua, that you don't stop studying on that account. Study is the first thing. Studying is like rowing against a current, once you stop rowing you are carried down stream. Accumulate knowledge, Shih-hua! Accumulate knowledge. I have sat here under a stranger's roof and speculated for many a month trying to find out what was wrong with our revolutionary movement. We did not have enough knowledge. We did not think that the Manchus would give up so easily. We were preparing ourselves for a long fight. We valued science less than the ability to make bombs and to handle rifles. We worked as soldiers and as wreckers, but when the time to build came we were crushed. I had many comrades who were studying politics, economics and law, but they evidently did not study them diligently enough. They still don't know what kind of government we should have. The revolution passed. The skillful politicians still hold in their hands the key posts in the bureaucratic machines. They have kicked out the unskillful revolutionaries. If you want to rule in the future, my son, you must study every science, not only its theory but also its practice."

"Our professor Li Tao-hsao organized a society for the study of Marxism at the university. Marx says that power should belong to those who produce, to the workers. Marx says that power expresses the domination of a class. Marx says that the political system cannot be changed without changing economic relations. For that reason we began educating the coolies in Peking."

"I don't know about your Marx. But what you say sounds reasonable. I never thought that suffrage for coolies and peasants could help them to improve their lives while they still were economically dependent on their masters. They would vote for their masters. How can a tenant vote against his landlord? He would lose his credit. As long as our peasants depend on pawn shops, on buyers and landlords, no matter how many votes they have, the masters will always win."

"But," I cried indignantly, "that is what we, the revolutionaries, exist for—to teach the poor how to use their rights."

"I don't know, Shih-hua. Perhaps things are different now. In our time you could count all the revolutionaries on your fingers. They were very few, and they were mainly students studying abroad. It is very good to have a circle for propaganda, but even revolutionary peasants need leaders, and only you, the students, can be their leaders. Who else will help peasants and coolies to build their government, who will explain to them the three principles of Sun Yat-sen—Nationalism, Democracy, Socialism?"

I did not argue. It was difficult for me to argue with my father. He had thought over these matters more than I. I was pleased with my father, and a little proud of this conversation of two revolutionaries—two fathers. I approached the most ticklish point of our conversation—I wanted to know father's attitude to the subject I had chosen to study.

"I have selected the Russian section of the philological faculty."

"The Russian section? Good, Shih-hua. The Russians are a revolutionary people. When I was studying in Japan the Japanese had a war with Russia and won the war. It was a stupid war. The people answered the defeat with a revolution. It was a fine revolution. Strong strikes. Peasants burned the estates of their landlords, workers built trenches in the cities. We, the Chinese revolutionaries, were happy over every victory of the Russian people. Study hard in the Russian section. Perhaps you will be able to go to that country and finish your education there."

"Only if I go there will I be able to grasp their literature fully."

At the word "literature" father made a grimace.

"Isn't there something more essential than literature? All right, you can study poetry and write stories if you want to so much. But couldn't you at the same time become an engineer, a chemist, a mechanic or a lawyer?"

"It is difficult to combine the two, but if you insist I study some practical profession also, I will do it. Perhaps law, perhaps military science, I can't tell right now because I don't know the educational plans for the next year." I changed the topic of the conversation. "Are you out of danger? Perhaps it would be wiser to go to a new place?"

Father reassured me as to his safety.

"What are you going to do in the future?"

"The same as I did in the past," laughed my father. "The Kuomintang of Szechuan is underground at present. People come over to see me at times. I keep in touch. I encourage some and remind others that we won't stay underground forever. I wish I could go and see Sun Yat-sen. I haven't seen the old man for so long. But it is difficult: we have no money and the war surrounds us."

And he looked at me with eyes that had grown much more gentle. The grey hair was now clearly noticeable in his beard and his moustache.

---

15. The First Russian

THE RUSSIAN DEPARTMENT WAS LOCATED IN A THREE-STORY building of the European type. It stood in an empty lot near the temple Ma-Schih-Mao. Through the window of our auditorium we could see the gilded bamboo of the Imperial Palace and the Corner Hill—a large green mound with a pavilion on top. Under the gilded bamboo lived Pu-Yi, the descendant of the Manchu Emperors. He had a large salary, a large harem and an English tutor. On solemn occasions the nobility, dressed in their mandarin garments, came to pay him their respects.

Our corridors were narrow and dark, our classrooms small. The building was not intended for lectures. It had been built originally as a dormitory. Then the partitions between the rooms were broken down, shelves built along the walls and long tables brought in. The air was filled with the rustle of newspapers and magazines: Chinese, English, French, Japanese, and German.

Our department also had a room set aside for a library. A few books stood on its shelves: a couple of anthologies, some fat dictionaries, and a few volumes of Tolstoy, Turgenev and Lermontov. On the wall we hung portraits of two bearded men, Kropotkin and Tolstoy. A little later we put up likenesses of Chekhov and Pushkin.

Fifty pairs of eyes watched a middle-sized man with a protruding chest and the sharp nose of a bird of prey. He was our first Russian professor. He spoke Chinese well. We were glad, it would make it easier for us. But what long difficult words! How can a Chinese pronounce a word like *rasprosterty?* And why should the endings of a word be different in different cases? Why not simplify the language as we simplify ours? The difficulty of the language troubled us. We had already spent a winter achieving nothing, and the following year we were supposed to study literature.

We began to press our professor. We interrupted him at every word and asked for an explanation. He did not like to explain and we did not like people who did not want to explain. Often his answer to our questions would be: "Look it up in the grammar," or "Don't ask me twice about the same thing. I have already explained it to you." One of us thought the professor had explained a rule incorrectly. We began to argue. The professor's face turned as purple as the back of a duck fried in pepper. The sharp notes of a man who does not like to be contradicted came into his voice. We quieted down, but a barrier had risen between us and the professor.

On the 31st of December, 1921, exactly on New Year's Eve, when the municipal workers were setting up forked posts along the avenues of Peking and hanging shabby red lanterns on them for the morrow's illumination, the secretary of the Socialist League received a letter addressed to the Union. He informed the members present: "The railroad workers of Chan-Sen-Tin have sent us five railroad tickets and ask us to send them five lecturers."

I was chosen as one of the five lecturers. I was proud and excited. Railroad workers—they were not like the coolies or furnace men who used to gather in our club at the sound of the bell. Railroad workers meant power. If we succeeded in convincing them that we were right, then we could stop the movement of trains in case of necessity or wreck any trains carrying the troops of our enemy.

I went to the library, I read newspapers, I made notes.

The following day was the day of the meeting. It took four hours to get to Chan-Sen-Tin from Peking. We were to meet at the south station at four in the morning. The tickets and the letter were left with the secretary who was the president of our delegation.

At three o'clock in the morning I was up. My eyelids felt heavy and yawns almost dislocated my jaw. It was dark on the street. The wind whistled in the blinds of the stores, throwing up dry, cold snow. Not a single yan-che was to be seen, no matter how hard I looked or how much I called. Wrapping my hands in the ends of my scarf which hung over my cheap coat, I walked to the deserted station and waited. I listened to every step. Here they are . . . No. . . . Well, now they are coming. . . . No.

Sleepy people passed by carrying blankets and packages. A short time before the arrival of the train I went to the entrance of the platform and stood near the ticket agent in order not to lose time in getting on the train. Had I had my ticket with me, I would have gone on alone without waiting for my friends. But the secretary had it.

The train left. I wondered what I should do. I learned that there was another train leaving two hours later from another station. Again I exposed myself to the snow storm and, protecting my eyes from the snow, walked to the other station. I waited for two hours. The train came and went but none of my comrades appeared. I went back home. I warmed myself with tea and drove the frost from my nose and lips. Then I went to see my comrades. Three of them were still in bed. They stretched their limbs, wrinkled up their faces and said gently: "Sorry, we overslept. The bad weather is to blame."

I went to the secretary. He had just gotten up and was going to take a walk. He was surprised to see me.

"Why are you here? Didn't the others go?"

"I am here and they did not go because you had the tickets. But even if I had had my ticket with me, my going would have been of no use, because I don't know the workers or where the meeting was to be held."

He shrugged his shoulders and spread out his hands. He stood by a table, turning over some books for no particular reason. Then he said, "Well, I am sorry . . ." and he went out, called a yan-che and drove away to attend to his private affairs.

My rage was boundless. I hated these people who could do nothing but talk and for whom a late morning sleep meant more than a great cause.

At the next meeting I came out with a furious attack on the secretary. I demanded that this rich mama's son be expelled. But he had the majority with him. He explained quietly that it wasn't really such a fearful crime and that my anger was easy to understand because I had caught a bad cold running from one station to another. The audience smiled at the picture.

I quit going to the league. When a blank questionnaire was given to me for the yearly registration I handed it back without a word.

---

16. The Manchus

IT IS NOT EVERY SUMMER THAT A CHINESE STUDENT CAN GO home for vacation, especially if he comes from Szechuan. He has neither the time nor the money. But in summer the dust on the streets of Peking becomes absolutely unbearable. It comes from the grey tile roofs, from the wind-eaten, dove-grey bricks of houses, from the dung of camels and horses, left on the pavements by street cleaners. It swirls up from avenues and unpaved alleys which have been badly sprinkled by the jugs of the lazy municipal workers or splashed with pails of slops by storekeepers. In addition to local dust, the wind brings dust from central Asia. In summer all true Pekingese are drawn to the western hills. The light blue chain of these hills stretches out within thirty li of Peking.

Many storied pagodas, castles of ancient courtiers, and temples bathed in the green of arbor-vitae, were scattered over the bare slopes and wooded valleys of these hills. There was the Summer Palace, with its artificial lake, in which the Marble Ship stood; there too were the hunting park of the Emperor and the hotels for foreigners. Donkey drivers and the carriers of tzaos milled around these hotels. They took tourists to the summit of the mountains from which the indistinct outlines of Peking could be seen.

But the western hills also sheltered small temples and broken-down houses. Here one could get a room for the summer and by making arrangements with the owners cooked noodles and vegetables might be had. In Peking board alone cost about twelve da yang, but in this summer place it could be had for six and a half da yang a month. We rented a couple of houses in the Manchu district. Intending to stay there for about two months we contributed ten da yang each. There were twenty of us, mineralogists, chemists, economists, philologists and musicians. As we did not want to waste our vacation time we resolved to organize a school for the vagrant Manchu youngsters. We proposed to teach them free; to buy the necessary textbooks, paper, brushes, and ink from what we saved on our summer expenses. Each of us was to take his turn teaching. There was to be a single daily lesson of two hours' duration.

The Manchus were the people who conquered China and introduced the braid, the present robe, and the ma-gua. During the three hundred years following the conquest, they lost amid Chinese surroundings their original characteristics and their native tongue. The families of the Manchu who formed the banner regiments of the Emperors settled around Peking. Extensive fruit orchards covered the western hills and the income from them was given to the Manchus. Every Manchu baby received from the day of its birth four silver lan a month from the government. The Manchus lived in idleness, got fat and lazy and lost a sense of the value of money. There were no more extravagant spenders in all China. The money came to them easily, and they let it slip easily through their open fingers.

For three hundred years the people had degenerated in idleness and luxury. When the revolution came and the streams of silver lan from the government dried up, their villages fell rapidly into decay. But their way of life and they themselves remained as before—carefree and lazy. Cold winds blow over the western hills in winter. The Manchus cut down and burned their fruit trees. The last source of their income turned to ashes in their stoves.

All twenty of us tried to advise our neighbors:

"You must get to work. Look, this room is falling down; the wind blows through the window. This brick will inevitably drop off tomorrow, if not today. It may fall into the cradle and kill your child. Why not fix it? You could stay a while in your other room while it is being repaired."

"Nonsense," they would answer. "Why should this brick fall? It has stayed there for a hundred years, why not another hundred?" And shrugging their shoulders they would leave us, who had suggested such strange things.

We got some instruments and climbed up on the roof. Without help of carpenter or of mason we mended their house. The Manchus laughed and wondered, but did not thank us for it. Obviously they thought we did it just to amuse ourselves.

It was even more difficult to deal with their children. They ran around with unwashed faces, they would not be taken care of, they would not sit still. In a few minutes they were bored with school and ran away. We could not persuade their parents that they would be better off if they knew how to read and write.

We tried to lure them with candy, we promised a reward for each hieroglyphic learned and for each sentence written. The children did not write their sentences and stole the candy. They entered the room in our absence, rummaged in our desks, went through our drawers, stole paper, ink, everything they could lay their hands on.

We wondered. Here we were on our vacations, we were supposed to rest, and yet now and then we took up a newspaper or a text book and read. But the Manchus—one might have thought that they were living in another world. The entire community would come out every morning, sit down on the long steps of the houses, lay their hands on their knees and talk slowly, mumbling their words, for one hour, two, three, four, six, sharing recollections, gossiping.

They could not get used to the fact that the government refused to feed them. The manners of a privileged class were apparent in their gestures and their walk. Their women, even of the poorest families who would have perhaps two grains of rice for breakfast, always came out on the street powdered and rouged and crowned with the glossy double semaphore chignon.

Manchu villages were falling down and the number of empty houses in them grew larger and larger. Those who did not die of starvation or winter cold went to Peking. Need and laziness drove the Manchu men into the shafts of Peking yan-ches and the Manchu women into the couches of second-rate brothels.

We were stubborn, but the Manchus were more so. Week after week passed and nothing was achieved. Our voices grew hoarse, our nerves tense. We were to illumine the whole world with our principles, and here we could not get control over a small bunch of ragamuffins. The little Manchus won. We gave up before the end of the first month.

"Lao Tan! Lao Tan! I have news for you." The comrade who called me was in a state of great agitation. "Do you remember Hu?"

"Which Hu?"

"The former governor of Szechuan."

How could I forget the man who had almost executed my father? Hatred gripped me. My comrade informed me that Hu now had an estate in the western hills where he grew cotton. He had a son in Germany, an idler, to whom he sent a thousand da yang every year. I could not wait. At last I was to see the man into whose body in my delirious dreams I had plunged a knife eight years ago. My countryman went with me. For a long time we sat by the road that bordered the stone wall of the estate, and waited.

A fat, rosy-cheeked old man passed along the wall. A grey robe fell in soft folds from his stomach down to his soft-soled felt slippers. The eyes of the old man were half-closed, piously. He was telling beads, counting them with his soft fingers, and mumbling like a monk. This was Hu. He passed by us, hardly glancing in our direction. Without changing his step, he disappeared around the corner.

I had nothing in my hands but a blade of grass.

17. Betrayal

AUTUMN AGAIN. THE UNIVERSITY COURTS BUZZED. THE bulletin boards which had been empty all summer were now covered with the autumn leaves of announcements. Dr. Sun instructed his Szechuan followers to begin working in the armies of the fighting generals. He ordered them to enter the fight and to attack both sides. It meant that father had to leave the castle. It meant that once again suspicious-looking, silent people would haunt our house in the middle of the dark night.

Father gathered his old associates into his group—former police officers from his Teh chien school, fighters from the Go-Lao and soldiers from Ming-Tuan who were wandering along the Szechuan roads. But recruiting was difficult now. People had lost faith in the revolution and were apt to regard father's group as just another of the bands that were fighting on Szechuan soil. They did not care to risk their money and lives for the whim of a Dr. Sun who lived in far-away Canton. They preferred the slogan of the cleverer people: "Who has milk is my mother." This was the slogan of my brother-in-law, a former member of the Kuomintang and an officer in my father's group. He came to the Li-U-Sianites and offered them his services. They knew that he was a member of the Kuomintang and did not believe in his sincerity. They wanted some proof. He had it ready.

"Here is a confirmation of my readiness to serve you. Tan Ya-pu, my sister's father-in-law, is recruiting troops by order of the Kuomintang. I helped him to the very last minute. If you want me to, I'll help you get him now."

An officer who had once in 1911 served under my father was present at this conversation. Loyalty to your chief, even a former one, is one of the virtues of the Chinese moral code. He managed to send a short note to my father: "They are after you, flee!"

On the eve of the New Year of 1923, when the house was all ready for the holiday rest, for dining and receiving guests, my father fled to an isolated peasant's farm that belonged to a comrade of his, who was perhaps related to my mother, as his name was Lao. On New Year's Day a detachment of soldiers arrived in Sian-Shih. They did not go to our house, they knew it was useless, they already knew he was gone. On the second of January my wife went to stay with her family and on the third the same detachment, without looking anywhere else, went straight to Lao's house, and broke into it.

It is the custom to visit the graves of relatives around the first of the year. Fortunately for him, my father had gone to the grave of my grandmother on this very day. Some peasants met him and told him about the search.

The soldiers turned the whole house upside down, threatened Lao, and went back to write a futile report. From that day my brother-in-law rose rapidly. A few months later the daoyin appointed him head of the municipal Ming-Tuan.

Silence hung over father's house. He started on his long-desired journey, without coming to Sian-Shih, travelling by indirect routes from dock to dock, from village to village.

The dust had not had time to settle on father's chair in our dining room when the mayor appeared at our house. My younger uncle received him politely and helped him to a cup of tea. He wondered what had brought this stout man to our house so soon after father's escape.

The mayor sighed sadly.

"Living is so terribly expensive now. If you only knew, esteemed Tan Tsi-pu, how poor I am these days. Literally not a single tung tze is left in the house."

"Yes, yes," said my uncle sympathetically, not yet knowing what the administrator was aiming at, but sensing that something was not quite right.

"And in the meanwhile," continued the mayor, "I must pay my debts. If I don't pay, I lose face. I know you are a very sympathetic person. I always respected your family. I hope that you will not refuse me a small loan."

My uncle figured out in his mind the financial situation of our family. "I am very much grieved over your situation, but I am sorry, we have no money, we are poor ourselves."

The mayor began to sigh deeply.

"Are you sure you can't spare anything? I came to talk things over in a friendly way. Why should we quarrel? Perhaps you also have troubles and I might be of some help."

My uncle, who was getting angry, asked guardedly, "Troubles? What troubles?"

The mayor searched in his inside pocket. Finally he pulled out a paper bearing a square-shaped seal. With a heavy sigh he looked at my uncle. The paper was an order issued to the mayor to make an inventory of the property belonging to the rebel and conspirator Tan Ya-pu, a fugitive from justice. It also ordered him to confiscate it.

There was no money in the house but it would have been disastrous not to pay. My uncle wrote a cheque for fifty lan— seventy-five da yang—while my step-mother and his wife brought out new silk dresses, baskets of fruit and jars of preserves. The mayor, his mood greatly improved, drank his tea and explained to my uncle how to go about the situation. He left, saying he would be back in two days to make the inventory.

During those two days my uncle rushed from lawyer to lawyer, preparing deeds in which it was made clear that the land under the house was heavily mortgaged, and that moreover it did not belong to the fugitive at all. On the day set the mayor came down with his clerk. He walked all around the rooms, examining the things and dictating. He dictated very well. All the best things in the house turned out not to belong to father. But even what was not of the best he listed incorrectly. He described a perfectly good table as a "table on three legs, unusable". All the deeds just acquired by my uncle were mentioned in the report. The five hundred trees of our tangerine orchards were called only a hundred. He might not have mentioned any, but that would have been dangerous. Too small a list might have aroused the suspicion of the daoyin, and he would have sent a controller.

Through with his inventory, the mayor again drank tea and ate preserves. Then he wrote a letter to Teh chien to accompany the inventory.

[271]

"Tan Ya-pu proved extremely clever. He sold almost all the good things belonging to him, and left only useless, broken-down objects. All that remains worth mentioning are the hundred tangerine trees. As to the house, it belongs to his younger brother, Tan Tsi-pu, a teacher in a public school in Sian-Shih."

The village service workers lifted tables, sideboards, benches, moth-eaten robes, and a couple of old blankets listed in the inventory and carried them to the town hall. There some of them were sold to second-hand furniture dealers. The rest fell to pieces and were thrown out. The hundred trees were sold at auction to a rich fruit merchant. This confiscation brought us altogether a money loss of a thousand da yang which added another load to the heavy burden of debt weighing down the family shoulders.

---

18. Russian Literature

Out of fifty people who had entered the russian department in 1920 only fifteen were left to continue the course in 1923. It was presumed that after three years we should know the language. A professor of the French department, Ih Fa-er, who had originally come from Russia, replaced our unlucky teacher.

Professor Ih Fa-er had lived long in Peking and knew the city better than we, the outsiders. He read the Peking newspapers much more diligently. I liked him. He was big and always very keen. His hair was light and soft like wool, an unusual sight for our eyes. His bright, extraordinary eyes were set so deep that, as one says in China, you could not cover them with soil. He paced the classroom rubbing his hands, his voice always elated. He would point at an object and ask: "Qu'est-ce que c'est?"

And when he asked a pupil to give the lesson he would add: "S'il vous plaît."

My comrades rustled their dictionaries noisily, looking for the meaning of these words. I explained to them that the words were not Russian but French and that they meant: "What is it?" and "Please."

Ih Fa-er spoke a good Chinese but it was not simple enough. Where we would have used one sentence he used three. He laughed at us and at our old text books. Instead of the tiresome anthology he told us to read the short stories of Chekhov. They were short, very funny, and easy to understand. After the stories we began to read longer things.

Chekhov interested us greatly. We outstayed each other in the library. We were dying to translate his works, although our vocabulary consisted only of a few dozen words which we could not decline and a few verbs in the infinitive.

The more we read Chekhov the more we were inclined to place him among the revolutionary writers of Russia, next to Tolstoy and Kropotkin. But here our professor made a sudden turn. He explained to us that Chekhov was a representative of the petite bourgeoisie and that he had very little in common with revolution, especially with the revolution that was taking place in Russia at that moment. We felt only bewilderment while he was denouncing Chekhov, but when he dared lift his hand against Tolstoy, we would not stand for it.

I had read not only the tales of Tolstoy but also his novel "Resurrection", which had been translated into Chinese long ago, not from the original Russian but from the Japanese. "Resurrection" was the most popular book in Japan. A folk song had been written there about the heroine.

Ih Fa-er denied the revolutionary character of the Tolstoyan philosophy. The intermissions between his lectures turned into debates. Ih Fa-er looked at us gaily and ironically and rubbed his hands like a chef who has put his vegetables in the pot and waits for them to cook.

I took "Resurrection" and read it again from cover to cover. Well, perhaps, the professor was right. Nekhludov, who gave his land so nobly to his peasants, was not real. Tolstoy was a Utopian. Things did not happen that way. Peasants should take the land themselves without waiting for all their landlords to turn into Nekhludovs.

During the arguments about Tolstoy I found two friends who shared my views. Their names were Hsao Tsu-chen and Tin Wing-ping.

During all these weeks of my exciting study my father was on his way to Canton. He reached the city only to receive an order from his teacher, friend, and leader, Sun Yat-sen, an order similar to his previous orders—to return to Szechuan, organize a military group and stand at the head of it. It was time for the new campaign. It was time to rejuvenate the Kuomintang intelligentsia with the vital blood of the coolies and the landless peasants of the rice fields.

My father went back North, at the time when Canton was getting ready for the congress of the Kuomintang.

19. Divorce

A LONG AND DETAILED LETTER FROM MY FATHER:

"The officer who sent me the note on New Year's Eve came to join my division. He told me certain things which I had suspected myself, but I had tried to suppress my suspicions as they seemed to me revolting and incredible. He repeated the conversation between your brother-in-law and the officers of Li U-sian. But that wasn't the worst. Your brother-in-law knew only that I was in Sian-Shih, no more. But who gave the address of Lao's house to the soldiers?

"I called your wife and asked her directly who could have told her brother where I was hiding? She looked down and did not say a word. It became clear that something was wrong. I let her go. Immediately she went to her room and locked the door. Later she hired a tzao and left the house. She went to stay with her family without asking permission either from me or from your step-mother. I began to have doubts—perhaps we had offended her by our disgusting suspicions. I tried again to verify the facts. At my instruction various people went around asking questions. They all brought back the same report: the soldiers had received their information from her brother.

"Such are the facts. I think you can judge them for yourself. I am sending you this letter by fast mail as I want to get your answer as quickly as possible. What do you intend doing about all this?"

I knew what to do. The thought of this terrible scandal in my own family made me tremble with anger. Why had it all happened? Why couldn't this dull woman have kept her mouth shut? Why hadn't she stayed quietly at home without making all this trouble? Then I felt a sudden joy—perhaps this base treason of my wife was all for the best. I could use it as grounds for a divorce, I could break our marriage and send my wife away, wherever she wanted to go. I would never again have to feel her breath over my shoulder when I came home.

I suggested to father that he begin the divorce proceedings.

My step-mother was against it. To her the divorce would come as a slap in the face. She was the one who had chosen Guan-in for me and who had insisted on the marriage. She suggested that we live apart without a formal divorce but father would not agree. For the first time in many years he flatly rejected her advice. He wrote to the family of my wife asking them directly whether they would accept a divorce by mutual agreement or prefer to go through the courts.

Perhaps it was Guan-in, tired of her disgusting and bitter marriage, who persuaded them, or her parents themselves who were uncertain of a favorable decision from the court and who were afraid of possible expenses, but at any rate they answered that a council of relatives of both families should decide on the divorce.

The Tans and the Guans met in our house. The mayor, not the same one who had confiscated our property, but a new one, stepped over our threshold to serve as a witness.

After dinner tea and preserves were served and the conference began. My wife was sent out of the room. My father spoke first. He described the whole matter and the way it had happened: 1. the conversation of the traitor with the officers; 2. the warning note; 3. first search in Sian-Shih; 4. the departure of Guan-in; 5. the second search in Lao's house. He asked them on what conditions the Guan family would agree to a divorce.

The merchants remained silent for a while. They undoubtedly had had their conference beforehand and were ready with their offer. The pause was only to make the bargaining look more important.

Their conditions were:

1. The couple to be divorced.

2. The family Tan to return the dowry given Guan-in to the family Guan.

3. The family Tan to pay 300 da yang yearly to Guan-in, the payments to stop only in case of Guan-in's remarriage. Or, instead of yearly payments, the sum of 3000 da yang might be paid at once.

4. The little girl Tan-tun to be left with her mother. The family Tan to pay a certain amount of money every year for the support of the child, the sum to be agreed upon each year.

Father listened to these conditions quietly and then rejected them all. His counter-proposal was: The child to stay with the father, and the family to pay the divorced wife 200 da yang a year, for not longer than ten years, the payments to stop in case of her second marriage.

The Guans were insulted. It was impossible for them to have a traitor in their family. All that was an invention. And moreover, they agreed to a divorce only because they wished to rescue their daughter from a family where she was treated so badly. But the solid front of the family Guan suddenly gave way when the uncle of my wife took our side. He recognized that Guan-in was obviously guilty and that the propositions of Tan were acceptable and that there was no need of turning such a painful conference into a bargaining match. This uncle was an educated man. His attitude toward us was the sympathy of one educated man for another in the latter's quarrel with a merchant.

The price set by the Guans went down slowly. They agreed that the dowry be returned, that we pay 200 da yang yearly, and that the child be kept by its father.

There were nineteen signatures to the paper: eight signatures of our family, eight of the family Guan and three signatures of witnesses present. My wife was brought back into the room. She made a cross in place of her signature.

The people left hurriedly. At the gate they snarled at each other for the last time. From then on there were no more bows, nothing but animosity, reproaches and spiteful gossip between the two families.

My step-mother, hysterical and crushed by the signatures, stood crying over the child. In her opinion the little Tan was now an unfortunate child, a half-orphan. Even my father grew emotional. Bending over the frightened three-year-old-girl and the sobbing middle-aged woman, he said, "Poor little granddaughter. My poor little granddaughter."

The letter from my father, describing all this, had set me free. But still . . . although I knew that my wife had taken almost no care of the little girl, it seemed to me that since the departure of her mother, the child might become a little forsaken homeless dog. I was troubled about her, remembering her face, her eyes, her dirty neck.

The loud greetings and congratulations of my comrades tore me away from the letter. My room-mate, Li, was the happiest of them all. Perhaps he was tired of the constant atmosphere of gloom that I always brought with me. My comrades dragged me out of the dormitory. We wandered along the streets and laughed. Finally we stopped at a small restaurant.

"Long live Tan Shih-hua the bachelor."

20. The Treaty

THE MONEY FROM HOME WAS UNCERTAIN AND INSUFFICIENT. Father was in hiding again and my uncle evidently found it difficult to provide me with the necessary money. My earnings in Peking were small and indefinite. I wrote stories for the Sunday editions of newspapers, much like the tales of Chekhov, Gorky, and Tolstoy. I was paid only a da yang a thousand hieroglyphics, but the stories were successful and the papers asked for more.

I was not the only one who wrote. There were a few other comrades from Szechuan who also wrote stories and wished to become famous Chinese authors. We organized a literary circle and decided to publish a magazine of which a group of our countrymen were to be the official publishers. We succeeded in persuading a printer to give us credit. The price was twenty-five cents a copy. We wrapped the fresh booklets in handkerchiefs, went to the book shops and laid out our magazines on the counters of the unperturbed book sellers. They condescendingly allowed us to place our creation among the colorful jackets of sensational novels, charged us twenty percent commission, and rarely paid us anything.

The war between the generals moved away from the walls of Peking. Tsao-Kun bought the votes of Parliament members and installed himself as President of the Republic. Chang Tso-lin was in Mukden, waiting for the day when he could begin his advance against Peking. Marshall U Pei-fu was drilling soldiers and writing refined poetry in Laon, pretending to be just a humble pupil. Actually he was the real head of Tsao-Kun.

"Lenin is dead."
The news of Lenin's death rolled like thunder over the pages of the newspapers. Journals which bore Chinese names but had foreign editors were joyfully prophesying the fall of the "State of the Poor". We listened anxiously, asked about Lenin and tried to get his books, his speeches and articles. Sun Yat-sen interrupted the congress of the Kuomintang in Canton and ordered three days of mourning in tribute to the memory of the wisest man of the present day and the greatest friend of China.

Li could not stand the arguments which took place constantly in our room. "Politics again," he would say, and in despair flee to his laboratory. We were arguing who would prove to be stronger—Ku Wei-chin or Wang Cheng-ting. Wang Cheng-ting and Karakhan were conducting negotiations for a treaty between China and Russia. There wasn't a thing the Peking newspapers didn't immediately know. The most confidential conferences in the palace of the President were described in the papers the next day in full detail. Ku Wei-chin, a rival of Wang Cheng-ting, was the Minister of Foreign Affairs and was tied up with the Americans. Afraid of a union between Russia and China, he was even more afraid of the popularity of Wang Cheng-ting.

All points of the treaty were already agreed upon. The majority of the cabinet was for it and even U Pei-fu had telegraphed his satisfaction. The first draft of the treaty was signed with the initials of Karakhan and Wang Cheng-ting, after the tense night of the last conference. All that was necessary to make it legal was the seal of the President. There was a rumor that this was to be affixed that same afternoon. Then it was changed to evening, then postponed till the next day, then till the council of ministers, then . . .

It was clear that Ku Wei-chin had upset the agreement.

The Students' Union called a meeting and decided to march to the palace of the President. We gathered at the university. The corridors and halls of the university boiled with our voices, but we did not succeed in getting out into the streets. A double line of policemen encircled the university and would not let the crowd pass.

We insulted the policemen, but not too openly, recollecting the muzzles of their guns were still black with powder from the recent shooting of the railroad workers.

I heard a conversation between an officer and a crowd of students near the stairs of a corridor.

"It is disgraceful, gentlemen, to make all this agitation. You know what people say about you? People say that Karakhan has paid you money on condition that you demand the signing of the treaty."

"Is that so, officer? And we hear people say that Ku Wei-chin is your brother-in-law."

To say that someone is your brother-in-law is to insult your family in the person of your sister.

The policeman's face turned purple.

"It's a dirty lie. Who dared to say so?"

"And who dared to say that Karakhan paid us money?"

Some skeptics reassured us:

"Just the same the Ministers will not be able to dodge the signing of the treaty. The thing is very simple: Ku Wei-chin doesn't want Wang Cheng-ting to sign such a splendid treaty, he wants to sign it himself."

They were right. On the 30th of May the news came, unforeseen even by the clever reporters: "The treaty between China and the Soviets is signed."

Again our crowd filled the courts and halls of the university to listen to a jovial man with a black beard—Karakhan. Over his head two flags were crossed—our five-colored flag and the red flag of Soviet Russia. From the faces of most students we could see that they needed an interpreter. We who knew some Russian were much more lucky. In the stream of indefinite sounds we could distinguish familiar words: "refusal . . . contributions . . . Soviets . . . treaty . . . railroad . . . equal . . . to break . . . people . . . Imperialists . . ."

We shouted together with the entire hall:

"Ten thousand years of life for the Soviets!"

"Ten thousand years of life for China!"

"Long live the peoples' revolution!"

---

21. Te-Ti-Ko

THERE HADN'T BEEN A FLOOD LIKE IT IN THE PROVINCE FOR many years. It looked as though the river had left its bed. It ran over the fields to the villages and washed away the clay foundations of the houses. The peasants floated from one village to another on gates broken from their own fences, using the boards as oars. A sea, which did not appear on any map, spread suddenly between Peking and Tientsin. The river Pei-Ho near Tientsin rose and threatened the city.

It had been long since Peking had witnessed so many beggars on its streets. The local beggars, among whom the city was divided by strict order, were furious when hundreds of starved and ragged people, neglecting the established rules, stretched out their dirty hands to the passers-by or ran after speeding yanches, clutching their fenders and moaning with feeble voices:

"Lao-e Da Lao-e, gentlemen, great gentlemen. To eat . . . bread . . ."

But the soldiers outnumbered even the beggars. They had red bands tied around their sleeves. The black-faced coal men passed along the streets under their guard pulling their carts filled with anthracite and ringing little bells attached to a spoke. The sound of these bells used to bring housewives out of their houses, but now they looked indifferently at the passing coal peddlers. Soldiers with rifles in their hands sat on the sides of trucks now loaded with ammunition. Groups of coolies recruited to dig trenches passed by under guard, like criminals being led to execution. Soldiers were seizing everyone who had strong muscles and a weak master.

The soldiers with red bands on their sleeves were the army of U Pei-fu. To the east of Tientsin were also soldiers, arresting coolies and guarding ammunition trucks. The only difference was that they wore white bands on their sleeves. They were the army of Chang Tso-lin who was allied with Sun Yat-sen. I did not like to see Dr. Sun lined up with the Japanophile against whom we, the students, had been fighting for five years. But I thought that right after their victory over the common enemy, they would inevitably split.

It was difficult to predict who was going to win. Peking officials and merchants were on the side of U Pei-fu, a man with a good name, not like the rascal Chang Tso-lin. U Pei-fu appreciated culture—he was unconquerable and noble. So thought the mandarins of Peking, the owners of antique shops and the gamblers at the race tracks.

I went with my countrymen to view an unusual place, the foreign settlement which up to that time no student had ever visited. We were bound for the Russian Embassy. The columns in front of the house were decorated with red material. A naked mast rose above the house. Hundreds of people surrounded the speakers' wooden platform, almost all of them Chinese—journalists, professors and many students. The Embassy had been transferred to Karakhan; the men in white uniforms had left. The lawn was bright with the green of the uniforms worn by the hired military band.

At the sound of a strange melody resembling a slow march a flag, as red as a New Year's card, was raised on the mast. A comrade tugged at my sleeve: "Do you hear it? Do you know what is it? It is the 'International'."

For the first time I lost my sense of being an alien in Peking. Joyfully I greeted the enormous banner which streamed across the street. It was embroidered with the golden symbols—a hammer and a sickle.

Only twelve out of the original fifty were left to attend the third year of our course. We were waiting for our new professor to come. His name was Te-Ti-Ko and he had just arrived from Moscow. We had not seen him yet and were a little afraid of him as he did not know a word of Chinese. What if we were unable to understand his Russian? If all his lectures were to turn out mere recitations in a strange language?

It was seven-thirty in the morning. The last few students hurried to their classrooms. The sound of sharp, quick steps came from the end of the corridor. An unusually tall, bald man appeared at the teacher's desk and said:

"Hello, comrades."

We answered slowly:

"Hello, how do you do."

He pronounced another sentence, which to our great horror

we could not understand—he spoke too fast. Then he asked a question. A student rose and began to pull out slowly the necessary words, as one might take things out of a suitcase. The professor listened and then said slowly, separating each syllable, "I will explain very slow-ly. If I be-gin to speak too fast (from the expression of our faces, he saw that we did not know the meaning of the last word), to hur-ry (we nodded), you must stop me. I will give my lec-ture be-fore hand . . . first . . . earlier to be printed, which will make it easier for you."

We were satisfied. Our knowledge of the language proved to be sufficient; we could understand him without an interpreter. We put our notebooks on the arms of our chairs and wrote down the new words.

At the intermission the class grew very noisy.

"Te-Chzu-Gan, Te-Chzu-Gan," we shouted and laughed. Te-Chzu-Gan was a long bamboo pole. We gave Te-Ti-Ko this name because he was so tall.

We talked about the manners and the character of Te-Ti-Ko, deciding that he was strict and touchy. A tall man is always associated with the idea of an officer. The tall people of Shantung are the best soldiers of China. And officers always have terrible tempers. People with tempers love to command, and one who loves to command is easily offended.

We were surprised and almost disappointed when Te-Ti-Ko in the same slow way, separating each syllable, began to smile and tell us jokes, and when he brought with him Moscow magazines and told us about that city, about Russian writers and about the burial of Lenin.

"Well, what's the news?" he would usually begin his lecture. When we had no news he would tell us his. He told us about a soldier Li E-yuan, who, in order to get back at a policeman for beating him up when he attempted to climb over the wall surrounding the foreign settlement, had attacked and thrashed a few foreigners. We were bewildered. What was so wonderful about that? The soldier was a ruffian, that was all.

[284]

He told us about the captain of a small American warship, who because an American was murdered by some bandit, trained his guns against the city of Fan-Sian, and demanded that two innocent boatmen be executed. And they were executed. We did not understand why the professor was so excited. Things of that kind had been happening in China for many decades.

Telling us these stories he would get excited and talk fast, but the minute he saw that we were making an effort to understand he would slow down again.

Te-Ti-Ko was interested in our lives, and I noticed that the clever and educated Li Shu-ling began to use this interest of his to get more intimately acquainted. It seemed to me that Li Shu-ling soon became a favorite pupil of the professor. He talked more about his compositions than about the compositions of other students and gave the most detailed answers to his questions. Li Shu-ling was standing in my way. I had always mistrusted him. I would have gone to visit the professor in his house but I did not want to meet the gold teeth of Li Shu-ling.

Once in October Lao-Te (as we called him respectfully), having received no answer to his usual "Well, what's the news?" told us how Sun Yat-sen had subdued the merchants' uprising in Canton and burned the entire commercial district of the city with fire from his guns. Lao-Te asked, "Was it right to do this?"

Ting Wing-ping was collecting words for an affirmative answer, furiously nodding, when Li Shu-ling interrupted him.

"It was wrong. How dare he destroy the property of the citizens of Canton. How dare his soldiers touch the stores of peaceful merchants?"

I saw that Te-Ti-Ko was surprised. I could not help feeling a secret joy over Li Shu-ling's mistake.

22. A Letter from Russia

THE VALUE OF THE SILVER DA YANG VARIED FROM DAY TO day. It reached the price of 180 tung tze, then of 210, then of 250. Soldiers were paid in copper money and in order to save some they immediately exchanged it for silver. The value of silver rose, the value of the tung tze dropped. All Peking lived on tung tze and grew poor and ill-tempered.

Peddlers carrying the long yellowish heads of cabbage were seen less frequently. Vegetables were bought directly from the gardeners by the cooks of the military kitchens. Thin-haired housewives, cooks, and owners of foreign boarding houses wandered down the market-stalls where bright ribbons of raw meat were suspended on the hooks, where dried vegetables were piled on the counters. They turned them over, feeling, smelling, moaning, and complaining at the prices.

Flour cost fifteen instead of five tung tze a tsin. Hot sweet potatoes, split in half, were steaming on peddlers' stands. A coolie stretched out his hand with a tung tze in it. Juggling the potato from one hand to another he mumbled, "A year ago I could get two potatoes for a tung tze, and sometimes three if they were small."

"Eat it and shut up. Soon, we'll have no potatoes at all. Wait until the soldiers pass through the fields."

One morning our professors who lived beyond the central city wall did not come to deliver their lectures. On street corners, under the painted pillars of wooden arches, barricades of coal carts had been built. White posters were plastered on the pillars. They were the manifestoes of general Feng Ui-sian. He had cut off his chief, U Pei-fu, from Peking, and so declared the war ended.

[286]

"Feng Ui-sian a traitor!" shouted crowds of servants around the houses of the rich. Shouts went up from the university students, especially from students who came from Henan, the native province of U Pei-fu. Feng Ui-sian was not popular with the people. He was too eager to spread the Christian gospel and he forced his soldiers to sing Christian hymns.

After spending a few days in his special railroad car in a futile effort to reach Peking from Tientsin, U Pei-fu fled to Shanghai on an American boat. The war ended with a victory for Chang Tso-lin (which meant the victory of Sun Yat-sen). In the meantime my father, defeated by Yan-Sen in Szechuan, plunged again into hiding.

There was a rumor that Sun Yat-sen was coming to Peking. Stores and shops which had closed their windows in fear of riots opened again. Red radishes filled the counters of the market. Theaters and restaurants began doing business.

Could it really be true? The paper said that in Moscow the writings of Leo Tolstoy had been put on trial. The judges had been Krupokaia, the wife of Lenin, and Sergei Mayakovsky. The court had decided that all Tolstoy's works were harmful, and ordered his books burned. Why was "War and Peace" "harmful"? Does not Tolstoy tell us to love the poor? Even if it was true that Tolstoy was not a revolutionary, was it necessary to burn his writings?

I was frightened. The other students who read Tolstoy and loved his country because of him might see this notice and turn away from Russia. I was so excited I was almost choking when I asked Te-Ti-Ko for an explanation. What if this were true? The professor laughed. He had already seen the story in the Russian émigré papers. He said it was probably published by the Whites—white, the color of death—to injure the cause of the Reds—red, the color of joy.

"Write to the newspapers," we said, "and tell them it is not true. We will translate your letter."

One morning a messenger boy brought us a letter in which he seemed to be very much interested.

"I have been to every other section of the university with this," he said. "They all say, 'This doesn't belong here.' You are the only ones left."

On the envelope was written in Russian: "China, City of Peking, University of Ta-hue-tang, To the Group of Students Studying Russian." That was all, but it had reached us. The postal service in China is excellent. But from whom could this strange communication have come? What was in it? We all crowded around and opened it. It was written in Russian. Twelve dictionaries were leafed over and twelve pencils followed the lines of illegible handwriting, pausing over unfamiliar words. After half an hour's work, we finished the translation. A Russian student, G. Schergin, was writing us proposing that we start correspondence with him so that information about the student life in our respective countries could be exchanged.

We plied Te-Ti-Ko with questions, talked it all over eagerly, and at length decided to send a reply. We tore from our notebooks the pages with our best compositions about the life of Chinese students. We resolved to have Schergin's letter translated and printed in our university gazette. We were very proud because neither the English nor the French sections had had letters from students in those countries. At our next lecture, we read over the draft of the answer.

> Comrade Schergin:
> When I read your letter I was overjoyed. I translated it at once and two days later it was printed in our university paper. I have long been deeply interested in your country. China is my native land, but Russia is my spiritual mother. My comrades want to answer your questions but unfortunately we do not know the Russian language very well. For the present, we will reply only to the following questions: the participation of students in the political life of China; types of Chinese students; their way of life. We are enclosing our papers on these

subjects. I decided a long time ago that I wanted to go to Russia to study, but I haven't the money. For that reason, I beg you to write me fully about Russian students and about their various political tendencies. Comrade, I believe that in the end the day will come when we can all gather in the same room and talk to one another.

My best greetings,

Then followed our signatures.

---

23. The Students and the Revolution

(*Not Related by Tan Shih-hua*)

TAN WAS SPENDING HIS LAST FEW DAYS IN MOSCOW. THE NEXT day, or the day after, he had to go back to China. He hadn't finished telling me about his life. Instead of giving me a day-to-day picture, he had skipped from one date to another. And still there was so much untold.

"You saw me in 1925," he said, "when Sun Yat-sen died and during the days of the Shanghai demonstrations. Why don't you write about it yourself?"

Very well. Let Tan remain silent; I shall try to speak for him.

At first, I didn't particularly single Tan out from my twelve students. He was very reserved and restrained. Racked by a terrible cough, he passed my table frequently to go to the spittoon. Sometimes at the end of a lecture he would come to me with a book in which he had underlined the words he didn't understand. He asked me tersely for explanations and when I had made them departed as austerely as ever.

[289]

One day I happened to visit his room with a few other Russians. It was furnished with two cots, a small table between them, and book shelves along the wall. The table was piled with notebooks and battered volumes. Over it hung a poster showing a girl holding a cigarette, sitting on the shore of a lake. This belonged to Tan's room-mate. Above the poster a photograph was pinned to the wall, a picture of a group of young people dressed in shimmering ma-guas. They were evidently school-mates and friends of Tan. Noticing my interest he pointed to one of them and said gravely, "This comrade has been executed."

During our visit he was very affable and pleasant. The girls who had come with me walked about the room, inspecting and handling all the objects in it as unceremoniously as housewives feeling cabbages in the marketplace. In the smile with which Tan watched them I sensed a certain pity, tinged with contempt for their lack of breeding. This attitude of his became more pronounced when the women began to ask him questions. Was he married? Had he a child? Were his wife's feet small? Was his wife beautiful? Among Russian women this curiosity is quite usual, but it is evidently regarded as improper in China.

The first half of the year 1925 I saw very little of Tan outside of my class except when I passed him occasionally in the halls. But I was with him and could watch his face during that tense and awe-inspiring moment when Sun Yat-sen, swathed in furs and green with cancer, got off the train and was greeted with a tumult of shouting and a waving of flags. Then the voices of the student-soldiers rang out, accompanied by the clash of bayonets, as they cleared a path for the aged revolutionary through the crowd of policemen on the platform. The policemen's swords rose and flashed in the air, but the students seized them and bent them across their knees.

The next night I was passing in front of the largest hotel in Peking, where a student demonstration was in progress. Tan

[290]

stepped up and pulled my sleeve fiercely. "See how they are afraid of us!" he cried. "They" were the mounted police who surrounded the field of bright red lanterns with a dark line of uniforms. The young people's faces were turned upward toward the façade of the building. Suddenly in one of the windows old Sun Yat-sen appeared. The crowd saw him, waved their lanterns and cheered.

Together with Tan and the other students I went to the apartment where Sun Yat-sen lay dead. Wreaths filled the room and overflowed into the sunny court. The members of the Kuomintang, subdued and clad in dark clothes, with white ribbons on their ma-guas, stood in line all the way from the entrance to the place where the portrait of Sun Yat-sen was hung. An enormous wreath sent by Chang Tso-lin flaunted its magnificence next to a five-pointed star from Karakhan. We approached the altar and bowed.

As we came away Tan told me how deeply grieved the students were at the death of the leader. Ting Wing-ping had dropped before the altar in convulsions and had had to be carried away and put to bed. Du Ge-hun and the Koreans had cried as they crowded into the little hotel room. But the cooks, Tan said, and the furnace man and the janitor and the waiters from next door had looked at the mourners and laughed. He also told me about the reactionary students who repeated the words of their rich uncles that Heaven had punished Sun Yat-sen with death because he overthrew the monarchy. From the furious, incoherent manner in which he told me about this, I gathered that he had had some kind of fight with these reactionaries. He ended his story by saying passionately, "I wish the revolution would begin. Then those people would go to the scaffold."

The little yellow coffin of Sun Yat-sen was followed by all of Peking. For a few days I could not tell who was a member of the Kuomintang and who was not. The tradition of respect for the dead compelled everyone, including the ceremoniously hypocritical noblemen, to wear the white chrysanthemum of mourning and utter the words of grief. Policemen walked next to students who carried placards with the slogans of Sun Yat-sen and shouted until they were hoarse, "Down with the traitors of the state! . . . Down with the lackeys of foreigners!" But the weeks of mourning passed. The coffin was taken from Peking to the topmost room of a distant temple and soon the artificial unity melted away.

At times it seemed to me that the interest of the students in revolution was subsiding. It had no outlet in action. The silent, sullen fury of the strikers at the factories in Tzin-tao, Shanghai, and Canton, a fury punctuated only by the rattle of police guns, aroused no kindred spark in them. The government was no longer afraid of them. It even went so far as to forbid the Fourth of May demonstration which was like forbidding one to commemorate one's birthday.

When the edict was announced the students poured through the streets and broke into the house of the Minister of Education who had issued the ban. The Minister escaped by the back door. The crowd rioted through the rooms, destroying tables, lanterns, chests of drawers and porcelain vases. Girls with tears in their eyes shouted, "Beat him to death! Beat him to death!" Then the police came with guns and sabres. The students seized the swords with their naked hands. Blood ran over their clothes. They carried the wounded on their backs to the hospital. The next day they marched through the streets of Peking, bearing the blood-stained garments of the injured on poles and shouting for revenge.

But their excitement soon died away. A few days later they paraded to the palace of Tuan Chi-jui, to demand the removal of the head of the police and the Minister of Education, but they were almost as listless and detached as people in a doctor's waiting room. A double line of soldiers stood in front of the palace. The marchers were not allowed to approach the entrance. They sat down on the curb on the other side of the street, in the shade of the trees, ate hard pears and drank sparkling water from bottles, stubbornly waiting for an answer from the President. Their powder was obviously getting wet. Even to my inexperienced eye it was evident that the revolutionary spirit was passing over from the students to the workers. It was descending on the strikers who were storming the gates of factories, demanding their jobs back or else compensation for the time they had been out of work.

24. Shanghai Days
(*Not Related by Tan Shih-hua*)

THINGS HAPPENED IN SHANGHAI ALL OF A SUDDEN.

On the 31st of May I came to my lecture but did not find my pupils. A student hurrying through a corridor waved me off with his hand without stopping.

"The English have shot and killed a crowd of people in Shanghai. We are preparing a demonstration; please excuse me, I have no time to talk to you."

The students flared up like a pile of lighted straw. "All to the demonstration! . . . All to the gates of the British Embassy! . . . Chinese blood must be avenged!"

I took my camera and went into the streets now crowded with students. The only foreigner in the crowd, I clung to the wall to keep out of the way of the passing people. The banners of the university headed the procession.

Two students, one of whom carried an umbrella and another a stick, were watching me. The moment I set up my camera, one of them lifted his stick, baring his white teeth threateningly; but

[293]

the other, grabbing him by the shoulder, placed his umbrella in front of my camera. I tried to tell them that I was a Russian, but it did not help.

Before reaching the gates of the Settlement the demonstration stopped. Good manners were in conflict with rage. Several students, evidently those in charge of the demonstration, ran to the head of the administration of the Settlement, to ask permission to march in front of the British Embassy. The crowd waited. It waited long, only to receive a curt, "No."

The students giving up the idea of entering the gates, were ready to turn and march around the walls of the Settlement, when several girls, grasping the faltering banners, rushed toward the steel gates, drawing the mass of the students after them. The head of the demonstration ran through the line of indifferent Chinese police. The gates were still open. The students ran, bending their banner forward. Through the open gates they saw the grey pavements of the Settlement streets, and the trees of its parks. A foreigner in a dress suit and a glistening silk hat commanded: "Shut the gates." The gates closed. The fists of the students battered heavy steel.

"Down with the foreigners!"

A detachment of French soldiers levelled their guns on the roaring crowd through the embrasure of the wall. Firemen were pulling their hose over the asphalt of the street toward the gates. The banners raised high on bamboo poles and fixed by the students over the gates flapped loudly like cracking whips over the emptiness of the streets on the other side. Suddenly the lone voice of a girl cut into the rattle of bamboo against the steel: "Down with the Christians!"

From morning until night, no matter where you were in the Settlement, you could hear the distant cries, growing ever more furious, of the crowd marching outside its walls. The government was silent. Students held meetings on every street corner. The foreigners were afraid to leave the Settlement. When an old Italian, who had spent almost all his life in Peking, passed by a crowd in a yan-che, the people shouted: "Murderer!"

He stopped his yan-che and asked, "Why do you call me murderer? I am an Italian," but without explaining, the crowd roared back, "Get out of here. Get out of here quick!"

The Europeans sat on their trunks. At the Christian missions sand bags were laid on the window-sills. If at night a red lantern was raised on the American radio mast, all Europeans rushed to the Embassy buildings and missions. The public square boiled with daily meetings. The yan-ches attached little flags to their carriages: "We do not carry foreigners." Messenger boys and janitors were leaving the British Embassy. Masons, working day and night, mended the breaks in the wall of the Settlement. Barbed wire closed the streets leading to it. Horrible photographs of maimed corpses plastered the pillars. At one meeting a Chinese teacher cut off his own finger and painted the words of hatred on his banner with his own blood. As in a religious procession, pictures of bleeding people, of a crowd running under gun-fire, of British soldiers commanding "Fire", were carried through the crowded streets.

One evening Tan came to see me. In spite of his aversion to the Settlement, he had come through a half-opened crack of the gates past colored French soldiers. He had not shaved for days. Black circles were around his eyes and his lips seemed purple. His mouth expressed anger, pain, and a thirst for revenge. Twenty hours every day he spent on the streets. All day long he stood on a platform, agitating, and at night he wrote plays about British bullets and Chinese blood.

Rebellious Peking pressed on the Settlement. The Settlement pressed on the President who, for his part, was biding his time, waiting to see how successful the students would prove in their attempt to compel the merchants to boycott British goods. But the merchants were against the boycott. They still remembered their losses in the anti-Japanese boycott. The Peking Chamber of Commerce debated the question. The tenth of June was the day of the decisive demonstration. The Chamber of Commerce promised to send the merchants to the meeting and close their stores. The merchants came to the square on the day mentioned but the stores remained open. The back-bone of the protest was broken. Policemen again appeared on the streets. The Minister of Foreign Affairs wrote a letter of apology to the Settlement.

I felt the change. Before, I had been able to walk safely along the crowded streets protected only by the name of my country. But on the tenth of June, the moment I appeared on the street, I was surrounded by policemen. They would not listen to me when I urged them to let me alone. I felt perfectly safe and sure that nobody would touch me. They repeated a sentence learned by heart: "Go back, we cannot guarantee your safety." And when the crowd attracted by our arguments surrounded us, asking what was the matter, policemen answered with one word "A foreigner!"; and their eyes flared up with hate, their breath quickened, their hands reached toward me. The ring of policemen protected me from the wrath of the people. Who knows but that perhaps the next day the "Peking and Tientsin Times" might have published a dispatch telling how a crowd of Chinese citizens had almost torn to pieces a hateful red agitator.

But day after day the tensity of the meetings slackened. You cannot march every day for a whole month. Either you have to break the grey walls of the Settlement or retire.

The July heat and the army of Chang Tso-lin were approaching Peking. Students were leaving for their provinces. I was getting ready to go back to Moscow and was saying good-bye to my pupils. We sat in a small room. On the table in front of me food was piled. The students laughed at my efforts to eat with chopsticks and moved various dishes toward me. We talked about Moscow and the Shanghai events, about the educational work in Russian villages, young pioneers, and libraries for peasants. The students sighed, "If only we could have that in our villages!"

Tan got up and said proudly, "My father is a rebel of

Szechuan. I go back with instructions to organize two revolutionary regiments in Szechuan."

He left Peking before I did. Here is a letter I received from him on the road.

June 18, 1925.

My dear Professor Tretiakov,

On June 13th I received instructions from our group to go to the southwestern part of China to carry on the propaganda of the Shanghai demonstrations. And now I am on the train in Hankow where the streets are filled with British soldiers and no Chinese can go out after dark.

My comrades and I have already talked with the head of the Uchan student committee and they are very glad to join the Peking students.

I get on the boat tonight and in five days will be in Szechuan. I'll write you a letter about my activity there. My play is finished and probably will be put on by my comrades in Szechuan.

Your student,
Tan Shih-hua.

---

25. On My Way

(*Tan Shih-hua Resumes the Story*)

To UNDERMINE THE BOYCOTT THE BRITISH STEAMSHIP COMpanies were charging a quarter less for their tickets than the Chinese. From Chungking to Ichang one had to pay only two da yang now. A few years ago the foreigners charged me forty da yang instead of eight for the same trip. Now it was two da yang instead of forty. Nevertheless the English boats were empty. The captains of Chinese steamers were supporting the

[297]

students' agitation not solely for reasons of patriotism. The boycott of English boats brought passengers to their steamers. The students were given free passage; we had to pay only for our food.

The sailors were the first workers with machinery I had ever met. They surrounded us, standing with folded muscular arms which gleamed blue against the whiteness of their sleeveless shirts. Their chests, which you could see through the open collars, and their biceps, were covered with tattooed fish and butter-flies.

We told them how the workers in Shanghai had gone to get money due them and had received bullets instead, how the Shanghai students carried their dead bodies over the streets of the foreign settlement and demanded compensation for their blood, and how the Britishers met the Chinese people in a Chinese city with bullets. We told them that we must chase the English out of our land, as the northern people had chased them out of theirs, to establish the "State of the Poor" which was now ruled by our brother-workers.

The sailors listened to us and then said: "And now tell us, gentlemen students, please, could we fight England? We know about the northern people. The union of stevedores in Shanghai and Hankow unloads only their cargo, and the boatmen near Nanking carry no one else across the Yangtze. But will they help us fight England?"

I was especially friendly with the boatswain Wu. He was thirty years old, bow-legged and strong. He wore canvas trousers and white slippers. When he took off his sleeveless shirt one might have thought him made of two different parts—his head was the color of strong tea and his body as white as white-wood. His face was darker than his lips which seemed painted white like the lips of a clown. He had a strong, happy voice and his trumpet, calling the sailors to a meeting, sang like a bird. We could not talk to the sailors without his permission.

After the meeting we collected money for the strikers, from

the sailors, cooks, stewards, waiters, stokers. Everybody donated willingly, even the captain and the passengers.

We changed twice before we reached Chungking. On each steamer we collected about three hundred da yang. The money, in the presence of other passengers, was sealed in an envelope. At the next port, a delegate from the sailors and I took the money to the post-office. Our central group had issued a strict order to mail at once all money collected.

The 15th of June found us on the boat. The 15th of June is the night of lanterns. According to Chinese belief there are homeless spirits in the other world, or to be more correct, the souls of childless people. Hungry and cold because they have no one to pray for them, these spirits wander through villages and towns, along the roads and canals, looking for food and annoying people. To protect themselves from these hooligans of the other world, people burn sacrificial fires on the 15th of June. They burn gowns, slippers, and paper money. It was necessary to placate these spirits, to let them have some money and so forget them. On that night the Chinese buy little, many-colored lanterns and float them on the water. All the rivers, lakes, and ponds of China blossom with bright, slowly vanishing fiery bubbles.

Everyone on the boat contributed for the purchase of lanterns —the captain and the sailors. Wu shook a bag full of collected money. Soon we were to dock and he was going to buy lanterns and sacrificial offerings. Wu shook the bag and said: "Listen, students, why should we feed the spirits when the living Shanghai strikers are starving? What do we want the silly lanterns for when we can mail this money to Shanghai?"

Several sailors egged him on: "Go and mail it, and then tell the captain that you lost the money."

But the others said gravely: "Don't do it. We might have a scandal. We might run aground on a sand-bar and the captain will accuse us of angering the spirits. And he'll fire you. Go and buy the lanterns."

I myself was very much tempted to send the money to Shanghai. We watched Wu running down the gangplank, pulling on his sleeveless shirt. He turned to look back at us for a moment. We saw his dark face and his bright, white teeth.

To me, who had seen only the slow peasant, it was amazing how much more alive, bold, gay, and intelligent the workers were.

---

26. Home for the Last Time

I LOOKED AT MY NATIVE VILLAGE, REMEMBERING WHAT IT WAS like twenty years ago when my uncle brought me to school for the first time. I could not recognize it. The stone streets were repaved with new flagstones and the flagstones were clean of tangerine peelings and pits. At the gates of houses stood boxes for rubbish.

In my childhood my grandmother used to buy me three tangerines for a tung tze. Now I had to pay two tung tze for one. The price had gone up five times during those twenty years.

New houses rose along the streets. I did not feel like entering the gates. In the old days every house meant friends, but now they were gone, scattered all over the world, studying, fighting. Some of them were in Chengtu, some in Shanghai, some in Nanking, others in France, in Japan or at Yale University in America. The youngsters who four years ago were beginning to learn hieroglyphics were now high-school pupils wearing white caps and grey jackets and waiting their turn to get aboard a steamer and go to the university. In the schools they were now learning foreign languages right from the start. The thin-

[300]

voiced little girls called each other "Miss". High-school girls, imitating Shanghai and Peking styles, bobbed their hair.

Not so long ago the girls had not dared to go alone in the streets. Now they were running to stores and marketplaces by themselves, or even with boys, holding hands and swinging their arms.

Could I ever have walked like that with Tsai-in?

The old go-betweens were dying out and there were no new ones to replace them. Parents consulted their children before beginning to negotiate a marriage. It was as though six decades and not six years had passed since 1919.

In my boyhood there were no more than ten university students in Sian-Shih and not more than forty high-school students. Now about a hundred of them went every year to Teh chien, and there were about thirty students from Sian-Shih in Peking alone.

Before, only three or four families used to get a newspaper; now even the school had its own newsstand. The old officials in charge of popular education were afraid to show up in the school, so strong were the present masters—the pupils.

I walked along the fields. There was something in them I did not like. Where I used to see wheat, or where the moist green of rice once glistened, tens, hundreds, millions of flowers lifted their heads. Pale-petalled flowers, the cursed flower, *ma-huei*— the poppy. When it loses its petals and a green ball begins to swell in their place, peasants come to the fields and make cuts in this ball, causing it to bleed. White blood fills up the cuts and coagulates. It is scraped off and rolled into sticky lumps. This is the raw opium. 400 grammes of it cost one da yang. The buyer melts it over a fire and makes a more expensive opium from it. One rain is sufficient to wash off the juice and ruin the harvest.

The peasants do not sow the poppy of their own free will. Wires are pulled in the yamen through the offices of the daoyin and the heads of the villages—"Sow poppy. Sow poppy." This is because the buyers are connected with the officials, because the opium houses are taxed by the dubans, because the duban gets taxes for the transportation of opium, because for every two poppy stems in his field a peasant is fined a tung tze. This fine was a measure taken by the government in its fake struggle against opium smoking. The government fined peasants, but whispered to them at the same time through thousands and thousands of its officials: "Sow poppy, sow poppy."

This meant the destruction of rice fields, for the poppy grows only in dry soil. For its sake the clay walls of many rice fields were destroyed, the irrigating ditches grew stagnant and the dams were broken. The pioneer poppy growers thought poppy-culture a profitable business. But more and more people sowed poppy and the price of opium went down. It was beyond the means of the peasants to reconstruct the old rice fields. Over-burdened with fines and failing to collect the necessary amount of opium from his field, the peasant was compelled to sell his field in payment of debts and go to the city to earn his living as a coolie or boatman. Eventually he perished in the dry dust of the docks. His only relief from long days of misery and starvation was the short hours of drunken dreams which came out of opium smoke. Thus did opium kill those who tried to grow it.

At home I was an infrequent guest. I came once in four years which was really not often enough. Moreover, when I went away I could never tell when I would be back, if at all. My family lived without much anxiety. Step-mother fed me with chickens and ducks and shook her head with pity as she noticed my hollow chest and skinny arms. What if they were skinny? They could still hold a rifle and pull a trigger.

Step-mother wrapped herself around me like excelsior around a fragile glass packed in a box. Perhaps she was trying to compensate with tenderness and attention for all the grief she had caused me in the past. I never mentioned my wife to her for fear she might begin to cry, thinking that I had done it on purpose to make her suffer. In the morning, if I were still asleep, after all were up, everybody would walk on tiptoe and speak in low voices: "Sh-h, Shih-hua is asleep." With gay malice I kept silent awhile after waking up, and then shouted loudly: "I fooled you, I am not asleep," and the voices in the house livened up like furniture polished with oil.

Gradually the little Tan Tun, now five years old, got used to me. I took her in my arms once but immediately put her down —she was too heavy. She didn't particularly like to be in my arms. She called me "uncle." and she called my cousin, who took care of her, "father". Tan Tun wasn't a bit afraid of me. Would I ever have dared to ask my father for anything, for a little attention, not to speak of candy or a toy? But I did not have time to turn around in the house before she had already asked me, "Uncle, buy me a toy and a foreign dress."

"What do you want a foreign dress for? It is not comfortable."

"Yes it is. Everybody wears foreign dresses now, even Aunt Shih-kuen."

I looked at Tan Tun with a certain respect. She wanted a foreign dress and she knew several hieroglyphics: "Onc, two, three, the sky, a man, the sun," the same hieroglyphics which twenty years ago I had read to my teacher on my first day of school. Soon my younger uncle, dark-haired and youthful, was to take Tan Tun to a girls' school.

Twenty years ago—why twenty?—five years ago—there were no girls from our village in the university. My sister kept looking at me hesitatingly as though she wanted to say something but did not dare, examined my books, asked many questions about Peking and then one day suddenly declared: "I want to go with you to Peking."

"What for?"

"I'll tell you what for. You are going to spend another year in Peking before going to Russia. During that year I can get acquainted with the city and the university. Then I could stay there alone after you go."

"What do you want to study?"

"The same subject you do, literature."

I laughed. "Our older uncle was right in foretelling your future as a famous authoress."

She also liked music and learned to play the piano in the school.

"Go ahead," I said. "Go and talk to step-mother."

Our step-mother did not reflect long. Her experience with me had taught her better than to oppose our plans. She folded her hands on her lap and said, "She may go. Only where will we find the money?".

The next day my smiling younger uncle again went around the village organizing a loan group for my little sister, Shih-kuen. He was as healthy as a bull. You could hear his laughter from a distance. The youngsters in the school loved him.

My older uncle was still living in the old broken-down family house in far-away Tan Tsia-Chen. He probably still drank warm wine and recited poetry and wondered what was going to happen to China. I had no desire to go there again or to turn over the dusty pages of the old family chronicle, so highly respected by me in my childhood.

I went to visit my father. I looked at him and wondered how many more divisions he would organize and how many more escapes he would be able to stand. Unlike my younger uncle, at forty-five he was stooped, grey-haired and old. His former austerity was replaced by gentleness and good humor.

"Good-bye. I am going back to Peking. The future may bring revolution and perhaps war with England."

"Good-bye, son," father said. "I am glad the revolution took some of your attention away from literature and poetry. If you seriously intend to go to Moscow, write to us and we'll manage to get the money for you somewhere."

"Thanks, Fu-tsin."

Money is a heavy burden. I had already a three-thousand
da yang debt on my shoulders—the four years at the university
and my divorce. When I would begin to pay it back nobody
knew. The years ahead were uncertain.

We went to Peking with a large group of relatives and countrymen, including my sister, a cousin of mine, Pen, and his wife
—a family with which I was very close in Peking.

Until we reached Chungking I was alone in my political talks
with the sailors. From then on my sister joined in. Where had
she learned to make such speeches? Her voice sounded firm
and there was not a sign in her of girlish shyness. The words she
used were significant and forceful. Her excitement showed she
had thought much about the Shanghai bloodshed, the generals,
and the grief of China. Sailors listened to her attentively and I
was pleased to hear them remark: "Students are our only leaders."

I was proud of her.

New people got aboard our steamer at Chungking. An anti-
British union of students, merchants and soldiers was organized
in this city. The student delegates were more experienced than
the others. We immediately arranged what we would say so
there would be no disagreement in public. We had to keep from
laughing as we listened to the officers, leaning on their swords,
their chests expanded.

"Damn the English who occupy our territory ("Right," we
encouraged them.)—in Korea and Weihaiwei. (Well, well, we
wondered, when did England occupy Korea?) We'll crush the
two dirty dogs, England and Japan, under our feet. They are
always engaged in a war with each other!" (What war was he
talking about? The poor fellow is all mixed up! We glanced at
each other, but did not say a word. It was not to our interest
to belittle the speaker in front of the audience. The map of China
was not very clear in his mind.)

He raised his shoulders adorned with stripes.

"We must fight England. We are not afraid. We will set the millions of Chinese people against the British cannon."

I turned my eyes away. I lacked his resoluteness. I remembered that all rebels in all times had thought thus, and always the British cannons proved stronger than millions and millions of tons of Chinese flesh.

---

27. Feng-Duban

IN PEKING, PEN, HIS WIFE, AND MY SISTER PLUNGED INTO STUDY for the examinations.

The city was in an alarming state. Soldiers of two hostile armies picketed its streets—the soldiers of Chang Tso-lin and of Feng. The latter ceased singing Christian hymns and wrote on the walls of the city: "No food for those who do not work." There was a rumor that Feng had submitted to the Kuomintang and was now getting ready to advance against Chang Tso-lin.

Feng organized three military schools in Kalgan similar to those organized by the Kuomintang in Canton—one for soldiers, one for officers and one for students. He invited Russian military instructors to lecture in his schools and needed translators.

I went to Kalgan as a translator. Many other students had scattered to other parts of China where struggle was eminent. Those who remained in Peking wandered along empty corridors. Conditions in the South, in Canton, among the peasants of Hunan, and the young soldiers of Feng, were in a state of high tension. The day of the great battle was drawing near.

The work in Kalgan was hard and tiresome. Russian instructors would deliver their lectures. We would listen, write them down, and then translate them into Chinese. Our translations were printed and distributed among the students. We worked all day long, our fingers grew numb, cramps tightened the muscles of our right arms. We did not know Russian very well but our knowledge seemed superb in comparison with that of other translators. After a day's work, with our eyes and fingers tired, we would fall into a heavy slumber. We had no time to go to a bath-house. We grew filthier and filthier every day.

General Feng was a shrewd man. He had the best soldiers and his officers of the lower ranks could have served as models. He himself dressed very modestly and lived a simple life and this modesty and simplicity became the rule in his army. His soldiers had to wash their feet and know their trade. No petty officer dared ride in a yan-che. But officers of the higher rank, the generals, with the exception of Lu Chun-ling, were all dull-witted, pompous, and mediocre—just clothes-horses for their uniforms. Perhaps Feng selected them on purpose—gifted assistants were dangerous as a rule.

Russian instructors were regarded by these generals as personal insults. If you tried to send one of them to a Russian instructor for advice he would answer: "What do they understand about Chinese military affairs?" Any private dressed up in a general's uniform would have been more intelligent.

Only two years before Feng had disciplined his soldiers with the help of a bible and a stick. Now the bible was gone, but the stick remained. Feng used this stick to strike his high officers in front of the soldiers. He slapped the face of the head of the military school in front of the pupils. As a result the officers had no authority in the eyes of the soldiers, but every word of Feng himself was law.

"Feng-Duban" the soldiers called him—and what Feng-Duban said was never contradicted. If he ordered them to sing

Christian hymns, they sang them. If the very next day he ordered them to shoot a Christian priest, they shot him. If he ordered them to raise the red flag one day, that flag would rise. If he commanded them the next day to open fire on the Communists, they executed that order.

The north of China was quiet with the stillness that precedes a storm. The two armies, trained to perfection, were ready to advance. In the meantime the staff officers of Kalgan were talking loudly about the coming war with Chang Tso-lin, discussing military plans and almost naming the place where the attack was to begin. We would say to them, "If you are preparing to launch an attack, you should keep it quiet." To which they would answer with great self confidence, "Don't worry, everything is in its place—police, secret service and . . . the telephones of the students."

"That's not sufficient. Information from Kalgan might reach Chang Tso-lin."

"How can it reach Chang Tso-lin when I have ordered every letter addressed to Mukden to be opened." The general probably was under the naïve belief that spies would send their information direct to the following address: "Mukden, Chang Tso-lin, Confidential."

The soldiers treated us ironically and called us "observers." But they came and asked us questions occasionally when they did not understand something in a newspaper or in a military order. The officers of the lower ranks would not ask us questions. They were almost as badly educated as the soldiers and were terribly conceited. The soldiers were all young people from eighteen to thirty years old. They had a great deal to do; building roads, learning different trades in the school, committing by heart, without understanding, the orders of Feng. What the soldiers liked so much about Feng was the fact that he paid them more regularly than the other generals.

My comrade Hsao Tzu-chen was as stubborn as a rodent, his

teeth gleamed challengingly and his hair stood up above his forehead like a thick brush. But I was sorry for U Shan-ming who was slowly wilting away under the strain of the work. In rare, free moments he would sit on his bed and tell me with bowed head about his woes. He did not want to have anything to do with women, but every night he would dream about them and suffer. One day he felt that he was getting very ill.

"Get leave and go back to Peking while you can still walk," I said.

He agreed with me without enthusiasm.

Next day he sat over his notebooks, a towel around his head. He could not stand the light—his head ached so—he was very thirsty and drank water constantly. From day to day his speech grew more nervous and more and more incoherent. A dark color spread over his pale cheeks. In two more days his neck blossomed out with a red rash. He was put to bed. For the first time in many months I heard U Shan-ming sing famous theatrical songs in a high clear voice, keeping perfect time. He was delirious.

The university sent us strict orders to come back, threatening to close the Russian section entirely if we did not return. We hurried back. U Shan-ming had to be left in the hands of servants. His breath came fast and with difficulty. After our departure he received his leave, but he was unable to read it. He no longer sang. A servant put the paper under a glass on the table at the head of his bed. The poor man, suffering with typhus fever, did not have even strength enough to toss.

28. Suffocation

Peking was terrifyingly quiet in the spring of 1926. Every day from nine to twelve the wind drove the sour, poisonous, cold dust along its avenues.

Kalgan could no longer hold its position. It was too early to hope for help from Canton. The generals of Chang Tso-lin were slowly pressing the divisions of Feng, cutting them off from the railroad. Chang Tso-lin had a division of White Russians. Their caps were adorned with the five-pointed, five-colored star of the Chinese army. Their names, as well as their citizenship, were changed to Chinese. Cruel and stubborn in battle, they hated Feng for his Russian instructors. Feng retreated to Tientsin.

Unknown hands plastered the walls of the university with posters and leaflets urging the people not to trust the Russians who would try to conquer China after taking possession of Mongolia. They stated that the Chinese Communists were working on money paid them by Karakhan, and asked all real patriots to fight the Red Menace.

The students of the Russian section had all returned except Ting-Ping. We spent evenings telling each other about our experiences in the different armies in which we had been working. Those who had not gone anywhere enviously inquired how big our salary had been.

"Well, well, a hundred and ten da yang a month—it's a fortune! You are wealthy men now!"

We did not deny that we had saved some money—about fifty da yang.

"Only fifty?"

"Yes. We lived next door to the Russian instructors and had to board with the Russians—it came to about forty da yang a month." Our clothes were all worn out and we had to buy new ones. Our savings came in handy.

The political scales were swinging slowly—Mukden was in one balance, Kalgan in the other. The fulcrum was Peking. To the west of Peking in the province Shangsi, famous for its old banks and the tiny feet of its women, Duban Yan Si-shang sat on the fence, unable to make up his mind which side to join— Chang Tso-lin or Feng.

The movement of the trains between Tientsin and Peking was disorganized. Military echelons and trains with ammunition would get out of the way only for foreign trains with locomotives all decked out in the flags of the seven nations which ruled China. Such trains might carry two or three hotel owners, a couple of diplomatic couriers, a missionary, and about five journalists (fulfilling at the same time the functions of military spies), all of them protected by seven different platoons of soldiers brought to China from every continent of the world.

It was difficult for Feng to fight with Mukden—British warships were helping Chang Tso-lin. The foreigners would not let Feng take possession of the river Pei-Ho connecting Tientsin with the sea.

The diplomatic corps presented an ultimatum to the Peking government demanding that no military action take place in Tientsin or its environment. For Chang Tso-lin it meant "Come in, the way is clear." For Feng it was equal to "Get out of here."

The President, Tuan Chi-jui, remained silent in his palace, accepting humbly as usual the shameful notes and insolent memoranda.

On March 18th I was lying in bed in my room. The students and the professors had started a demonstration in the morning at the gates of the palace of Tuan Chi-jui. They had taken along high school boys and the youngsters from preparatory schools to demand action by the old man against the ultimatum. For two days I had not been feeling well. I was expecting my comrades to come to my room and tell me laughingly how they had argued with police officers and how the palace master of ceremonies had explained to them smilingly that old Tuan had hurt his feet wearing new shoes and so was unable to come out himself to meet the crowd.

Suddenly Hsao Tzu-chen rushed, or to be more exact, fell gasping into my room. He tore the paper frame off the door and almost took the door itself off the hinges. I jumped out of bed, lifted him from the floor and put him on the mattress. His eyes were rolled back. He was clutching at his face with shaking hands and smearing it with blood. I began to stroke his chest trying to quiet him and saw that my hands too became red. He tossed and turned on the bed and bit the pillow. I tried to give him water but he could not drink it. He breathed hard and groaned. Neighbors came into the room. Many minutes passed before Hsao could tell his story.

The delegation had been met by palace officials who announced that the Tuan was not at home, and that in any case there was no reason for him to talk such matters over with a mob. Students pushed the officials aside and their cries resounded over the streets.

"Death to Tuan!"

"Death to the lackey of the foreigners!"

Before the cries had time to rise over the gates an officer's whistle pierced the air and a line of soldiers fired into the crowd. One volley, two, three . . .

The street was narrow. The crowd rushed back. They stepped over the fallen, treading on their throats. Those who were still alive crawled out from under the dead bodies, their clothes sprinkled with human brains.

"There were women and children with their skulls cut open. I climbed from under a pile of bodies and crawled along the

[312]

street. Bullets were whistling all around me. The whole crowd crawled away on their bellies."

Hsao was talking and shaking. I wiped his face with a wet cloth. There wasn't a scratch on it—he was covered with the blood of others. We sat on the bed wringing our hands and suffering from a feeling of helplessness. Our eyes glistened, the teeth of Hsao continued to chatter and he whispered, "Many bullets . . . whistles . . . we ran . . . feet and poster poles are sticking up from piles of human bodies. . . ."

We could not go on staying in a little room, shaking and shedding tears. If the police fired, we would fire. If generals laughed at us we would find words to arouse our great country and spur it against the generals.

A new professor came from Moscow, a stout, rosy-cheeked, curly-haired man whom we called "pretty maiden". We put literature aside and demanded explanations of Marxism, Leninism and dialectic materialism. I learned from him that a Chinese student could live easily on 400 da yang a year in Moscow. I asked my father, who was again the head of Ming-Tuan in Sian-Shih, to collect the money. From my Russian comrades I got letters of introduction to people in Moscow.

My sister watched my preparations.

"Take me to Moscow with you."

"But you don't know the language."

"You could teach me."

"I am going away too soon. I have no time."

"Well, just teach me as much as you can."

My sister agreed with my argument but she was disappointed. She made me promise that as soon as I got to Moscow, I would find out how a young girl might get along there, and write her about it. She came to me with a notebook and the Russian alphabet and learned a few Russian letters. That exhausted our first Russian lesson.

[313]

A few of my acquaintances left for Russia. I would have gone with them but my money had not yet arrived. Enviously I watched the train carry away the lucky persons from the corrugated iron awnings of the station to a country where one could talk loudly about revolution, where one did not have to hide the writings of Lenin in fear under other books.

The days grew warmer in subdued and blood-stained Peking. Feng retreated to Kalgan. The enemy circle tightened around the walls of the city. Hsan Tzun-chang entered Peking with his guard of hired White Russians. Peking shrank like a dog before a threatening cane. Merchants closed their stores, expecting riots. Newspapers did not dare say a word about the new ruler. A rumor went from mouth to mouth about Russian officers drinking in Chinese saloons, breaking glasses, threatening people with revolvers, riding around in automobiles with screaming, drunken women.

People spoke under their breath about Hsan Tzun-chang. He was enormously tall and lusty and had a colossal harem where the women had to wear numbers because he could not remember them all by their faces. His guard began its activity by increasing this harem. They broke into the houses of noblemen of the best Chinese families and dragged the young women away—the best-looking daughters-in-law and the most beautiful concubines. A daughter of the former Minister of Agriculture and Commerce was kidnapped by them. The secretary Huan-Fu lost his daughter-in-law. The soldiers of Hsan Tzun-chang even broke into the house of Ling-Su, the famous poet and enemy of Hu-Shih and Chen Du-su, and carried away the wife of the poet's son. The husbands of the kidnapped girls talked indignantly to their relatives and promised to complain, but then they secretly packed their trunks and left Peking to save their own hides.

The last news I received before going to Russia upset me most. Li Shu-ling, who had just returned to Peking from Canton, Li Shu-ling who had worked in the People's Army and with the followers of Sun Yat-sen, took a job on the staff of Hsan Tzun-

[314]

chang. Well, he got a double salary. He knew not only Russian, but also many other valuable things.

Some of my comrades tried to justify him: Li Shu-ling came from Shantung and so did Hsan Tzun-chang. But I felt that I could never forgive him. Even though a thing like this was to be expected of Li Shu-ling, I felt ashamed of my old comrade.

I kept the promise I had given to my father and joined a group organized by our President at the university, Tzai Yan-pei, for the study of the military profession, its theory and practice.

Postscript

ONE DAY TAN SHIH-HUA FAILED TO VISIT ME. A WEEK PASSED AND he did not show up. It became clear that he had left.

Telling me the last chapters of his life, he had often said:

"Chang Kai-shek betrayed the revolution. But I know a man who will never betray either Moscow or the revolution. This man is Wang Ching-hui. I believe in him. I believe in him as I do in my father. If somebody told me that my father had betrayed the cause, I would not have enough strength to renounce him. I would have to go and see him myself to make sure that it was true."

Wang Ching-hui betrayed the revolution sixty days after the departure of Tan Shih-hua.

Two years have passed since Tan Shih-hua left Moscow. He plunged into China and disappeared. My letters to him have remained unanswered. I do not know where he is or what he is doing. Perhaps he is editing literary pamphlets, perhaps he works as a clerk of Feng or teaches in Szechuan. Or perhaps, after looking closely into the split face of the Kuomintang he has become a Communist, and like his father, who once wandered from village to village with his insurgent army, continues to carry on guerilla warfare around the populous villages of Hunan and Tzian-si. Or perhaps he has fallen into the hangman's hands, and his head with its sparse black hair and its quiet eyes, is peering through the bamboo bars of a prison-cage in some marketplace far in the interior of China.

THE END